The World of *Aufbau*

The World of
AUFBAU

Hitler's Refugees in America

Peter Schrag

The University of Wisconsin Press

The University of Wisconsin Press
1930 Monroe Street, 3rd Floor
Madison, Wisconsin 53711-2059
uwpress.wisc.edu

Gray's Inn House, 127 Clerkenwell Road
London EC1R 5DB, United Kingdom
eurospanbookstore.com

Printed in the United States of America

This book may be available in a digital edition.

Library of Congress Cataloging-in-Publication Data
Names: Schrag, Peter, author.
Title: The world of Aufbau: Hitler's refugees in America / Peter Schrag.
Description: Madison, Wisconsin: University of Wisconsin Press, [2019]
Identifiers: LCCN 2018045754 | ISBN 9780299320201 (cloth: alk. paper)
Subjects: LCSH: Aufbau (New York, N.Y.) | Jewish newspapers—New York (State)—
New York. | German American newspapers—New York (State)—
New York. | Jews, German—United States—History.
| Jewish refugees—United States—History.
Classification: LCC PN4885.G34 A947 2019 | DDC 070.47/1—dc23
LC record available at https://lccn.loc.gov/2018045754

*   *   *

Aufbau was a major presence among the refugees in New York. It created its own community and aroused emotional attachments among its readers. It was *Aufbau* that first impressed upon me the power of journalism among my elders and neighbors.

Max Frankel

The readership was a community of fate; in large measure, the exiles of Europe wrote their paper themselves.

Hans Steinitz

Contents

Illustrations

Preface

A few words about language, style, and usage: After a long debate with myself, I finally chose to use the name of the paper, *Aufbau*, without the article "The" since that is what it called itself on its masthead. All quotations from the paper and other German texts, except where noted, are my translations of the German original (and, where *Aufbau* mixed languages, I usually quoted literally; e.g., "cookies und Milch"). Where the *Aufbau* text was in English, that is indicated where it's quoted when it's not obvious from the context. My favorite bit of Gerglish is "Onkel Sam."

As to structure: major issues and themes in *Aufbau* and in the era it covered often recurred and evolved through different times—as did the mounting brutality of the Nazi attacks on Jews and their other political and cultural enemies. So, too, did the conflicting (and changing) feelings about Zionism, the capricious demands of American immigration policy, and the treatment of post-Hitler Germany, among many others. And because many issues had simultaneous effects on others, it was necessary to compromise between the basic chronological structure and the topical portraits that cut across chronological boundaries. Conversely, some things in this period in U.S. immigration history and those who made it—the need among new arrivals to learn the language, find work and housing, and acculturate, for example—hardly changed at all. Necessarily also, compromises had to be made between the need to provide the background of events abroad without recounting the details of every campaign of World War II and every debate in Parliament and at the United Nations about the future of Palestine. Accordingly, the book is roughly divided chronologically into five sections, with the first serving as an overall portrait of the paper and the Hitler refugees who arrived before Pearl Harbor, and the succeeding ones following the story through the war and postwar years. But again there had to be compromises with recurring issues—anti-Semitism, for example—in new contexts.

This book was begun long before the 2016 presidential election campaign got under way—and thus even longer before its stunning end. But when the end came, questions like these—and the many others that the story of this generation of Hitler refugees and Holocaust survivors raised—have been given even more searing meanings. No, the present era is probably not like the Europe of the 1930s, but reviewing the legacy of Hitler's refugees in America now makes those questions even more troubling.

The World of *Aufbau*

Introduction

In the long history of American immigration—Irish, German, Italian, Polish, Greek, Hungarian, Japanese, Chinese, Latino—one generation has rarely been portrayed in the larger narrative. While there are countless books and articles about the European intellectuals and artists who fled to America in the 1930s and early 1940s, the broader story of the Hitler refugees and the displaced people and concentration camp survivors who arrived after the war is a major chapter in the history of immigration that deserves far more attention.

Not all were Jews, even by the Nazis' racial criteria. The largest numbers were Germans and Austrians; others came from virtually every country in Europe. America was not the first place of refuge, nor sometimes was it the last, for many of those fleeing the Nazis who had once thought they'd found safety in Belgium, Luxemburg, Czechoslovakia, Holland, France, or North Africa. Between 1933 and 1945, roughly 130,000 German and Austrian refugees immigrated to the United States—the figures in these categories are a little uncertain, even the definition of "refugee" was unclear—and some 150,000 came from other European countries.

In the eight years after the war (1945–53), while many went to Palestine, 140,000 Holocaust survivors arrived in America, most of them Jews, in addition to the thousands of other displaced people, many of them fleeing communist dictatorship in Hungary, Poland, Czechoslovakia, Russia, and Romania. Compared to the millions in prior generations of immigrants, those were small numbers, due to the tight U.S. national origins immigration quotas—quotas that, though low, were rarely filled. Between 1929 and 1965, immigration, as a percentage of the total population, was the lowest in recorded U.S. history. But because of their education, skills, and cultural background, and because of the circumstances that brought them, their impact was far greater than their numbers suggest.[1]

Some émigré names were already famous: scientists, academics, writers, and artists with international reputations who found posts in American universities and other institutions. Most were less well known: small businessmen and craftsmen, many of them, proud professionals in Europe who, if they wanted again to practice their profession, had to start all over, and some never could. For lawyers, certification in America was harder than for physicians, since U.S. law was totally different from German law; medicine, in comparison, was similar. But little was easy. After Pearl Harbor, there were a variety of jobs. In the Depression years before the war, things were worse for immigrants than they were for Americans citizens. Many struggled, and it was not just in finding jobs.

But the Hitler refugees were not like the huddled masses of classic American immigration history. By and large they were an urban middle class: from petit to haut bourgeois, from little shopkeepers and notions salesmen to proprietors of large department stores, from cabaret musicians, clerks, and nurses to corporate lawyers. And for them, the thousands of people who were not celebrities and had few connections, one of the most accessible introductions to their new world and, subsequently, to Americanization, was the New York–based German-language paper *Aufbau*, which, as Will Schaber, one of its former editors, later said, became "a document of a culture in exile." Or as Tekla Szymanski, another former *Aufbau* editor, put it, "It was home, helper and support— the speaking tube—for German Jews in America."[2] For formerly provincial Jews from different parts of the German-speaking world, it also helped forge a common identity.

There's no way to know how many Hitler refugees hated Germany so much, or were so embarrassed by the language, that they never went near anything published in German, but for most, *Aufbau* was a major avenue into American life. At its tenth anniversary in 1944, it had a healthy weekly circulation of over thirty thousand, with each copy, according to Ludwig Wronkow—who doubled as cartoonist and circulation manager—reaching ten people.[3] In 1946–47, with a new wave of postwar immigrants, its audited circulation would briefly reach forty-one thousand.[4] As such, it was a window into a whole generation of immigrants—or more accurately, maybe, two generations—the voice, as someone else described it "of the silent majority of the refugee middle class." Its long-time editor, Manfred George, said that the readership "sought spiritual and material shelter against the storms of the times" within *Aufbau*.[5]

In its early years, the editors, like many of their German émigré readers, were troubled by uncertainties about, and conflicts over, identity, which sometimes generated heated arguments: How German, how Jewish? How German, how American? And there were arguments about the future: a possible return to a post-Nazi Germany or a future in Palestine, as against whole-hearted Americanization; between complete assimilation into American culture or retention of a German or Jewish cultural identity, which in turn raised questions about the melting pot and conflicts between Zionists and anti-Zionists. Hannah Arendt later recalled that in the early Hitler years, Zionism seemed to some German Jews to dovetail nicely with the Nazis' efforts to get rid of them—"dissimilation" as an antidote to "assimilation." In the spring of 1933, shortly after Hitler became chancellor, the Zionist Berlin editor Robert Weltsch even urged his readers to wear the yellow Jewish star, the Mogen David, "with pride."[6] Sometimes there were *ex-post facto* recriminations from individual writers, as from Bruno Bettelheim and Raul Hilberg: if upper-class Jews hadn't been so unrealistic about assimilation in Germany, or so ready to get along, maybe they would have been more ready to resist the Nazis and help their fellow Jews before it was too late.[7]

But by the late thirties, the paper would unequivocally celebrate American ideals: democracy, religious tolerance, due process, and civil liberties. In a piece in *Aufbau*'s tenth anniversary issue in 1944, editor Manfred George wrote a "letter" to his son who was then serving in the military in Italy outlining his conviction that *Aufbau* and its readers embrace "the freedom of American society and its democratic world view, and the freedom to be what our forefathers were: sons and daughters of the Jewish people."[8] Americanization therefore was the only reasonable course for the Hitler refugees, and *Aufbau* encouraged Americanization in countless ways, not least by trying whenever possible to highlight the best of the nation. Anyone who wants to cause trouble for himself, in the words of one item on a list of "commandments for new immigrants" in 1936, need only begin a sentence with the words "in our homeland in Germany."[9] For a time *Aufbau* carried the phrase (in English, no doubt as a counter to American nativists and xenophobes) "Serving the Interests and the Americanization of the Immigrants" at the top of its front page. At the same time, it dedicated itself to "saving the values of our European past from destruction."

Hitler cannot and will not remain a symbol of Germany, wrote the German-born psychiatrist Wilfred C. Hulse, who would be a regular *Aufbau* columnist. "The time will come when German-speaking people will become ashamed of the barbarity of this regime."[10] In the meantime it was important, wrote George, who would soon be named editor, to resist the "tendency to ban the German language completely from one's consciousness and to treat it, for all intents and purposes, as if it were an enemy language."[11]

Through most of its existence, *Aufbau* was consistently mindful of the challenges facing new immigrants. There was hardly one among its readers who was not in some way beholden to *Aufbau* for help, advice, leads, or general information, wrote Steinitz, who was *Aufbau*'s editor from 1966 to 1984. And it provided a sense of community. In the first years of its existence, as Steinitz later said, "it also was virtually the only paper on earth where exiled anti-Hitler German writers could be heard."[12] Steinitz, who immigrated to the United States in 1947, said that the first time he saw the paper was when he was an inmate in the French concentration camp at Gurs in 1942. He and many of his fellow prisoners found it "a revelation."

*

Aufbau began in 1934 as the occasional newsletter of New York's German-Jewish Club, later renamed the New World Club. It evolved, first as a monthly, then fortnightly under a string of editors until in 1940, under George, born Manfred Georg Cohn, a prolific liberal journalist and theater critic in Weimar Germany and Czechoslovakia, it became a hefty, vigorous weekly tabloid.[13] George—a Zionist who had written an early biography of Theodore Herzl, had reported from the Loyalist side in the Spanish Civil War, and had been an active opponent of the Nazis before Hitler came to power—had arrived penniless in New York in 1938. He served as editor from 1939 until his death in 1965.

As the paper grew under him, its main financial support would come from its advertising and subscriptions, and its financial dependence on the Club diminished, though the Club remained its legal owner and the paper continued to run regular announcements not only for its parent organization but for Jewish clubs, synagogues, and other organizations in New York and many other U.S. cities. In 1941 it also began running a supplement every other week called "The West Coast," reflecting its growing readership in California, especially the Los Angeles area. Nonetheless, like other New Yorkers, on occasion it still regarded southern California as something of a weird place. One article headed "A Walk Through Hollywood—City without Pedestrians" said the busses, those they still had, would serve better as trash bins. The nearest thing to a big

Manfred George, *Aufbau*'s editor from 1939 to 1965. (courtesy of the Leo Baeck Institute, New York)

city in Los Angeles, *Aufbau* said, were "the mighty drug stores which over-shadow their New York colleagues . . . and whose owners are mainly film di-rectors or stars."[14] But in May 1943 it also ran an interview with the journalist and labor organizer Carey McWilliams, at the time an associate of California governor Culbert Olson and later the long-term editor of *The Nation*, headed "California—Land of the Future."[15]

From the time of his appointment, George not only built his paper but was among the many authors of the powerful and often moving essays in *Aufbau*'s pages about what was happening in Europe. Those authors were struggling with deeply troubling questions—What could we have done? What should we do now? Why, how could it have happened? What did it mean? How could the world not have known?—questions asked long before most Americans were awake to, much less cared about, the lengthening shadows overseas. What re-sponsibility did the Jews have? Could they have resisted instead of emigrating or even collaborating with the SS, as the Jewish Councils in Hungary, in their efforts to protect Jews from deportation, were later accused of?[16]

Aufbau tried to cover everything of interest to its émigré readers, from Wall Street to the Nuremberg laws, from all the aspects of immigration and natural-ization regulations to events in Europe and Palestine, much of it in signed ana-lytical essays. It was staffed primarily by émigré journalists, many of them po-litical liberals (in the American meaning of that term) from the Weimar era, but occasionally featuring pieces by other well-known immigrants, among them Albert Einstein, Hannah Arendt, Lion Feuchtwanger, Franz Werfel, Oskar Maria Graf, a socialist, who was Manfred George's brother-in-law, and the Nobel laureate in literature, Thomas Mann, probably the biggest name in Euro-pean letters of his time. Occasionally it would also run pieces by other major literary figures, among them the playwright and novelist Stefan Zweig and Franz Kafka's friend and literary executor Max Brod. Because of newsprint shortages, it reduced its type size during the war almost to the point of illegibility to cram in more copy, giving it a badly crowded look. It averaged just thirty pages in the midwar years, then climbed to a hefty forty pages on average after rationing ended, sometimes more. But despite wartime rationing, it continued to report from all the places in the United States and abroad and on all the issues it had been covering before.

Mainly *Aufbau* relied on its own staff for its news summaries and analytical pieces, on the wire services and other mainstream media for its hard news, on reports from the JTA (Jewish Telegraph Agency), and on contributions from what one editor called "volunteer co-workers" from all over the world, many of them recognized German-language journalists who recently escaped from Europe themselves or were still living there. Until the American landings in

North Africa in November 1942 prompted the German Army to occupy all of France, it often ran items on the concentration camps in the south of France where many German and Austrian Jews were imprisoned and ran appeals for help—for food, clothes, and other aid—for their inmates. Its lead story in 1942 on the Nazis' decision to strip all Jewish emigrants of their German citizenship ran under the headline "You're Not a German Anymore." (In fact, by then it was mostly old news to many refugees; Hitler had denaturalized many Jewish expatriates long before.)[17] *Aufbau* also pointed again and again to the senseless-ness of the fact that while the Nazis had denaturalized all its émigré Jewish citi-zens, once the United States entered the war in December 1941, it classified German and Austrian Jews as enemy aliens.

In *Aufbau*'s reporting agenda before VE Day, Lisbon, as the last European port from which most refugees could depart for the United States after the fall of France, was of particular interest. Additionally there were reports from else-where in Europe, and many other places abroad and from other U.S. cities, Los Angeles particularly. A lot of actors and film directors, who had been driven out of Europe by the Nazis, as many articles in *Aufbau* reported, found work in Hollywood—Weimar in Hollywood, they sometimes called it—as di-rectors, technicians, or actors playing Nazis and German officers.

Some European writers, any sort of established writers, got their immigra-tion visas by contracting with Hollywood studios for one hundred dollars a week—if you had a job, you could get a visa. After the war, the émigré literary agent Felix Guggenheim told an interviewer that every studio was persuaded to offer about ten such jobs—a good deed benefiting Hitler refugees but a poor salary by Hollywood standards, and thus a good investment for the studios as well, even if only a few ever produced a usable script. The novelist Heinrich Mann, Thomas's older brother, was one who never did.[18] Some also got help from the European Film Fund, founded by, among others, the German-born (Jewish) Hollywood actor and director Ernst Lubitsch. Most of the acting jobs would vanish after VE Day, when Hollywood stopped producing war films, but for many European movie-related and theater people Hollywood was a safe haven.[19]

Aufbau's success, said Steinitz later, was rooted in the fact that its readership shared (broadly) a common past and a common destiny. But in columns such as "From the Grapevine," it also compressed a potpourri of material from other publications (mostly credited) and tidbits of information and gossip gathered from all possible places and sources. In the later years of the war, it also ran German translations of Joseph Alsop's and Walter Lippmann's *Herald Tribune* columns. The latter was introduced to *Aufbau*'s readers as the ultimate insider in the world of politics. After the war, it carried former Interior Secretary Harold

Ickes's column "Yes and No." Sometimes *Aufbau* also ran pieces, or translations of columns, by figures such as Eleanor Roosevelt, who, because of her strong advocacy on behalf of Hitler refugees and other liberal causes, and the flurry of personal letters of congratulation she sent those who had had some significant success in America, was deservedly a great favorite in the émigré community. And, as the occasion arose, it also published commentaries by American politicians, New York officials particularly (not surprisingly), on issues dealing with immigration and the status of refugees and, when available, essays and interviews by celebrity journalists such as John Hersey.

It also published fiction on occasion, including long excerpts from new books by noted émigré writers—chapters from Franz Werfel's *April in October* and, in forty-three weekly installments, much of Lion Feuchtwanger's novel *The Day Will Come*, the final volume in a trilogy about (in Feuchtwanger's telling) the historian Josephus's Roman-Jewish identity conflict. It published poems in almost every issue, many by well-known German and Austrian émigré writers such as Ernst Waldinger, and sometimes more than one, including some in English (and at least one, Waldinger's "I Saw Vienna Lovely in the Moonlight," in which some lines were in German and some in English). It ran excerpts from memoirs such as Anna Freud's *Recollections of My Brother Sigmund Freud*. That, too, was a sign of its commitment to keeping alive "a culture in exile."

And so, of course, was its decision, the war and the Nazis notwithstanding, to publish the paper mostly in German, with occasional pieces in English at first, and, as the war reduced the flow of new arrivals in 1942–44 and as its readers Americanized, more later, including, among other English-language features, Art Buchwald's columns and Herblock's political cartoons. (Sometimes the heads were in English and the stories in German.) More telling, maybe, pieces that sought to resist American nativism—reports on the low numbers of immigrants coming to America, for example, or one headed "Roosevelt Lauds Patriotism of Jews"—were often in English.

And it regularly covered and reviewed books, plays, films, concerts, and opera, especially those by refugee writers or that, like Lillian Hellman's play *Watch on the Rhine*, were on subjects that had a particular relevance to its readers. By the time of World War II, American concert halls were famously associated with the names of European Jewish artists—Horowitz, Schnabel, Rubinstein, Heifetz, Walter—and with the names of anti-fascist gentiles, like Toscanini, who had also fled Europe, so the performances at Carnegie Hall, the Metropolitan Opera House on 39th Street, and the 92nd Street Y were often doubly relevant.

Aufbau was hardly the only German-language paper in America, much less the only foreign-language paper. There were hundreds—French, Spanish,

Italian, Polish. One of the nation's great newspaper chains, Knight-Ridder, began as a nineteenth-century German-language paper. (In the 1930s, before the war, there was also a roughly similar anti-Nazi paper for German-speaking exiles in France, the *Pariser Tageblatt*, some of whose writers, Oskar Maria Graf among them, were later associated with *Aufbau*. The Parisian paper folded at the start of the war in 1939, when the French interned many of its staff.)[20] Through the war years, in the *Jewish Way*, *Aufbau* also had a direct, aggressive competitor in New York's Washington Heights, which asserted that it was more faithfully Jewish.

Nor was *Aufbau* ever as large as the *Forverts*, the *Jewish Daily Forward*, the Yiddish-language democratic-socialist paper that, though down from its halcyon era a decade before, still had a daily circulation in 1939 of over 150,000, most of them immigrants and children of immigrants from the great era of immigration between the 1890s and the 1920s. But the editors of *Aufbau* uniquely committed their paper to the integration into American society and culture of the Hitler refugees, in many respects a very different class of people from the *Forward*'s readership. It also served as a German-Jewish hometown paper to thousands of exiles, not only in New York, where the largest number settled, but in Los Angeles and in countless other places both in the United States and abroad to which this twentieth-century diaspora had scattered. The death notice in 1948 for one Kurt Rosenberg—one of the thousands of such notices that relatives bought in the pages of the paper—listed relatives in New York City; Cape Town; Buenos Aires; Mexico City; Batavia, New York; and Haifa. Another for Ilona Klaber, formerly of Vienna, listed loved ones in Hartford; Forest Hills; Los Angeles; Kensington, Maryland; Vienna; and rural France. One writer reported admiringly from Sacramento, California, where he found twelve German immigrant families comprising some forty people. In 1942 it got a letter from a man named Leo Bauer who was about to be commissioned a second lieutenant in the Army at Fort Sill, Oklahoma, and who asked the paper to publish his news. Ordinarily, he said, the Army notified the individual's hometown paper of the new commission but, Bauer said, as a refugee he had no other hometown paper. There must have been many like him.[21]

As the "hometown" paper to Hitler refugees, *Aufbau* ran a regular feature, headed "Looking For," which comprised small classified ads placed by émigrés looking for relatives lost in the chaos of the war and later others newly liberated from the concentration camps—for example, "Eidinger, Nathan and Bertha (formerly of Vienna) by Heide Weil-Fluss, 155-01 90th Ave., Jamaica, L.I., N.Y." Often the ads were placed by people in one part of the world (Shanghai or Capetown or Mexico City) looking for friends or relatives in another. Many appear to have been successful. One such notice, *Aufbau* reported, brought

answers from Brooklyn, Johannesburg, and Auckland, New Zealand. Until the
Germans occupied southern France at the end of 1942, *Aufbau* also ran lists—
twenty-three according to one count—of prisoners in the French concentration camps and, later, long lists of the names—hundreds of them—of those
who had been deported from them, among them mothers with their young
children, all presumably to the Nazi death camps in the East. For some indication of the numbers, on the fourth list of deportees from the French camp at
Gurs *Aufbau* published on December 4, 1942, there were twenty Levis or Levys.
Next to it was a partial list of deportees from Rivesaltes. It included one Blum,
three Blumenfelds, one Blumenheim, one Blumstein, one Blumenstein, and
two Blumstejns. By the time those lists appeared, the industrialized genocide
that would become known as the Holocaust was well under way. But few in
America then knew of it.

Toward the end of the war and well after, in addition to many stories about
the liberation of the camps, it ran the names of thousands of people who were
liberated from them. An *Aufbau* headline in March 1945 about the efficiency of
the Red Cross in finding places for newly liberated internees inadvertently reflected the magnitude of the horrors: "Only thirteen thousand Jews," it said,
"still in Theresienstadt." The liberation then generated yet another kind of
search list: refugees in America, Palestine, France, and South America looking
for friends or relatives who had been deported by the Nazis, listing the places
they had been deported to. Since the lists ran after the camps had been liberated
at the end of the war, they probably served more as memorials than reflections
of the hope that people such as Moses and Frieda Toch, formerly of Vienna, or
Hilda Frank (née Nussbaum) and her son Lajos, formerly of Miskolc, who had
been deported to Auschwitz, could be found alive. In December 1945, not long
after one of those lists appeared, U.S. prosecutors submitted it as evidence at
the War Crimes trial in Nuremberg. And beginning in 1947, *Aufbau* also ran
requests from survivors looking for witnesses to testify and people who had evidence against individual perpetrators of crimes in the concentration camps.
Among the more macabre documents sought was a sixtieth birthday album for
Hermann Schmitz, the CEO of I.G. Farben, with photos of the company's
slave labor installation at Auschwitz.

✳

In the years before Pearl Harbor, there were ads for shipping lines and other
travel services running ships from the declining number of European ports
where refugees might be able to embark to the places to which they might still
have a chance to go: Cuba, the Dominican Republic, Mexico, Argentina,

South Africa, Shanghai, and Palestine. In June 1939, a travel agency calling it-self "the official authorized agent" advertised "Emigration from Europe through Russia via Trans-Siberian Train to Vladivostok, and then to Japan and North and South America." The next summer, there was a lengthy ac-count of one such trip—a nine-day rail journey from Berlin through Russia, then by ship to Yokohama, another ship to Seattle, then by bus to New York.[22]

Aufbau ran articles on the U.S. labor movement—here the big unions, it said, were not part of the political party organizations. It translated German idioms into American expressions ("Take it or leave it," "Nuts to you"), ran vocabulary lists and phonetic tips on American pronunciation, and defined commonplace American facts and expressions—what was a nickel, two bits, a hot dog? It ran lists of guided "behind the scenes . . . tours and trips (around New York) introducing newcomers to America and the American Way": in-cluding parks; Hunter College and other local campuses; one to Harlem, "New York's Negro Quarter," and another to the Savoy in Harlem, "Birthplace of renowned black dances like the Lindy Hop." (In those days, notwithstanding *Aufbau*'s discovery of "Negro Jews in Harlem,"[23] it was always more a local curiosity or maybe a place for some vaguely exotic entertainment than a neigh-borhood where real people lived and worked.)

There were excursions to the Metropolitan Museum of Art, local high schools, the Astor and the Waldorf Astoria Hotel, men's night court, the Brook-lyn Borough Gas Works, Rikers Island prison, the Jacob Ruppert Brewery and Kraft Cheese Factory in New Jersey, the newsroom of the *New York Herald Tribune*, the offices of Western Union (at the time "the world's largest telegraph facility"), Bloomingdale's Department Store (then catering to a more modest class of shoppers than the upscale clientele it serves now), "Scenic Staten Island," LaGuardia Airport to watch planes (most of them two-engine DC-3s) land and take off, and historical monuments and other local landmarks. And often there were weekend excursions to the attractions of the region, such as "Wir fahren in die Bear Mountains."[24]

Aufbau urged readers to walk across the Triborough Bridge and take in the Manhattan skyline, announced lectures and tours, among them a talk featuring Albert Einstein at Princeton University. It also ran weekly lists of services at more than a dozen New York synagogues, as well as many other items from the Hebrew calendar. And for a time during the war years, it ran a fortnightly section, "The Jewish World," devoted "to the knowledge and study of Judaism." It listed sporting events sponsored by its parent organization, the New World Club—mainly hikes in the country, soccer, gymnastics, swimming, track, bowling, and Ping-Pong—as well as bridge, chess, bingo, and skat tourna-ments.[25] It ran ads for excursion cruises and dinner dances on tour boats around Manhattan Island. It explained the workings of the New York subway system (the fare, a nickel, which went up to a dime in 1948), listed German-speaking physicians and nurses, and gave guidance on filling out income tax returns. Its regular women's page offered everything from advice on proper lady-like behavior—be a giver, not a taker (not stuff that would pass muster today)—and some predictable reporting on department store events displaying new lines of clothes, accessories, and jewelry. One piece was headed "Easter Parade in the Clothes Closet." There were leads on where women could sign up to become civil defense volunteers, postwar appeals for care packages to Europe, and shrewd insights into the key role that women played in American cultural life. In America, wrote Vera Craener, who for many years ran the women's page, it's the women who sustain that cultural life, much of it through college courses and afternoon appearances by circuit-riding guest lecturers at women's clubs, a time, presumably, when their husbands were at the office. Culture was women's business. (On occasion, Craener would also celebrate the families of earlier German-Jewish immigrants, such as the philanthropist Julius Rosenwald, part owner of Sears Roebuck, whose father arrived in 1854 and began life in America as a peddler.)[26]

There were many articles outlining the requirements and explaining the tight quotas set by the Immigration Act of 1924.[27] On January 1, 1939, it reported there were 234,000 applicants for the 27,000 places in that year's German quota (counting Austrian and Czech Jews). The number waiting for visas later that year exceeded 300,000. In July, a front-page item (in English and obviously directed at the complaints that refugees were flooding the country) headed "The Truth About Refugee Immigration" pointed out what would become a big black eye for the United States in later years, the insouciance that historian David S. Wyman would call "The Abandonment of the Jews":[28] that immigration restrictionists at the State Department never admitted more than a fraction of the Hitler refugees that even the already-tight quotas allowed. On the basis of the official records of the U.S. Immigration and Naturalization Service, *Aufbau* reported, in the six years since Hitler became chancellor in 1933, "the quota laws permitted an immigration of 922,444, whereas only 241,962 were admitted for permanent residence, about 26 percent of the quota allowance."[29] America's historic pride as a nation of immigrants—the welcome on the Statue of Liberty—would become an embarrassment in the twentieth century.

Other pieces on immigration regulations and the naturalization process explained how to get what were called "first papers," the formal declaration of an individual who had been in the country for two years on an immigration visa of his intention to become a citizen, how to fill out visa and naturalization applications, how to secure documents for friends and relatives still abroad, and where to get the registration cards that every alien was required to file. After the declaration of war in 1941, it provided information on the lengthy questionnaire that all German, Italian, and Japanese noncitizen residents, including the Jews who had been denaturalized by the Nazis, needed to register as enemy aliens. They then got a registration card they were required to carry at all times identifying them as an "Alien of Enemy Nationality." (And of all ironies, shortly after the war, the Army and Air Force ran ads—in German—in *Aufbau*, seeking veterans wanting to re-enlist.)

Aufbau's thousands of ads may have been as indicative of who the readers were and what they needed as was its editorial content: ads for accountants, lawyers, beauty salons, drug stores specializing in familiar European remedies, watch and radio repairmen, menders of men's shirts, shipping lines, travel agencies, language schools, driving schools, nursing schools, dancing schools ("Waltz, Foxtrot, Peabody, Rhumba, Tango, Conga, Lindy Hop"), translation services, car dealers, movers and truckers, optometrists, exterminators, typewriter repair shops, dealers in second-hand sewing machines and vacuum cleaners, camera shops and stamp dealers (buy or sell), art dealers and antiquarians, and dealers in foreign books—such as Adler's on West 47th Street, Gerard J. Fuchs on Broadway at 72nd Street, and Friedrich Krause (German books) on West 177th Street.

The ranks of *Aufbau* advertisers also included dealers in Oriental rugs and in Meissen and other quality china (buy or sell again), vendors of shoe inlays for flat feet, currency exchanges, upholstery repair and slipcover refitting, seamstresses, and furriers—where to buy a mink coat or sell one—some of them working in shops, others out of their homes. Among the typewriter repair shops was Osner Business Machines on Amsterdam at 79th Street in Manhattan, begun by one concentration camp survivor and then run by another, which, as one of the last of its kind—it closed in 2001—serviced the typewriters of a long list of literary celebrities, from Isaac Bashevis Singer and Erich Maria Remarque to Philip Roth and Joseph Heller. Its last owner, Mary Adelman, died in 2017.[30] Part of the story of that first generation was illustrated in those little businesses, as well as the many who were trying to sell the treasures they managed to bring with them.

Also part of the story was the hard work of fitting in while still holding on to something of the past. "Americanize yourself," said an *Aufbau* ad from Richard Lippmann tailors. "Also your wardrobe."[31] At about the same time, *Aufbau* ran a piece headed (in English) "Swim American" that urged its readers to learn the crawl—the breaststroke favored by Europeans was slower and harder to learn (and in any case, though the ad didn't say so, embarrassingly European).[32] By the end of the war, a restaurant on the West Side that claimed "First class Viennese and Hungarian cuisine" also advertised a "Special Thanksgiving Turkey Dinner" (in English) for $1.75. Coffee and sweet shops such as Café Vienna on West 77th Street and the Éclair on 72nd Street, boasting genuine Viennese pastry on New York's West Side, advertised regularly. As one sign of assimilation, *Aufbau* would later carry recipes, complete with a detailed calorie count, for the Thanksgiving Day turkey dinner: "Truthahnbraten zum Thanksgiving Day."[33]

*

Among the other regulars in *Aufbau*'s advertising columns were children's summer camps with "American counselors" and language lessons, and summer hotels in Fleischmanns, New York, and elsewhere in the Catskills and at Lake Placid that catered to refugees, with waiters, clerks, bellboys, and other help who spoke German. Sometimes ads for a dressmaker, a watch repairman, or a bakery would list the European city where the proprietor had his or her previous establishment. Leo Bauer, who proclaimed himself the founder of the German zipper industry in Saxony, and later in Prague, was now doing business as Victor Slide Fastener, Corp. at 1170 Broadway. Auto Cappel, "Ford dealer since 1908," now selling new and used cars in Queens, advertised he had previously been in business in Düsseldorf, Aachen, and Krefeld. Prior to the war (and, of course, before Castro) there would be travel service ads for tours to Miami and Havana, eighty-nine dollars for four days.

There were long columns of classified ads for apartments and furnished rooms to sublet, and ads seeking skilled workers of one kind or another, or seeking jobs or business opportunities, as well as for domestic help. After the war— and occasionally before—the back pages were crammed with ads placed by commercial outfits that would ship almost anything—food, cigarettes, clothing, nylons, shoes—to Germany, France, Austria, or Hungary. A package of butter, sugar, coffee, cocoa, honey, canned ham and bacon, and condensed milk (depending on quantity) would cost anywhere between twelve and thirty dollars (the equivalent of roughly three hundred dollars today). And later that list would include kosher food to Israel—and still later refrigerators and other household appliances.

One frequent advertiser was a Park Avenue psychiatrist named Arnold Hutschnecker, a refugee from Vienna and passionate critic of Hitler when he was still there, who touted the beauty and comfort of his European-style country sanatorium. Later Hutschnecker would be consulted by Richard Nixon—it was never clear for what ailment—and after Nixon was in the White House urged him in a famous leaked memo to create a program to test young boys for violent or homicidal tendencies and, if they had such tendencies, to send them to camps for treatment. His sense of irony appears to have been fatally underdeveloped.

And then there was the North American Travel League, Inc., which in early 1941 offered everything: passage on ships from Lisbon to North America (always provided that the passenger had the visa and other necessary documents), food packages to England and Gurs, money transfers and information on immigration to South America. Gurs, the huge concentration camp in southwest France, where thousands of Jews, Arendt for a time among them, were interned, became a particular subject of concern to many U.S. immigrants. Groups of émigrés ran advertisements in *Aufbau* soliciting funds to help the Quakers feed the internees in "the hell of Gurs" and the children interned in the French camp at Rivesaltes.[34] After the French surrender in 1940, *Aufbau* collected what information it could on the conditions at the Vichy French internment camps, observing in one piece that the good intentions of some camp commandants was nullified by their powerlessness.[35] One article reported that the Vichy French offered to release any Gurs prisoner for whom someone would guarantee a minimum of twelve hundred francs, roughly twenty-four dollars, a month in support. It wasn't quite like a ransom, but close enough.[36] Another reported that the Swiss were allowing the monthly transfer of 550 French francs per person to prisoners at Gurs. Another said the French would release anyone who had fifteen thousand francs, roughly three hundred dollars at the time, in a Vichy French bank.[37]

Feuchtwanger, the popular German-Jewish novelist in Europe, who, with the help of the American Varian Fry and the New York–based Emergency Rescue Committee, escaped from one of those French internment camps, acknowledged after his arrival in the United States in 1941 that because he had money to buy food and other necessities, and even to hire other prisoners as servants, life in his camps was not all that uncomfortable. But he knew that he was an exception.[38] In 1964, as part of a "Baden Evening," where many Gurs inmates came from, the New World Club held a commemorative ceremony for those who died in Gurs. One of the speakers was the mayor of Karlsruhe.

*

Inevitably, *Aufbau* analyzed and reported on the conditions in Europe. Long before the United States entered the war, the paper became a cheerleader for the battle against Hitler. It leveled sharp attacks on Hitler sympathizers, American isolationists such as Charles Lindbergh and anti-Semites, often inviting respected outsiders—New York District Attorney Tom Dewey, journalist Dorothy Thompson, even the jingoist publisher William Randolph Hearst—to fire the shots. It warned about Nazi agents and propaganda in the United States, sought to persuade its readers, some of them still skeptical in the late thirties, that the stories about Nazi atrocities were true, and tried to organize help for the Jews who were still in Germany. That touched on troubling prewar questions, often raised in letters to the paper: If the west boycotted Germany, as many were proposing, wouldn't it also damage Jews and other anti-Nazis who were still there? And if a Jewish paper like *Aufbau* attacked Hitler, a few readers asked, wouldn't that prompt the Nazis to attack Jews in Europe even more savagely? *Aufbau* flatly rejected those complaints. The only way to help the Jews of Europe was through the defeat of Hitler. "The tragic fate of the Central and Eastern European Jews," wrote *Aufbau* columnist Wilfred Hulse, "cannot be ameliorated by treating National Socialism lightly and by glossing over or covering up its crimes."[39] With Pearl Harbor, those all became moot questions.

Perhaps sensitive to the possibility of an anti-Semitic backlash against "warmongering Jews," *Aufbau* avoided any call for direct American military involvement in Europe until the United States officially began to move away from its policy of strict neutrality. But by the spring of 1940, after the Germans invaded Belgium, Holland, and Luxemburg, the paper was unequivocal in its calls for American aid to the Allies. The only fear was that if war came, the U.S. would intern all Germans as enemy aliens, as Britain had briefly done—and as the U.S. would do with the Japanese after Pearl Harbor. That same spring it published a piece headed "Refugees, Not a Fifth Column."[40] And while it carefully avoided taking sides in domestic partisan politics, it left little doubt that it was a strong supporter of FDR and the Democrats and in making clear that the issue was one of freedom against dictatorship, especially after the German sweep through northern Europe and the fall of France and after it reported on the internment of tens of thousands of German Jews in Belgium. The safety of the Jews required an Allied victory, though even that was not sufficient. Only when Europe's Jews had a place of their own would it be assured.[41]

The next year, when Pearl Harbor and the ensuing German declaration of war formally made the exiles' enemy America's enemy, *Aufbau* published a new "Statement of Policy" (in English) loaded with stars-and-stripes rhetoric that oriented the paper more emphatically toward the American future and less to the past of European culture. The whole front page of its tenth-anniversary edition in 1944 was a drawing of the Statue of Liberty and a quote from the

Emma Lazarus poem ("Give me your tired, your poor / Your huddled masses") on the pedestal under it.

Aufbau's editors greatly admired Roosevelt, despite his unwillingness to try to loosen America's tight immigration quotas at a time when hundreds of thousands were trying escape from Hitler, and notwithstanding the paper's strong protests against the government's ongoing wartime classification of German-Jewish immigrants as enemy aliens. Eleanor Roosevelt probably was much more sympathetic to Hitler's refugees than her husband was—and even better liked—but that didn't keep the paper from running a Thomas Mann paean to the man who had become a hero to its readers when he died or from marking the anniversary of FDR's death for many years after 1945. In 1946, 1947, and 1948, hundreds of people made pilgrimages to Roosevelt's grave in Hyde Park sponsored by *Aufbau* and the New World Club. *Aufbau* also took note of the fact that in Jerusalem the chief rabbis said Kaddish for FDR, one of the rare occasions, the story noted, when the prayer of mourning was said for a non-Jew.[42] In 1950, it serialized, in thirteen installments, a German translation of Roosevelt's long-time secretary Grace Tully's memoir of "the great president."[43] Even in the paper's declining years, the pictures of its three iconic figures still hung in its offices at 2121 Broadway: Einstein, Mann, and Roosevelt.

But despite the war, and all the attention the paper was giving it, it had to negotiate through its divided American/Jewish/German sensibilities and those of many of its readers. Though formally dedicating itself to the cause of all central European émigrés, not just Jews (which almost necessarily meant German-speakers), it devoted considerable space to Jewish events in New York, the Jewish calendar, and other items dealing with Jewish issues. It campaigned consistently against anti-Semitism in America, often through pieces by non-Jewish writers, and after the war, in Europe. That also required addressing, often through sharp debates on its pages, the old biases of German Jews against the *Ostjuden*—the Eastern, mostly Polish and Russian, Jews—(and often the reverse), reaching out to their organizations and publications, and trying to reconcile "estranged brothers," efforts that weren't always successful. There were the familiar questions about the dangers of Jewish conversions, apostasy, and intermarriage. And there were the endless unresolved questions about what should follow—in Germany and Europe, in Palestine, in the possible return of refugees from America—when the Nazis were gone.

The end of the war made it possible for *Aufbau*—though still relying on reports from news agencies, returning travelers, letters, and refugee military people abroad—to appoint new correspondents, many of them refugees themselves, in Amsterdam, Paris, Ankara, Tel Aviv, Vienna, and elsewhere overseas, and to greatly expand its coverage of events both in Europe and in the

Middle East. It also saw it as a business opportunity: to enlarge its circulation abroad and become not only an "American Jewish organ but also to expand into the liberated countries." In that effort it invited readers to name acquaintances overseas who might become subscribers. That, too, seemed to reflect its belief in its essential role as the heart of what it regarded a widespread closely knit community. (It was widespread, but sometimes not so closely knit.) At the same time, it continued its mission to instruct readers in American history, ways, and culture. In an article in April 1943, the bicentennial of Jefferson's birth, it noted (in English) that American Jewry has a special reason for taking an active part in the observance of "the father of religious liberty in America."[44] In 1951, it ran a translation of Dale Carnegie's biography, *The Unknown Lincoln*, in fifteen installments.

★

Aufbau's prewar attacks on the Nazis differentiated it from the long-established *New Yorker Staats-Zeitung und Herold* with its older German-American (largely Aryan) readers, which, until the coming of the war, vacillated between defense of Germany as a "friendly nation" and condemnation of the Nazi persecution of Jews. In December 1935, *Aufbau*'s editors prided themselves on the fact that the Nazis had banned their paper in Germany. The *Staats-Zeitung*, they pointed out, had never been so honored. In the prewar years, they missed few opportunities to hammer the *Staats*.

Almost necessarily, *Aufbau* straddled the line between, on the one hand, the old-world culture and the nostalgia of its immigrant readers and, on the other, their need and often their eagerness to Americanize as quickly as possible and its mission to help them do it. Those who were recently naturalized took enormous pride in their new American citizenship. So beginning in 1943, *Aufbau* began running an occasional feature called "Our New Citizens," naming the recently naturalized. (When my mother's cousin Trudel was naturalized, I recall her proudly telling friends that the policeman on the street was now *her* policeman.) This was a generation that prided itself on becoming and being Americans. And the paper itself never left any doubt about which side of the line it was on. In the summer of 1940, Hulse devoted a piece headed "Homesickness" to the democratic system and the natural beauty of the immigrants' new country. He wrote about a drive through the Smoky Mountains, Virginia, and the Carolinas, and visits to national parks that, because of the care of the government, were made accessible even to people who had to watch their pennies. And then, on the car radio on his way home, he heard a conversation about democracy between Eleanor Roosevelt and two new young citizens, one from Italy and one from Germany. "Sun and woods and freedom and space for all,"

Hulse concluded. "Where else in the world could you find all this? He who doesn't learn to love this land doesn't deserve to be here."[45] It was all so hokey and wonderful, too. Yes, one letter said, "many of us were homesick, but anyone's who's not homesick will never learn to love this country."[46]

And just as necessarily, the paper would address the vexing question of what should happen to Germany after the defeat of Hitler, including pieces by Mann, Arendt, the prolific biographer Emil Ludwig (born Emil Cohn), and the Lutheran theologian Paul Tillich, also a refugee from Hitler. Would the Germans who had so enthusiastically supported Hitler ever be able to become citizens of a democratic state? And, as might be expected, there was much discussion—in the pages of *Aufbau* as elsewhere—about how Germany should be governed after the war, some of it acrimonious, about who should be tried as a war criminal, and how broadly to define the term. Most *Aufbau* readers, judging by their letters, favored a very broad definition. Some distinguished Jewish émigrés became personally engaged in addressing those questions, among them the highly regarded constitutional scholar Karl Loewenstein, who was teaching at Amherst and served as an advisor on de-Nazification to the American Military Government (AMG) in Germany after the war. Others worked for the AMG in the German de-Nazification process.

From time to time in the later years of the war, *Aufbau* published pieces from émigrés in the U.S. military who had returned to Europe as soldiers with the invading Allied armies, sometimes as officers, to the country they had fled not many years before, and talked about how they could never have imagined such a moment when they traveled the same routes in their flight from the Nazis. In 1943, five years after he arrived in America, at the time as fifteen-year-old Heinz Kissinger, Henry Kissinger would be among them, going back to Germany as an Army rifleman. There, according to his commanding officer, Sergeant Kissinger's "exceptional knowledge of the German people and his linguistic ability enabled him to capture many high ranking Nazi officials, including at least a dozen Gestapo agents."[47] But in assimilating, Sergeant Kissinger would be no more able to break the embrace of *Realpolitik* than he could shed his German accent.

Well before the end of the war, even before the full picture of the Holocaust began to emerge, *Aufbau* had resolved its uncertainty about Zionism and the importance of creating a Jewish homeland in Palestine. The Holocaust also prompted the paper to call for enlarging the American immigration quotas with even more urgency to allow admission of thousands of displaced people in Europe to the United States, many of them concentration camp survivors, a course fiercely resisted by the anti-Semites in the State Department and by many members of Congress. When one member of the Senate warned that many displaced persons (DPs) were Jews from Eastern Europe and thus might be communists, *Aufbau*'s editorial caustically suggested that the senator seemed to regret that they'd survived the Nazi terror.

Everything that had happened in the Nazi era seemed to make the creation of a Jewish state a moral imperative. *Aufbau* devoted a great deal of space to the issue in the years immediately after the war, when the millions in European DP camps, some not much better than the German concentration camps in which they'd been imprisoned not long before, made the need all the greater. There was intense coverage of the debates in Britain, the reports of one commission after another, and the hearings at the United Nations: Should there be a new Jewish homeland? Should Palestine be partitioned between Jews and Arabs and, if so, how soon? Or (a still unsettled question) should Palestine become a single binational Jewish-Arab state? There was the bombing of the King David Hotel and other terrorist acts by Irgun terrorists and the terrorism of the Stern Gang and other Jewish militants; there were the unauthorized landings of hundreds of Jews from rickety ships on the coast of Palestine and the ensuing British blockade. "There is no illegal immigration into Erez Israel," George wrote in November 1945. "It is a return of Jews to the land of their fathers."[48] By the time the British seized the ship *Exodus* with its forty-five hundred passengers in July 1947, the eventual outcome of the debates about Palestine seemed all but certain, but the ensuing drama and the symbolism of Whitehall's bizarre decision to send its passengers back to Europe and intern them in Germany pretty much clinched it. On May 14, 1948, following violent Arab resistance and facing attacks from all its Arab neighbors, and overcoming the U.S. State Department's opposition, mainly over oil—in one piece George called it "The Dance Around the Oil Barrel"—Israel proclaimed itself an independent nation. President Truman formally recognized it the same day.

Aufbau devoted ten pages to celebrating Israel's founding in 1948 behind the front-page head "The Great Goal: Rebirth of the Jewish Nation."[49] But it marked Israel's decisive victory in June 1967 in the Six Day War with caution. It was a victory—"their finest hour," which "shook the world"—and it generated enormous pride among Jews everywhere—and maybe some sense of closure for Europe's émigré Jews. No one, *Aufbau* said, quoting *The Economist*, "who witnessed the events of the past week can question the maturity, competence and passion for life of this people." It also ran columnist Max Lerner's piece of admiration for Israelis' skills, courage, and sense of duty. But as the paper pointed out, Israel was not out of danger. Its headline a week later summarized it: "After the Blitzkrieg, no Blitzpeace." Already the Arabs, "behaving as if they'd been the winners, not shameful losers," had launched a diplomatic offensive. "The peace process [in the understatement of all understatements] will be long and complicated."[50] The end of combat was not the end of Israel's crisis. As it turned out, it was not even the end of combat.

The paper also ran a great deal about the Eichmann Trial, about the failure of Pope Pius XII and the Vatican to vigorously oppose the Nazis, and about the alleged collaboration with the Nazis of great artists such as the symphony conductor Wilhelm Furtwängler, who, though he helped Jews and was never a Nazi, continued to conduct at Nazi functions in Germany, as well as the pianist Walter Gieseking. As his de-Nazification hearings were in progress, *Aufbau* ran two long pieces on the Furtwängler case, one an excerpt from the conductor's defense (he said he was trying to preserve Bach, Beethoven, Mozart, and other German high culture), the other by the poet Fritz von Unruh, which ended with a telling quote from St. John: "He who does no more than greet the devil participates in his evil work."[51] The panel's decision, allowing Furtwängler to resume his post at the Berlin Philharmonic, was essentially political, similar to the decision lifting the ban on the other great German conductor Hebert von Karajan, who was a Nazi. It was never about Furtwängler's compromising behavior. The Russians had offered him a post in the East Zone. The Americans wanted his prestige in West Berlin.[52]

Aufbau also devoted many pages to the postwar restitution of Jewish rights, including pensions for jobs lost through Nazi decrees and expropriated property. For a time after the war, *Aufbau* ran a column every other week about German reparations—the *Wiedergutmachung*. And it wondered whether Germany's "renewal" in the first years after the war was, as one head suggested, "a fairytale." Most of its readers of that time would probably have agreed that it was.

Aufbau attained its greatest readership, and possibly its most important functions, with the arrival of the camp survivors and other displaced persons—and later a wave of refugees from Eastern Europe—after the war. When the first shipload of Holocaust survivors arrived in New York in May 1946, *Aufbau*, under a front-page headline "Welcome to Freedom," ran column after column of personal stories of narrow escapes and lost loved ones, and photos, including one on the front page of a grim-faced mother and young daughter showing the Auschwitz tattoos on their arms. There was another on the same page of happier people still on the ship holding copies of *Aufbau*, which, the caption said, they had already become familiar with in postwar Berlin. *Aufbau*'s editors were hardly the first journalists to crow a little.

Those were the years when the full extent and horror of the Holocaust was first confronted—the years of the Nuremberg trials (1945–46), which *Aufbau* covered in great detail, including much verbatim trial testimony,[53] and later again the Eichmann Trial (1961)—and to which it devoted many columns of sharp debate about the scope of culpability. Was the prime purpose at

Nuremberg to exact justice or to impress on the Germans the magnitude of the crimes that had been committed in their name and, implicitly, with their consent? Where did culpability end? It ran many articles, including one by the German psychiatrist-philosopher Karl Jaspers (one of Arendt's teachers at Heidelberg and, after the war, her close friend) on the importance, rightness, and impact of the Nuremberg trials—would they end German militarism?— and of the new concept of "crimes against humanity." It campaigned intensively for compensation and restitution of rights and property to the victims of Europe, something that continues to be an issue to this day. It ran many pieces about the shortcomings of the AMG in the years immediately after the war and the failings of the de-Nazification process, which allowed too many Nazi-era officials, judges among them, to again take official positions.

When the American authorities turned the task over to the Germans themselves, *Aufbau* said it became "a farce." In one story published four years after VE Day, it counted hundreds of mayors and other local officials who were former Nazis. The story didn't make clear who did the count or what definitions were used, but there can't be much doubt that many ex-Nazis occupied those posts. There was, in those early postwar years, no one else to do it.[54] At about the same time, *Aufbau* was also among the first to call attention to what it called the "sins of omission" of the International Red Cross for its wartime failure to be more vigorous in helping the Jews in the concentration camps and in reporting on their condition, as it had with prisoners in some other wars.[55]

Like most Jewish refugees from Hitler in the first years after the war, *Aufbau* was not comfortable with the effort to establish an economically revived and (ultimately) remilitarized Germany as a bulwark against the Soviets. And like many, it faced a dilemma about the Marshall Plan when it was first proposed: Support it as Americans, or simply as good humanitarians, to get Europe back on its feet, aid millions of desperate people, and reduce conditions that might allow the Russians to dominate Germany? Or oppose it as Jews because it provided aid to a country deserving punishment and still full of Nazis? By the mid-1950s, as the prospering new German democracy developed, the fear of resurgent Nazism had somewhat abated (and *Aufbau* became a strong backer of the Marshall Plan) despite the continued existence of neo-Nazi groups and continuing waves of anti-Semitic events. But in the rubble of 1946, 1947, and 1948, the old shadows still loomed. *Aufbau* occasionally carried stories about conscientious Germans who protected Jews in the Nazi years, sometimes at considerable personal risk—in one case saving and protecting the Torah and other precious items from a synagogue. But even decades after the war, a lot of German émigrés, like a lot of other Jews, wanted to have nothing to do with Germany ever again.

If *Aufbau*'s pages were any measure, its postwar readership, bolstered by the new wave of immigrants, allowed *Aufbau* to enjoy two or three prosperous decades, running into the 1970s. Through those decades its readership, perhaps predictably, was becoming more economically and socially comfortable. Many had settled into better jobs—a reflection both of their own rise and of the growing U.S. economy—moved to the suburbs, and became citizens. The ads, now for TV sets and air conditioners, were pitched to higher incomes. The ratio of houses for sale in Queens and beach cottages on Long Island to furnished rooms for rent on the Upper West Side had increased markedly; there were ads for Jewish restaurants in Brussels and hotels in London.

Yet by the early 1980s, as its immigrant readership became acculturated and moved into the mainstream, or died, and as thousands of other institutions proliferated—the establishment of Brandeis as a Jewish university in 1948, the same year as the founding of Israel, and the creation of new Jewish day schools, synagogues, and countless new social service agencies—and as the things that it had once uniquely provided gradually ceased to matter as much, *Aufbau* inevitably began to shrink. Some Jewish exiles moved to Israel; some, such as Mann, Marc Chagall, and Bertolt Brecht, went back to Europe; others, who were less successful, returned to Germany or Austria to try to reclaim the businesses and other property that had been aryanized under Hitler.

To survive, *Aufbau* tried various devices to broaden its readership, including a misconceived "Young People's Column." It solicited voluntary contributions from grateful former readers to supplement its dwindling income. But eventually it succumbed to its own success. The Americanized children of immigrants, as the magazine *Fortune* noted, "seldom read their parents' native language" and for the most part had moved beyond their parents' world. After it died in 2004, it was taken over by JM Jüdische Medien AG, a Jewish media company in Zurich, which published it as *Aufbau: The Jewish Monthly Magazine*, a left-leaning, beautifully illustrated periodical that ran compelling articles, some in German and some in English, on a broad range of global issues. Most recently, its contents ranged from articles about the revival of Histadrut, the confederation of Israeli labor unions, to one about presidential candidate Bernie Sanders in 2016 reintroducing social democracy to American politics, to the civil war in Syria and the European refugee crisis.

✱

The *Aufbau* community, the mostly Jewish German-speaking immigrants who arrived in the half century after 1933, was often fractious, with countless class, ethnic, religious, and cultural divisions, people who came from a great spectrum of places and backgrounds and thus constituted a melting pot within a melting pot. From time to time they held their own separate events — "*Zusammentreffen*" of Jews from Austria, or from Baden or Bavaria, with song recitals and poetry readings followed by old-home schmoozing (maybe just to hear familiar accents). Churchill famously said that wherever you come on three Poles, you will find two prime ministers and one leader of the opposition. That could as easily have applied to the often-disputatious émigré Jews (and maybe was so intended). There were events like the "Austrian Weekend in Boston," a two-day bus trip for $11.85 sponsored by a group called "Austrian Action," and an evening at the YMHA on "Forbidden Art" — talks on and performances of Felix Mendelssohn, Gustav Mahler, Karl Krauss, and other composers and writers banned by the Nazis.

From the start, however, it left no doubt about its nature as a publication addressed to Jews, listing synagogue services and holiday events and, soon, ads for competing temple services: For the high holidays in September 1939, there was a piece by a rabbi headed "Are you still firm in your beliefs?" In the same issue, Congregation Beth Lechem advertised its forthcoming presentation of Leib Glantz, "the world's most famous cantor" and the Nadler Chorus. (Reserve your seats soon.) And immediately next to it on the same page, the Central Synagogue announced that it would feature a rabbi formerly of Essen and a cantor and organist from Berlin. There was the Austrian Jewish Congregation and not surprisingly, perhaps, services for certain groups — for Jews, for example, from Cologne and the Rhineland.

From time to time, *Aufbau* ran recipes for kosher dishes: gefilte fish, kosher chow mein, lukschen kugel. Manischewitz advertised its kosher wine, gefilte fish, matzos, and dehydrated borsht. Pepsi Cola, with the blessing of the Union of Orthodox Jewish Congregations, advertised that it was kosher for Passover. Likewise, for those keeping kosher, Heinz advertised its "vegetarian baked beans" as suitable for either milk or meat dishes. All its foods, it said in another ad, were "endorsed by the Union of Orthodox Jewish Congregations of America." And, in an indication that not all its Jewish readers had been totally Germanized, in back pages crammed with entertainment ads, the Yiddish Art Theater just off Columbus Circle promoted plays like Maurice Schwartz's production of Sholem Asch's *Salvation*. At the 2nd Avenue Theater on the Lower East Side, there was Menasha Skulnick in Herman Yablokoff's great Yiddish musical success, *Live and Laugh*; nearby at the Clinton Theatre, there was Jewish vaudeville with Leo Fuchs and the Medoff Stage Family. In addition, *Aufbau* and the New World Club themselves presented a monthly programs of folk music and dance by Jewish performers, including Yemeni, Assyrian, and East European music and dance. By the mid-1940s, it occasionally ran its own "Yiddish

Theater News" column (itself something of an indicator of an intra-Jewish rap-prochement), including the announcement early in 1943 that Molly Picon's hit musical *Oy is dus a leben* was about to go on a twelve-city national tour.[56]

There were other platforms for Jewish émigrés. Beginning in 1938, WEVD, the left-wing radio station of the *Daily Forward*, whose call letters were an acro-nym for the socialist Eugene V. Debs, collaborated with the German Jewish Club to air a program every Saturday afternoon (later changed to Friday eve-ning, times that may themselves have excluded the strictest Orthodox Jews) about and for the Hitler refugees. There were weeklies and monthlies in French, Spanish, and countless other languages — for a time two French-language papers, *Amerique* and *La Voix de France*, even advertised in *Aufbau* — and there were hun-dreds of synagogues and other community institutions catering in one way or another to immigrants. One regular advertiser was the Jewish Conciliation Board, which evaluated and mediated conflicts within the Jewish community.

"Telling the history of *Aufbau*," George said, "would mean telling the story of German-Jewish immigration through its many changes and circumstances." But the same would be true in reverse. The histories of the two are intertwined, with *Aufbau* sometimes going a little far in its assimilationism. Readers lambasted it for a sympathetic article by a contributing columnist on American Christmas celebrations, what one reader called "assimilation madness." This, they re-minded the editors, is a paper for Jews. In response, the paper explained that it was only the opinion of the writer.[57] But it was also probably a not-altogether unconscious reflection of the culture that many of its refugee readers brought with them or sought to join. (The complaints didn't keep Elizabeth's Bookshop in Washington Heights from advertising Christmas cards in *Aufbau*.) And as one writer in *Aufbau* remarked, one of the drawbacks of assimilating is that you also had to give something up.

For all those reasons, *Aufbau*'s mission inevitably also carried within it the seeds of its own demise. For a time, it described itself on its masthead (in English) as "An Independent Weekly Journal to Serve the Americanization and the In-terests of all Immigrants and to Combat Racial Intolerance." Once those im-migrants assimilated — when those immigrants had learned the language and began to read the *Times*, the *Post*, the *Herald Tribune*, the *World-Telegram*, or *PM*, and became fully Americanized and/or died — it would no longer have a reader-ship or a mission. Given that the migration of Hitler refugees would not end until the postwar flow of survivors from the camps — however many America would allow in — had also stopped, that would take some time. Not quite coinci-dentally, *Aufbau* lived, and for a time thrived, as a major institution for just sev-enty years, in its era a good human lifetime — 1934 to 2004. The dates could be part of its epitaph, engraved on a tombstone.

✳

My parents and I, who arrived in New York in June 1941 after a set of narrow escapes from Europe, were part of that generation, though in some ways not a typical part because my father had an American mother and knew English. In any case, this is not about us but about the tens of thousands of others who arrived in those years. But like many other immigrant kids in the two decades after Hitler's accession in 1933, and particularly during the war years, I avoided all things German. I recall *Aufbau* showing up in our house from time to time (read, I think, mostly by my mother), as it did in the homes of my immigrant friends, and being vaguely embarrassed by its German presence. Now, as I look back three-quarters of a century later, and after considerable reading of U.S. immigration history, I'm newly aware of the importance of the *Aufbau* years in that history and of the centrality of *Aufbau* both as a bridge between worlds and a reflection of the lives of those immigrants. In a way, this may also be an attempt to catch up with, and make up to, the world I once wanted to have nothing to do with.

As suggested above, most Jewish refugees of the Hitler era were unlike the stereotypical masses of struggling people who arrived in the decades of mass immigration between 1870 and the late 1920s, when the nation's tight immigration quota laws went into effect: The majority were urban, cosmopolitan professionals or reasonably skilled men and women. Many were bilingual or even trilingual because of the two or three places they had lived in their effort to escape. If you were poor and without connections, your chances of escaping Europe were much lower. Thus many of those who came could soon make cultural, scientific, and economic contributions to the nation: at New York's New School for Social Research or Princeton's Institute for Advanced Study (both of which became havens for émigré intellectuals), at Los Alamos, Carnegie Hall, Hollywood, and, once the war started, in the military, at the Office of War Information (OWI) or as language and intelligence officers at the Office of Strategic Services (OSS). But many of those who didn't get professional jobs struggled to overcome the blow to their lowered social status and to regain their footing—for men the adjustment appeared to have been harder than for women—and some never did adjust. As one German scholar later pointed out, for most bourgeois immigrants, the American notion of the self-made man was totally foreign.

Aufbau frequently ran pieces trying to calm the fear and depression or, in some cases, assuage the distrust, bordering on paranoia, of older immigrants traumatized by the collapse of the world they'd lived in most of their lives. Hulse, who was also on *Aufbau*'s editorial board, devoted a series of columns to the issue, under headlines like "Don't Lose Your Head" and "Social Problems of Immigration." In another article, he would ask for understanding for the misbehavior of some immigrants: No one ever said, he wrote, that Hitler and Mussolini drove out only nice people. He made himself, in essence, a sort of emotional counselor to the Hitler refugees.

At the same time, in the words of one team of scholars, "the transatlantic vantage point—and the forced nature of their migration—helped European migrants in postwar America to transcend parochial and national perspectives and to regard Europe as a more encompassing social, cultural, and political entity."[58] It may even be possible to suggest that the transatlantic perspective nourished and helped shape the idea of a postwar European union. What European migration certainly did was to leave a deep and lasting impression on American civilization—made it more cosmopolitan and worldly—one so deep and now so integral that it's rarely noticed at all.

1

A Community of Fate

* * *

Their common language was German, though they'd been born in a score of countries in every part of Europe—Germany, Austria, Czechoslovakia, Italy, France, Poland, Russia, Hungary, Romania, Yugoslavia, the Baltics—and had lived in countless others in their attempts to get out. The general preference among German and Austrian Jews trying to escape Hitler in the 1930s had always been for some neighboring, and thus relatively familiar, European country, not for America, which most didn't know anything about—or knew things that were mostly wrong or out of date—and which many thought was coarse and uncultured. Some were natives of places that were in a different country when they arrived in the United States, because of the boundaries that had been redrawn at Versailles in 1919 or Nazi annexations in the early years of World War II. They had stood, sometimes for days, in the same lines outside the U.S. consulates in Berlin, Vienna, Antwerp, Luxemburg, Brussels, Paris, Lisbon, and Amsterdam in the hope of getting a visa; had sluiced up and down the Canebière in Marseille and through its cafés in their pursuit of documents, real, forged, stolen, or some combination of two or even three of them.[1] At some consulates, as one immigrant said about the U.S. consulate in Stuttgart, "Everyone had to be bribed. From the lowest level doorman to the senior functionaries issuing the visas, this consulate was on the take."[2] One of the things they had brought with them was an acute sense that without papers—an identity card, passport, visas, residence permits, affidavits, travel permits, tax stamps—you were a nonperson. If you were stateless you had no rights. If you were stateless, as Hannah Arendt would observe, and there was no place to which to deport you, the easiest recourse for the authorities was to intern you. In *Aufbau* articles such as her "Guests from No-man's-land," she'd touch on the theme again and again.[3]

They had huddled in cellars as bombs crashed into buildings overhead, stood in lines outside bakeries hoping there'd be some bread left when their turn came, been interned in the same camps (Auschwitz, Dachau, Mauthausen, Buchenwald, Theresienstadt, Saint Cyprien, Les Milles, Rivesaltes, Argelès, Le Vernet, Gurs), walked the same roads, sat on their luggage in the same railroad stations waiting for trains that would never run again, had the same "J" stamped on their German passports and/or the same "Juif" on their French identity cards. They had been seized by the same fear when the douaniers or the Gestapo, or both, came through the train; been taken by *passeurs* across the Line of Demarcation between occupied and Vichy France; waited for news, funds, and documents in the same places (Perpignan, Toulouse, Marseille, Lisbon); had hiked across frontiers and over the Pyrenees, as had Franz Werfel, his wife Alma Mahler, Thomas Mann's son, Golo, and Mann's older brother Heinrich Mann, sometimes in the dark of night. Some had been the beneficiaries of the courageous Aristides de Sousa Mendes, the Portuguese consul in Bordeaux who lost his career for issuing thousands of visas to refugees in defiance of the instructions from the repressive Salazar government, most of them to Jews (one notable exception was the surrealist painter Salvador Dali), as the Germans were invading in the spring of 1940. Some had fought in the German army in World War I. Others had fought with the loyalists against Franco in the Spanish Civil War. A few probably had done both. Some fortunate ones, roughly ten thousand children and teenagers, had been chosen for the Kindertransports and received asylum with families or at institutions in England until their American quota numbers came up. Many of those children would never see their parents again.

The luckiest, or the wisest and the wealthiest, had come before the European war on the British Cunarders, the United States Lines, American Export Lines, or the Holland-America Line. Those who were less lucky—and if they had the necessary money and connections and negotiated the nerve-wracking chaos of changed schedules and canceled sailing dates of the early 1940s[4]—had come on the rusty, cramped, fetid ships of the Portuguese Line, some of which never arrived at their advertised destination or weren't allowed to land their

AUFBAU

RECONSTRUCTION

Published Weekly by the New World Club, Inc., 67 West 44th Street, New York City

TODAY: 28 PAGES

Vol. VII - 36   Member of Audit Bureau of Circulations   New York, Friday, September 5, 1941   Entered as second-class matter January 26, 1940, at the New York Post Office under Act of March 3, 1879.   5¢

In dieser Nummer des "Aufbau"
ERSTMALIG
DIE WESTKÜSTE

Die Toten der "Navemar"
Die Namen der fünf auf der Ueberfahrt Gestorbenen waren bisher nicht zu erfahren. Auf dem Büro der Linie Garcia & Diaz wurde die Bekanntgabe der Namen unserem Berichterstatter mit der Begründung abgelehnt, dass dies "no good publicity for the line" sei.

Der Fall "Navemar"

Wie lange noch Wucher mit Schiffskarten?
Ueberfüllte teure und billige leere Schiffe

Letzte JTA-Depeschen

Budapest: ...

London: ...

Jerusalem: ...

Bukarest: ...

Jerusalem: ...

Antwerpen: ...

New York: Edmund I. Kaufmann, der Präsident der zionistischen Organisation Amerikas ...

London: David Ben Gurion, ...

London: ...

Lissabon: ...

Jerusalem: ...

Paris: ...

Ab Ende September:
"Die Jüdische Welt"
14TÄGIGE BEILAGE DES "AUFBAU"

Loyal Germans and Illoyal Nazis in U.S.A.

By ROBERT F. WAGNER, JR.
President of the "Loyal Americans of German Descent"

Bemerkung in Vichy

Grynzpan von der Gestapo zu Tode gebracht?

The crowd seeking U.S. visas from the consulate in Marseille. Most waited in vain. (photo by Hans Cahnmann, courtesy of the U.S. Holocaust Memorial Museum)

passengers when they got there—the *Nyassa*, the *Guinea*, the *Navemar*, which an anonymous writer in *Aufbau* called a "floating hell,"[5] the *Winnipeg*, the *Serpa Pinto*, the *Mont Viso* (sunk by a U-Boat in 1943), or the German ship *St. Louis*, which became a *cause celèbre* in May 1939 when she was not allowed to land her 908 German-Jewish refugee passengers either in Cuba or in the United States and had to turn back to Europe. Some two hundred of the passengers would eventually perish in the Holocaust.

Some refugees, such as the playwright Bertolt Brecht, accompanied by wife and mistress, made it out by train through Russia and then by ship from Vladivostok. A lifelong Marxist, having fled from the McCarthy-era Red hunts, he would die in East Berlin in 1956. Some had gotten from Marseille to Martinique or Cuba and from there to the United States. For a number, the first stop in America had been Ellis Island, where over a period of more than a half century some twelve million prior immigrants had, in the words of Henry James, stood "appealing and waiting, marshaled, herded, divided, subdivided, sorted, sifted, searched, fumigated, for longer or shorter periods."[6] Liane (Kayser) Gutman, born in Mannheim, who came as a teenager with her mother in 1941, recalled that it "was utopian compared to Gurs particularly in terms of

Top left: *Aufbau*'s front-page story about the dangerously overcrowded ship *Navemar*. (courtesy of JM Jüdische Medien AG, Zurich)

Bottom left: Passengers sleeping in a lifeboat on the *Navemar*. (courtesy of the Leo Baeck Institute, New York)

cleanliness."[7] Ellis Island would finally close in 1954. They were among its last waves of arrivals.

For some, said the Czech émigré writer Hans Nanotek, the departure from Europe had been easy, "like leaving a bad movie—it's gone, not worth talking about." But for many others, the parting was a mix of "resignation and panic . . . as if we were in an overloaded lifeboat that couldn't get away from the sinking ship, or rather the sinking shore. Panic encourages more the use of your elbows than your altruism."[8]

Most were Jews, though hardly all: Among them were former labor leaders and socialists, communists, writers, politicians, lawyers, theologians, café singers, comedians, academics, and other activists who had been attacking Hitler or lampooning him in the decade before 1933. Some of those who had fought for Germany in the first war thought their service would immunize them against Nazi persecution. Two leading left-wing politicians from the Weimar period, the Social Democrat Rudolf Breitscheid and the Marxist economist Rudolf Hilferding, who fled to France after Hitler became chancellor, thought that for men like themselves it would be "undignified" to cross the French-Spanish border without documents, even when the American Varian Fry of the Emergency Rescue Committee (more to follow) urged them to and could have helped them. In any case, they said, Hitler would never "dare" extradite them.[9] Eventually they were arrested by the Vichy authorities and delivered to the Nazis; neither survived. And there were countless German Jews who, when the French and the Belgians ordered them to report to the police as enemy aliens after the start of the war, quickly obeyed (and were promptly shipped to internment camps). It was their German training, some explained: When you were ordered to do something by someone in authority, you did it.

Even after the passage of Hitler's Nuremberg laws, said one émigré, his grandfather, who would die at Auschwitz, "could not conceive of the possibility that his German compatriots would ever turn against a decorated veteran of WWI and his family." Many more had thought themselves safely assimilated in Weimar Germany, which the cultural historian Peter Gay, himself a German refugee, called "a republic of outsiders." "Only Hitler made me into a Jew," he would say, "and, it turned out, not a very good one."[10] But for Hannah Arendt, who said she never considered herself part of the German *Volk*, only a German citizen, "Indifference was no longer possible after 1933."[11]

The political and social prominence of some Jews during the Weimar years, the brief fifteen-year period of social democracy between the end of World War I and the ascendancy of Hitler, had made other Jews uncomfortable. Germany, they argued (correctly, as it turned out) wasn't ready for that. When Walter Rathenau accepted the job of foreign minister in 1922, Albert Einstein and Kurt Blumenfeld, the leader of Germany's Zionist movement, urged him to resign. "A Jew," they reportedly told him, "could at most be the minister of Posts, not Foreign Minister." All it would do was fan anti-Semitism. Rathenau countered that he was a fully assimilated German.[12] A few months later, a right-wing fanatic assassinated him. The symbiosis of the German and the Jewish, said the cultural historian Paul Mendes-Flohr, always existed more in the heads of Jews than as a real cultural dialogue.[13] "I never felt particularly Jewish," the quantum physicist and future Nobel laureate Max Born had written to his friend Einstein soon after Hitler became chancellor and Born was about to flee to England. "Now, of course, I am extremely conscious of it."[14] The shock of that discovery and all that came with it was part of the baggage that Hitler's refugees brought with them.

Many other German Jews, fleeing Hitler, had thought they were secure in Belgium or France, countries that, needing workers after the devastation of World War I, had welcomed them not long before. Although Hitler, after first imposing on all Jewish males the middle name "Israel" and on all females the middle name "Sarah," had eventually denaturalized them—rendering all Jewish émigrés stateless—that didn't keep their new countries, America among them, from declaring them enemy aliens once war came and, as in France and Belgium, interning them all over again.[15] And as Arendt later pointed out, once they became stateless, were technically citizens of no country, they became that much more vulnerable. For a time, until the United States created the category "Involuntary German (or Austrian) Nationals" late in 1941, refugees from Hitler seeking extension of their expired passports or other official papers were also in the impossible position of having to go to the consulates of nations that no longer recognized their citizenship.[16] (One who sensed early on what was likely to happen was my maternal grandfather Ludwig Haas, a lawyer and politician in Weimar Germany and a German officer in World War I who urged his son Karl to get as far away as possible, which he did. Karl emigrated to New Zealand, where this son of the urban Jewish bourgeoisie became a sheep rancher.)[17]

The estimate cited earlier for the number of refugees who had managed to make it to America between 1933, when Hitler came to power, and 1944 has always been uncertain, and the count for Jews even more so. Until World War II, as required by U.S. law, the manifests of ships arriving in the United States always listed each passenger by "race or people." The "race" listed for those who declared themselves to be Jews was "Hebrew" (others were "German," "Spanish," or "Slovak"). What is certain is that the number who did make it was well below what even the tight immigration quotas enacted in the 1920s would have allowed, thanks in part to a rigid State Department bureaucracy suspicious of all refugees—how many were Fifth Columnists, spies, or communist agents?—and thanks in part to its deep strain of nativism and anti-Semitism. Under officials like Assistant Secretary of State Breckinridge Long, who headed the Visa Division, the State Department was laced by animosity toward Eastern Europeans and Jews in particular. Immigration restrictionists in the 1930s warned about a Trojan horse of foreign agents posing as Jewish refugees; Donald Trump would use the same words about Syrian refugees eighty years later.[18]

As many historians have pointed out, before 1941, when the Nazis blocked emigration, a lot more Jews might have escaped had other countries, the United States and Great Britain especially, been willing to take them.[19] What's certain is that most of those who came in the early and mid-1930s—before the *Anschluss* in March 1938, when Hitler seized Austria; before *Kristallnacht* that November, when Nazi mobs smashed windows and looted synagogues and Jewish-owned shops all over Germany and often beat up their occupants on the streets outside; before Hitler seized Czechoslovakia in 1938–39; before the invasion of Poland and the beginning of the war in September 1939; before the German invasion of Belgium, Holland, and Luxemburg in May 1940—had it easier than those who tried to get out later. "Going to America," said the journalist and political scientist Henry Pachter, born Heinz Pächter in Berlin, who had also been interned by the French at Gurs, and came to the United States in 1940, "was in itself an admission of defeat."[20] (During the war, however, Pachter would work for the U.S. Office of Strategic Services, the forerunner of the CIA, and the office of War Information, and would later become a co-founder of the influential liberal quarterly *Dissent*. He taught at the City University of New York until his death in 1980.)

To this day, there's debate about how many more could have been saved had Roosevelt been more responsive to the pleas of Jewish organizations and humanitarian groups, both before and during the war. But in the years before Pearl Harbor, Roosevelt had other (and politically more difficult) problems to worry about. He faced stiff resistance from groups like the America First Committee and from members of Congress, among them progressives like Senators Robert La Follette, William Borah, and Hiram Johnson, in his effort to engineer help for Britain in its desperate battle and to prepare the United States, still in the Depression and mired in its ocean-protected isolationism, for the war he was sure would come. Nonetheless nearly all Hitler refugees idolized FDR. Given Republican isolationism and opposition to liberalized immigration policies and, as an election eve piece in *Aufbau* in 1936 noted, the tilt of Nazi sympathizers like Fritz Kuhn's German-American Bund toward the GOP—and the Democrats' embrace of immigrants, something that went back nearly a century and had, for nearly all that time, been a source of the party's political strength— nearly all the German Jews would remain lifelong Democrats.[21] Werner Gundersheimer, who had arrived with his parents at the age of three and later became a distinguished Renaissance scholar, recalled

Roosevelt's death came as almost a physical blow to my parents. I had never seen anything like their grief. It was as though they had lost a beloved relative, as though all of the losses and sorrows they had stoically endured during the past decade could now find expression. They had never known an America without Roosevelt, so his loss also felt profoundly destabilizing. For the first and only time in my life, I saw my parents weeping. I don't know how long their mourning went on, but it certainly lasted several days, as they sat by the crackly radio in the living room.[22]

Most of those who made it must have been fully aware that, given the tight American immigration restrictions, they were the lucky ones. Thousands more came on visitor's or transit visas in the hope that later their quota number for immigration would come up, as well as a thousand children who were brought over by various relief organizations in the 1930s and early 1940s. They were unaccompanied by parents, many of whom had already been deported to concentration camps and would be murdered there. In 1939, the Wagner-Rogers Bill, legislation with bipartisan sponsorship and wide support, would have allowed the admission over the existing quotas of some twenty thousand refugee children from Nazi Germany in a two-year period, but after it was amended again and again it died in committee and never came to a vote. America, opponents argued, should first look to its own neglected children.[23] And in the first years, those who made it and had jobs and their first American homes were besieged by those who hadn't. "They get torn to pieces," one émigré wrote to a friend, "by all the demands for help."[24]

Some owed their visas to the few American consuls who disregarded orders and issued visas too liberally. The one who later became known and would be honored for it was Hiram Bingham in Marseille, who, with his colleague Myles Standish, in effect defied Washington and would soon be reassigned for it. Other refugees had managed to get to Palestine, many without documents; to England (though often on the condition that their stay would be temporary and they wouldn't take jobs for which British citizens were available); to South Africa, Cuba, Mexico, Argentina, Bolivia, Brazil, Chile, Haiti, the Dominican Republic, Panama, New Zealand, Shanghai, or Canada. Perhaps the biggest hero among the diplomats, though little recognized at the time, was de Sousa Mendez, the Portuguese consul in Bordeaux.

After the war, another wave of immigrants arrived who may have been equal in number to those who came in the 1930s—displaced people, many of them survivors of the Nazi death camps, including thousands defined as "unrepatriable" because they were stateless or because the place of their birth was now in a different country, "people without a country."[25] But in some ways most were as different from the prewar generation of Hitler refugees as that generation had been from the classic "huddled masses" of American immigrants—Italians, Poles, Russians, Hungarians, Greeks—who arrived between 1880 and the late 1920s, when the National Origins Quota Immigration Act Congress passed in 1924 became fully effective and America slammed shut its golden door.

Most didn't come for economic opportunity, much less to earn money and then return home as many prior aliens did, but for safety and freedom from fascism. Many had been professionals in Europe, among them many scientists, writers, artists, actors, musicians, and academics who were already well known or soon would be. As a cosmopolitan middle class, they prided themselves on their *Bildung*, a status word without an English equivalent for a cross of education, civility, and cultural enlightenment. Among the best known: Albert Einstein, Enrico Fermi, Hans Bethe, Wolfgang Pauli, Edward Teller, Leo Szilard, John von Neumann, Walter Gropius, Marcel Breuer, Victor Gruen, László Moholy-Nagy, Mies Van der Rohe, Marc Chagall, George Grosz, Jacques Lipchitz, André Masson, Max Ernst, André Breton, Otto Kallir, Alfred Eisenstaedt, Robert Capa (born Endre Friedmann), Kurt Weill, Lotte Lenya, Bertolt Brecht, Franz Werfel, Bruno Frank, Heinrich Mann, Thomas Mann, Sigrid Undset, Alfred Döblin, Vicki Baum, Lion Feuchtwanger, Hannah Arendt, Hans Morgenthau, Paul Tillich, Theodor Adorno (born Wiesengrund), Erik Erikson, Karen Horney, Rudolf Serkin, Roman Totenberg, Alfred Adler, Kurt Herbert Adler, Arthur Rubinstein, George Szell, Vladimir Horowitz, Arnold Schoenberg, Erich Wolfgang Korngold, Darius Milhaud, Bruno Walter, Otto Klemperer, Erich Leinsdorf, Fritz Kreisler, Fritz Lang, Billy Wilder, Max Reinhardt, and Peter Lorre. Many knew one another and had worked together (e.g., Lorre and Brecht, Weill and Brecht, Lang and Lorre, as well as many of the musicians) before they came to America. It was an impressive list.

They had places to come to. When the New York–based Emergency Rescue Committee (ERC) sent the young editor Varian Fry to Marseille in 1941 with a list of cultural stars that he was commissioned to help get out of Europe, it was because, as one of his sponsors then said, "there was a fire sale on brains" in Europe and America should pick up as many as possible. Working with Bingham and Standish, the American consuls in Marseille, and with the resourceful and courageous Lisa Fittko and her husband Hans, who led countless refugees from the French coastal town of Banyuls-sur-mer over the Pyrenees into Spain, Fry helped save more than a thousand—Arendt, Werfel, and Feuchtwanger among them. Fry and his colleagues in Marseille codenamed Feuchtwanger "Wetcheek," a rough literal translation of his German name.[26] When the Vichy authorities drove Fry out of France in 1941—he was told he was helping too many Jews and anti-Nazis—*Aufbau* dubbed him "the good angel of Marseille."

Nonetheless, Fry's commission later raised a troubling question. In effect, was the ERC very selective about whom it would help, screening its clients, demanding, as a later critic put it: "Show us your art work and we'll try to save you"? But at places like New York's New School for Social Research, where Alvin Johnson, its director, grabbed émigrés like Pachter, the political philosopher Leo Strauss, and many other refugee intellectuals for his University in Exile (some of whom left for other institutions as soon as their names became known in America), they soon made an impact.[27] Columbia welcomed the psychoanalyst and social theorist Erich Fromm, the social theorist Max Horkheimer, the sociologist Leo Löwenthal, and other colleagues from the influential Frankfurt School of Critical Theory. (Horkheimer and his colleague Theodor Adorno would soon move to Los Angeles where, Adorno said, "the beauty of the landscape is without comparison, so that even a hardboiled European like me is overwhelmed.")[28]

At the New School, Princeton, and other American universities in later years they and other émigré academics would have a significant impact on American scholarship. The American sociologist David Riesman listed Fromm, Löwenthal, the Vienna-born émigré empirical sociologist Paul Lazarsfeld, and Hannah Arendt among the major influences on his work, and there surely were others who would have named one or more of the same people. The highly regarded Austro-Hungarian economic historian Karl Polanyi, a Jewish émigré, wrote his most important work, *The Great Transformation*, at Bennington College in Vermont and later was recognized as an important influence by the Nobel laureate Joseph Stiglitz and other leading economists. Ironically, Polanyi, perhaps the most prescient critic of the destructive effects of unchecked capitalism and its relation to incipient fascism, was never able to settle permanently in the United States because his wife, who had been a communist in Hungary, couldn't get a visa. After the war, Polanyi taught at Columbia, commuting to his job from his home in Canada.[29]

It's often been said that without those émigré scientists, and Einstein's famous 1939 letter to Roosevelt impressing on him the potential of the atom in the development of an entirely new and radically more powerful weapon, the United States might not have decided to build its atomic bomb until much later, maybe not until after the Nazis had developed their own. But the concentration of émigré brainpower that was driven out of Europe in that Nazi-era fire sale—then no longer available to the Germans and now engaged in designing and building the atomic bomb in the Manhattan Project (Fermi, Szilard, Stanislaw Ulam, von Neumann, Teller, with occasional help from Niels Bohr, who had fled Denmark for Sweden and then England)—certainly made an enormous difference.

One study, headed by the Yale University sociologist Maurice R. Davie, was clearly intended to counter the anti-Semitic backlash against Jewish refugee immigrants. Published shortly after the war, it listed twelve Nobel Prize winners who came to the United States between 1933 and 1945, 150 in *Who's Who*, and some 220 identified as refugees who were named in the 1944 edition of *American Men of Science*.[30] Many on those lists were refugees only in the broadest sense; they were people who had sponsors and institutions—universities, Hollywood studios, musical organizations—that had invited or welcomed them, or those such as the highly regarded Russian-born French publisher Jacques Schiffrin, a Fry client, who soon reestablished themselves in the United States (Schiffrin as the founder of Pantheon Books). Some, certainly many of the eager-to-assimilate young, didn't want to be regarded as refugees at all. "We declared," wrote Arendt, that "we had departed of our own free will to countries of our choice, and we denied that our situation had anything to do with 'so-called Jewish problems.'"[31]

But most were not well known: they were small business owners, low-status professionals, mechanics, and artisans—lawyers, bankers, accountants, clerks, doctors, dentists, ceramicists, chemists, pharmacists, nurses, social workers, teachers, salesmen, jewelers, diamond cutters, glass manufacturers, haberdashers, leather workers, shoemakers and shoe manufacturers, furriers, tailors, printers, tool and die makers and other machine tool craftsmen—educated and literate, but men and women of no particular distinction or renown. (Among them, it appears, was virtually the entire diamond industry of Antwerp and Amsterdam, some of whose craftsmen and merchants, nearly all Orthodox Jews, most of them Yiddish-speaking, fled to Palestine ahead of the Nazis, but most of whom came to New York, to West 47th Street, which became the Diamond District and where many of their successors remain to this day.)

Many refugees, few of them celebrities, had gotten help from American and international organizations: the American Jewish Joint Distribution Committee (the "Joint"), which paid for the cost of some of the Portuguese ships that brought refugees over; HIAS, originally the Hebrew Immigrant Aid Society; HICEM, the anagram of the three Jewish organizations that formed it; the National Refugee Service, another Jewish-funded umbrella organization, which was established in 1939 specifically to aid European émigrés; the Quakers of the American Friends Service Committee; the American Federation of Labor; the YWCA; the Unitarians; the National Council of Jewish Women; the American Christian Committee for Refugees; the Catholic Committee for Refugees; Selfhelp; and countless other church and social service groups. Of all these private groups, what would now be called NGOs, the Joint and the Quakers, who provided aid of every conceivable sort to refugees and other war victims all over the world, were probably the most warmly supportive, providing everything, as one of the Friends reports said, from "clothing, temporary maintenance, food parcels, travel money to reach jobs; assistance with legal formalities of all kinds; counseling and referral; job placement" to help in finding relatives. It's impossible to know how many Jews, having been given temporary housing or a temporary job in a Quaker facility, found themselves on many a Sunday in the stillness of a Friends meeting.[32]

A few got out in the grand bourgeois style, as in the case of one family that had first settled in France and arrived in New York with thirty boxes of linen, fine china, silverware, jewelry, rugs, furs, and enough cash to start a new business, and some others who had packed what were called "lifts," huge containers with sofas, tables, armoires and other furniture and art. "There's a well-to-do class of immigrants in New York," said a lead piece in *Aufbau* in 1937, which, consistent with its liberal/social welfare DNA, implored those well-off immigrants to honor a tradition going back to the first days of New York when, it said, Peter Stuyvesant urged the affluent to look after their less fortunate peers (as indeed many would). As to that class of fortunate émigrés, "God knows how they got their money to America—who live as thoughtlessly here as they did in Germany. They read the same books, live in the kind of same elegant apartments . . . give the same 'parties.' . . . They didn't emigrate, they simply moved to New York."[33]

But many more, allowed to take virtually no assets out of Germany, even the proceeds from things that had not already been smashed, burned, "Aryanized," or simply stolen by the Nazis, were dirt poor when they arrived. Their luggage, such as they brought, was sometimes still covered with the stickers of the grand hotels in St. Moritz, Arosa, Grindelwald, Wengen, and the other Swiss Magic Mountains they had once vacationed in, but often that was all they brought.

Inevitably they were shocked by a loss of status almost as great, and more sudden, than the one that hit them when the Nazis came to power. Once proud members of the European bourgeoisie, most could no longer practice their professions without retraining and re-certification, which usually also meant literacy in English and learning American idioms—and for some those challenges were insurmountable. (The one thing immigrant lawyers could become without certification, *Aufbau* reported, was tax consultants.) So many, especially in the Depression years, were in fact unemployable in their old occupations, or in anything but unskilled jobs. "I may not do what I have learned," said the writer Johannes Urzidil, who was born in Prague. "What I may do I have not learned."[34]

Formerly high status lawyers and business people worked as door-to-door salesmen of Fuller brushes, neckties, magazine subscriptions, or household appliances—or as waiters, janitors, dishwashers, elevator operators, or in dirty factory jobs like the twenty-four-year-old Henry (formerly Heinrich) Bierig who began as a busboy at Longchamps in New York, then took a job in Chicago mixing bronze powders at the Illinois Bronze Powder Co. ("not one of the healthiest jobs," he would later recall). Still, he thought himself lucky. In his letter to a reunion of fellow immigrants from Mannheim, he listed the names of eighteen relatives, his and his wife's, who had perished in the Holocaust, thirteen at Auschwitz, one at Sobibor, one in the French camp at Rivesaltes, one in Minsk, one in Zasavica, and one "declared dead, camp unknown."[35] And as officially designated enemy aliens once the war began, German and Austrian immigrants were also disqualified from working in some defense-related jobs.

Aufbau ran ads for schools offering training in diamond setting, pressing ("pressers always find jobs"), the needle trades, and for jobs in the "fur industry" (and, of course, in "American English"), but it's not likely that many former lawyers or accountants ever took advantage of them—or could. In the words of one study conducted in the mid-1940s: "Many an intellectual worker became a hand worker, an employer became an employee, a housewife became a wage earner, and a person of independent means became dependent on others. The need of doing hard physical labor, to which they were unaccustomed, was especially trying to the middle-aged and older people. The loss of status as well as the disruption of the former mode of life caused further distress."[36] In that respect, the bourgeois refugees from Hitler were probably less prepared and less fit than the classic huddled masses who arrived in the last decades of the nineteenth century and the first years of the twentieth who were used to physical labor and had no high social status to lose. In October 1942, *Aufbau* ran an article reporting that there was plenty of work in the fields of California—"housing and camp sites available on most jobs"—an opportunity that not many German immigrants were likely to have even thought about.[37] In effect, they were wanted to replace the Okies who, with the coming of the war, had found better jobs at Lockheed or at Henry Kaiser's steel mills and shipyards. Thousands of those farm jobs would be filled by Mexican workers under the Bracero Program, many of whom would become the vanguard of a much greater wave of immigration a half century later.

Not surprisingly, resources at the social services agencies were tight. Selfhelp, originally called Selfhelp of Émigrés from Germany and Austria, then de-Germanized to Selfhelp of Émigrés from Central Europe, the modest organization started in New York in 1936 by a small group of émigrés, mostly women, to assist both the refugees who arrived after them and those still in Europe, often met at someone's Manhattan apartment. In the early meetings of the board there was one crucial set of questions: Should Selfhelp use its very limited resources, sometimes doled out in amounts of fifty dollars or less, to help German Jews get out of Nazi-occupied Europe, later broadened to include all refugees "regardless of national origin, not just Germans," and to aid the thousands in French concentration camps? Or should it just concentrate on helping the refugees who were already in the United States—finding jobs and housing for new arrivals, schools for their children and, more broadly, lightening the load that those new arrivals often put on the last arrivals, and, still more broadly, easing the "problems of despair"?[38] The questions themselves told a lot.

I had a school friend in Queens whose father had been a lawyer in Munich and who was now going door to door as a typewriter repairman looking like a beaten man, but there were many others. Selfhelp—it's now a vastly larger social service organization called Selfhelp Community Enterprises, Inc.—found that it was easier to find jobs for the women, perhaps because they were more flexible, perhaps because loss of status meant less to them, than for the men.[39] They were not fancy jobs—jobs primarily as seamstresses, cooks, nannies, and other domestic help. One, typically, got a job as a cleaning woman in B. Altman's department store (through "connections"), even though she was a trained stenographer and knew English and German. Often, as an *Aufbau* writer pointed out, it was the women who had gotten the men out of the (French) concentration camps and began their escape from France "carrying their children and the sick on their backs across the Pyrenees."[40] Through the whole refugee saga, the women often appeared to be tougher and they seemed to learn the practical elements of American life faster than their men—in part because chores like shopping and getting the wash done had always been the woman's job, but also in part because of that toughness and the practical flexibility that came with it. There are no statistics, but it's quite probable that even when a refugee family could afford their first car, it was the wife who drove it.

Nonetheless, given the traumatic impact on people who had never known anything like the blows that war, fascism, and internment inflicted, some women may have been almost as emotionally devastated as the men. One, who was formerly well-to-do and now worked as a domestic in a Park Avenue residence, wrote *Aufbau* in 1939 that her employer, though a nice person, just didn't understand her or her situation, to which Hilde Scott, *Aufbau*'s women's columnist at the time, reminded the letter writer to think of how the Polish Jews who worked as maids and nannies for the German bourgeoisie in the old days must have felt.[41] For some, taking a job also meant an indefinite separation from spouses and children. One letter in *Aufbau* (in German) remarked on the fact that in English, the paramount passage in the Bible about the torment of mankind was called "The Book of Job."

Aufbau's psychiatrist-columnist Wilfred Hulse tried to address some of the trauma of people who had to deal not once, but often more than once, with the struggle of locating loved ones among the millions of refugees in Hitler's Europe, then getting affidavits, visas, and countless other documents, and securing passage for them, and, when those loved ones finally arrived, facing the question: Now what? In a piece headed "Disappointment in New York," Hulse has his everyman, Albert Lehmann, who had been a lawyer in Germany, now selling hosiery door-to-door and after two months on the job discovering that his employer was not living up to what had been promised. Meanwhile his wife had just lost her fourth job as a domestic when the family she worked for went off on summer vacation and, not being used to constant physical labor, is unwell, feels it in every limb, and sleeps badly in New York's summer heat.[42] The general message, always in the most understanding terms: be patient and, in the meantime, suck it up.

And as ever in American history, before and since, unemployment reinforced the arguments of immigration restrictionists: aliens were taking jobs that should go to Americans. One third of American families in the mid-1930s had an income of less than $780 a year. The median was just over $1,100, and many couldn't live on that income. Writers in *Aufbau* and elsewhere made great efforts to undercut the argument that immigrants were taking jobs from natives. In fact, they argued, immigrants created as many jobs as they took, maybe more, as entrepreneurs and as consumers. It ran stories about new enterprises launched or managed by refugees—a rubber manufacturing plant in Charlotte, North Carolina, soon to employ two hundred people; in New Jersey a refugee who not long before had arrived with four dollars in his pocket had created a plant for the processing of smoked meats. Refugees had started new glass works; a manufacturer of cotton gloves, formerly of Cologne, now employed fifty people, all but four of them Americans. A leading toy manufacturer reported that America's share of the global toy industry had grown substantially thanks to the expertise of immigrants.[43]

The paper also ran tables showing that the states with the highest percentage of foreign-born residents (New York, Massachusetts, and Rhode Island) also had the highest per capita income.[44] (Which, of course, was no evidence of causality. If there was a causal relationship, it was more likely the reverse.) America was full of major industries that had been founded by the immigrants of prior generations.[45] Alongside such pieces, *Aufbau* ran invitations to readers, in conjunction with a group called the Non-Sectarian Anti-Nazi League, to provide information on jobs created by immigrants and other employers in response to immigration. It was one of the ways of "counteracting reports that refugees are injuring American industries."[46] On its part, *Aufbau*'s parent, the

German-Jewish Club, later renamed (for reasons that should be obvious) the New World Club, sponsored countless talks on American industry and employment opportunities. Yet even when refugees found decent jobs or created growing businesses, the loss of status seemed to rankle. In El Paso in the 1950s, the mother of an immigrant who had become a successful scrap and junk dealer became locally famous for saying her son was in the steel business.

Beyond (and sometimes before) the challenge of finding employment, immigrants faced the often-difficult problems of adjustment to a new culture, new language, and new customs, which may have been more difficult than for prior generations, many of whom tended to start their lives in America in the secure cocoon of their own ethnic enclaves. "We German-Jewish refugees," said Rabbi Alfred Gottschalk, the former president of Hebrew Union College, "were fish out of our linguistic, economic, and cultural waters."[47] As a result, as another émigré told an interviewer, "The immigrant must learn anew how to stand, walk, eat, sleep. You are at once dead tired and excited. Only a few grasp that so tremendous a readjustment resembles a state of physical illness. Ignorance of the simplest customs and formalities, the difficulties of communication, uncertainty as to your own situation and worry about those for whom you are responsible—all these only serve to heighten your state of confusion." For the man who, hoping to quickly regain his status, tried to "mingle at once with native Americans, his European manners and ideas were all the more conspicuous, with the result that he attracted undue attention, much of it unfavorable."[48] And as always and everywhere, parents worried about their children, reflected in events such as the Immigrants Conference focusing on "The Refugee Child—Problems of Adjustment and Placement" at the Child Study Association of America.

Others took their new status philosophically. "Here in America," said a letter to *Aufbau* in 1940, "I'm a doorman at a movie house in a fancy uniform with gold buttons, silver cords and a red general's stripe on my pants. I'm doorman number seven, and with that I must be satisfied. . . . But with that doorman position I can rescue wife and child from the wreckage and send them the necessary documents."[49]

Aufbau, whose parent, the New World Club, offered all manner of classes—"Salesmanship," "American Business Correspondence," "Stenography"—but English classes most of all, constantly encouraged its readers to learn the language and acculturate. In the 1950s it also published and sold booklets such as "How Good Is Your Business English?" for sixty cents a copy. It got a nice vignette from its correspondent Richard Dyck of one language class, composed of immigrants from almost every country in Europe—Germans, Poles, Hungarians—who, "judging from their manner, their dress, their looks, hadn't been in the country long. But without exception had been through Hitler's hell. Do these people, men, women, children, who had been through this inferno still have the strength and focus to learn a difficult foreign language? Yes, they indeed do, and how. One has to see with one's own eyes how the doctor, the craftsman, the child, the old person, sitting side by side at the same school desks, struggle to repeat the words sounded by the teacher. . . . As if by magic carried away into the free, New World, these Jewish new immigrants learn English with an enthusiasm that's heart-rending."[50]

The struggles in learning the language and absorbing the culture became a minor classic of American literature with the publication in 1937 of "The Education of H*Y*M*A*N K*A*P*L*A*N," by Leo Rosten, a Jewish native of Lodz who was brought here in 1911 as a young child, writing under the name of Leonard Q. Ross. First published in the *New Yorker*, "Hyman Kaplan"—a series of sweet, satirical stories about a night school class for new arrivals, most of them Yiddish-speakers, overseen (if rarely actually taught) by the kind, ever-patient WASP Mr. Parkhill—was sometimes condescending and never recognized the influx of Hitler refugees or the horrors that drove them here. Yet it may have done almost as much in recognizing the cultural travails of the new immigration as any earnest tome of serious scholarship.

✳

For many refugees, moreover, there was the underlying ambivalence, what someone called "the searing wound of exile," between the imperatives of learning and assimilating to the new and nostalgia for the old culture—generally clung to longest in the Seder and Sabbath dinners and other religious rituals among those who came with them, and for many others in the kitchen, the *Sauerbraten* with potato dumplings, the *Spätzle*, the soups and the *Suppenfleisch* that went into it, and the cakes and pastry. (And it may be well here to remember that when it came to nostalgia and *schmaltz*, from Schubert and Strauss to Schnitzler, Schiele, and Schlag, the Viennese had long been second to none.) For some, wrote Helmut Pfanner, a scholar of German exile literature, "New York City was more important as a place of remembering than as a site of new experience."[51]

The ambivalence was often sharpened by their European disdain for what they regarded as American materialism, crudeness, and the fuzzy and often altogether wrong picture of the United States that they brought with them. It was part of their baggage, the former German playwright Carl Zuckmayer wrote, even though few of them had ever been to America.[52] They had grown up with the belief that this was a country "without tradition, without *Kultur*, without any passion for beauty or form, a country of chemical fertilizers and can-openers. Should we divorce ourselves from the slavery of European mass dictatorships, to subject ourselves to the tyranny of dollars, of *business*, of advertising?" For some, as noted earlier, that attitude probably contributed to the delay in emigrating until it was dangerously late. Zuckmayer again: "American consulate? Quota numbers? Questionnaires? Affidavits? Why should we rush to a country in which we don't belong, which has nothing to give us, from which we have nothing to learn and to which we have nothing to say?"[53] And it was what drove their contempt, during the months, and for some, the years, after they arrived, for the tackiness of household goods from Woolworth's; the cheap china; the gum-chewing; the awful packaged white bread and the processed cheese at the grocery store; the commercialization of everything, the public rudeness of New York, where many of them lived and which many others regarded as representative of all America. Did they really want to become part of this? (In the early war years, Zuckmayer was a farmer in Vermont, which should have given him a slightly different perspective.)

It sometimes took years to shed it. Many, as one of them later said, imagined America "to be full of rich people and gangsters."[54] For the biographer and drama critic Ludwig Marcuse, emigrating to America had been the choice of desperation. "What did we, the sons of high government officials and the affluent, the pupils of a humanistic *Gymnasium*," he wrote, "have to do with the 'buy me' countries? . . . The foundation for my conception of America? The image of skyscrapers lining sunless chasms in which untold numbers of people crawled about looking for dollars." The center of the intellectual universe of his time had been Paris. "New York and the colonial territory surrounding it were further away than Africa."[55]

And as they became acquainted with their new country, some, especially those in the South and Midwest, also began to discover what the American-born daughter of refugee parents who had grown up in Kansas called the country's "virulent prejudice against blacks and communists—against any and all who deviated from a narrow and confining white Protestant norm."[56] This was the land of the free, but not for all.

As the paper for Jewish refugees still unsure of their own standing in America, *Aufbau*, perhaps not surprisingly, didn't delve deeply into the matter of discrimination against blacks, or into any other of the nation's historic problems, until after the war. But once race became a national issue, the editors, many of whom had searing memories of racism and fascism, covered the civil rights movement and endorsed its objectives—the Brown decision in 1954, the Civil Rights Act, the Voting Rights Act in the 1960s, among others—with a passion. The refrain, in the words of one *Aufbau* headline, was "Now or Never." *Brown v.*

Board of Education would not immediately end segregation, but under the head (in English) "All Men Are Created Equal," it said in almost Biblical terms, "the word has been spoken and the word is now the law."[57]

Jews, immigrants, and others, many of them acutely conscious of racial discrimination, later became a mainstay of the American civil rights and civil liberties movements. Some, among them the German trained sociologist Werner Cahnman, went south to teach at Atlanta University, Fisk University in Nashville, and other black colleges. In an *Aufbau* piece titled "A German Jew in a Negro University," Cahnman wrote not only about the dismal conditions he found there but the profound inequality in American society—racial, economic, social—that belied its noble professions about freedom, equality, and opportunity.[58] Rabbi Joachim Prinz, a Hitler refugee who came to the United States in 1937, became president of the American Jewish Congress, a leader in the American civil rights movement and an organizer of the 1963 March on Washington, where he spoke just before Martin Luther King Jr. gave his "I Have a Dream" speech. The German refugee Aryeh Neier, born in Berlin, was the national director of the ACLU from 1970 to 1978 and later headed Human Rights Watch. In 1962, the immigrant actor and journalist Hertha Pauli, who, in the words of the literary scholar Guy Stern, "had never seen a black before coming to America, undertook out of a moral impulse and in recognition of a parallel minority fate," to write the first biography of the abolitionist and former slave Sojourner Truth.[59]

Conversely, some young refugees also embraced historic American prejudices as proof of their Americanization, told ethnic and misogynist jokes, and, like most other Americans, demeaned homosexuals. Some Americanized by becoming New York Jews or, if they were lucky enough to get into an Ivy League college, by becoming or trying to become all-American WASPs. More than one must have sat in morning chapel at Amherst or Williams singing "Praise God from whom all blessings flow." New York's liberal, humanist, socially engaged Ethical Culture Society, founded in 1876 by the son of a nineteenth-century immigrant German rabbi, drew scores of earlier German-Jewish immigrants beginning in the late nineteenth and early twentieth centuries—the Seligmans, the Oppenheimers—and probably still does. And while some Hitler refugees of the pre–Pearl Harbor years said that their experience had made them avow their Jewishness, to quote the émigré dramatist Bruno Frank, "wherever one can, and as loud as one can," others, according to a survey, said their Jewish consciousness had not become stronger—and had never been very great to begin with.[60]

For many refugees, however, acceptance and, often, embrace of American culture came hand-in-hand with the rediscovery of the Jewish identity (cultural, if not religious)—food, history, literature, idioms, humor, even a few Yiddish phrases, and later support of Israel—that had been buried under their German cosmopolitanism.[61] "I look upon Jewish nationality as a fact," Einstein said (in English) in 1940, "and I think that every Jew should come to definite conclusions on Jewish questions on the basis of this fact. I regard the growth of Jewish self-assertion as being in the interest of non-Jews as well as Jews. That was my main motive for joining the Zionist movement."[62]

They came as reluctant *exiles*, but in considerable part through the resources of *Aufbau*, and through its encouragement, if not its influence, most soon became *immigrants*: the Americanization (almost always as liberals) of the old anti-American Weimar left. Many, like religious converts in other contexts and times, became more committed Americans than the natives. They learned to believe that if there were class lines in America, they were less rigid than those in Europe, that there was more social mobility, and that government officials were, as one said, "public servants, not petty tyrants," as they had been in Germany. If they read any daily English-language newspaper other than the *Times*, or maybe the *Herald Tribune*, it was the unabashedly left-wing *PM*, and, in the years after the war, the relentlessly muckraking *I. F. Stone's Weekly*. For those who tried to believe America could do no wrong, it must have been an eye-opener.

Along the way, assimilation sometimes also included a gradual intra-Judaic rapprochement, maybe inevitable, between German and East European Jews, another double melting pot. "Our prejudice against 'Eastern Jews' did not evaporate at once, nor did their reciprocal one," wrote the historian Manfred Jonas, a native of Mannheim. "But over time a degree of mutual adjustment took place which reinforced, as it reshaped, our Jewishness."[63] And because of their admiration for FDR, because of their Weimar-era liberalism, and because the Democrats, as with prior generations, had been more hospitable to immigrants than the Republicans—the great Democratic political machines in Boston, New York, Chicago, Milwaukee, and other cities had long thrived on immigrants—most would also become lifelong Democrats. The New Deal itself was based in part on those urban machines. In the same vein, *Aufbau* celebrated Lincoln, who, it said, had close Jewish friends, among them the banker Joseph Seligman and the publisher Adolphus Salomon, welcomed the Jews, and, in the words of a rabbinical eulogy after his assassination, "embraced them with his whole heart." Lincoln, the piece also pointed out, had quickly countermanded General Ulysses S. Grant's order barring Jews (most of them presumably salesmen offering materiel for the Army) from the sectors under his command.[64]

Manfred George, the long-time editor of *Aufbau*, would observe that it "was the privilege of the so-called first generation to see things with double vision." But often that doubleness, compounded by the pain and bitter personal memories of the Nazi period, generated unbearable tensions. What one had been one could no longer be: but in the first years off the boat—and for some, many years after—there was little to replace it, except an unbearable sense of loss. And given the depressed, disoriented, and often lonely state that many had sunk into, it was hard for them to understand the optimism and cheerfulness of the Americans they saw around them. Some, who had defied all risks and danger to escape with a child or an older parent and come to America, never overcame what might now be called PTSD, Post Traumatic Stress Disorder, which overwhelmed them after they escaped. The great philosopher Walter Benjamin had committed suicide following his arrest by the Spanish police after strenuously hiking across the Pyrenees from France. (His guide on that hike was the indefatigable Lisa Fittko.) The writers Stefan Zweig, Klaus Mann, son of Thomas, and Ernst Toller committed suicide (Zweig in Brazil after a few months' residence in the United States), and there may have been many others. As early as 1939, a writer in *Aufbau*, using Toller as an example, referred to a "suicide epidemic" without further names.[65]

Rabbi Gottschalk, who was born in Germany and brought to New York when he was nine, recalls how some kept their spirits up:

> Although we lived in Brooklyn, my mother and I would travel to Washington Heights on the weekend and visit family. We would exit the subway at 168th Street and walk to 180th Street and Fort Washington Avenue, where our relatives and friends lived. It would sometimes take hours for my mother and me to walk the relatively few blocks because she would stop along the way every few yards to greet people, have a cup of coffee in a cafe, and discuss in German the events which masked the discontinuity of upheaval [in their lives]: births, deaths, bar mitzvahs, and marriages.[66]

Zuckmayer, writing in *Aufbau* in the grim days after Pearl Harbor, told his fellow exiles to buck up. "Throw the mantle over your shoulders, and delay not to go further into the night. Toss a schnapps down your throats and gaze without fear into the horrible darkness. Love and hate, be men, ready to breathe, to fight, to witness, and to die."[67] The piece was wrapped around the poem "Psalm of Courage" by Lion Feuchtwanger that was not quite as grim but no more cheering.

*

And, as the Marxist philosopher Ernst Bloch noted, there also were émigrés who, out of bitterness, disillusionment, or simple embarrassment, never wanted to think about the old country again, in some cases refused to speak German, and in their hatred of all things German came to the point of self-hate.[68] The avoidance of anything having to do with the old country was, as with prior generations, especially true of the children and adolescents, and emphatically during the years of war with Germany, when nearly all of them wanted to become one hundred percent American as quickly as possible. A German speaking German loudly to an acquaintance on the street would leave the acquaintance pretending not to know the person speaking to him. "This small town habit of many of our countrymen of standing around in front of cafeterias and on street corners in little gossip groups," said a letter-writer to *Aufbau*, one of several who wrote with similar complaints, "is a terrible phenomenon. The American regards it first with surprise and then with disgust and the collectivity suffers the damage."[69] *Aufbau* agreed. But reading that letter now, it may also have been an expression of the endemic internal class discomfort—an urbane, upper-crust *Deutschjude* looking down on the bad manners of a bunch of uncouth low-class Jews.

In Los Angeles in the 1930s there may have been an additional incentive: Many of the German-speakers appeared to be Nazi-sympathizers, people the refugees didn't want in any way to be associated with or to be taken for. One refugee, Heinz Pinner, recalled "that when he arrived in Los Angeles in 1940 'every German, former German, who was here, was more or less a Nazi' and that the relationship between the 'old German Americans' and the refugees was troublesome."[70]

Predictably, *Aufbau* would sometimes lampoon immigrant snobbery. It would repeat what may have been a common joke of the time: As two Jewish refugees were watching a Memorial Day parade on Fifth Avenue one says to the other, "in Germany the marching was better." There was too much of "In Germany this, in Germany that," *Aufbau* complained.[71] (Maybe the better quip was the one about the dachshund who tells an American dog: "In Germany I used to be a St. Bernard.") Among some people, so many remarks began with "Bei uns" (meaning "among us") that users of the phrase became known as "byunskis."

Conversely, as in most prior generations, the children of immigrants, whether foreign born or native Americans, were often embarrassed by their parents' old world manners, speech, and dress. Boys resented still having to wear short pants and chafed under their German names. (I was born Peter Ludwig Schrag, the middle name was my maternal grandfather's. It was the name on my birth certificate, and thus on my naturalization document and my passport; it's a name I tried for most of my life to shed.) Sometimes our parents obliged us: Heinz became Henry, Fritz became Fred, Günter became Gordon, and Hans became John. The German names of an earlier attempt at assimilation thus gave way to those of a later one. But as always, as one wrote much later, even "at the age of four, I was already at a different level from my parents in colloquial American speech, nuance, humor, and slang." And, as ever, last names were sometimes changed as well: Kohn became Cole, Levine became Lewis; some, like Manfred George, simply shed the Cohn and Anglicized the Georg. It was part of an honorable tradition: if the noble Battenbergs could become the still nobler Mountbattens, why couldn't Kohn become Cole?

But if this generation of Hitler refugees had much in common, the first generation was divided by at least as many differences: Were they German or Jewish; Conservative, Reform, or Orthodox; and if Orthodox, what kind? Zionist versus anti-Zionist; West European Jews (*Deutschjuden*) versus East European Jews (*Ostjuden*); and what one observer in the early 1950s called "the great gap" between Germans (whom some Austrians called Yeckes) and the Austrians whom the Germans called "Wiener." "They have their separate clubs and congregations, and their members rarely mix socially. They don't even live in the same neighborhoods."[72] In addition, there were all manner of differences in class, professional, and educational status, region of origin and dialect, Hochdeutsch versus Plattdeutsch, Hamburg versus Munich. There was considerable overlap among the categories. Eastern Jews, with a long history of pogroms and other persecution in their backgrounds, as Walter Benjamin said, had no choice but to seek a Jewish state, no more choice than "a person fleeing a burning building."[73] For Western Jews, who thought (or imagined) themselves assimilated into secular society, the outlook had been, or seemed, very different.

Eastern Jews tended to be more Orthodox than the German, assimilated, urban Jews, many of whom had hardly been Jewish at all—they had never been to a Seder let alone to any Shabbos service at a synagogue and had been as likely to observe Christmas as Hanukkah, assuming they knew there was such a holiday. Some, such as former Secretary of State Madeleine Albright, born Marie Jana Korbelová in Prague in 1937, whose family first fled the Nazis, then the Russians, didn't know until she was in middle age that, although raised Catholic, she was Jewish and that three of her grandparents had died in Nazi concentration camps.

The postwar concentration camp survivors and other DPs were more Orthodox, more unreservedly Jewish, than those who arrived in the decade just before Pearl Harbor. Because they came disproportionately from Eastern Europe and because they'd had fewer resources, economic or cultural, they had much less chance for timely escape. Led by Rabbi Yosef Yitzchak Schneersohn, the Lubatvitcher Rebbe, who escaped from Europe in 1940, and his successors in the Crown Heights section of Brooklyn, they brought with them a Hasidic strain of

Orthodox Judaism that was nearly crushed in the Holocaust but has thrived in America. But even among the German Jews there were those divisions and that ambivalence.

The questions haunted the pages of *Aufbau*: To what extent should all things German be rejected? To what extent did the Jews themselves—through their failure to make common cause with the *Ostjuden* before it was too late and their faith in their (perhaps) illusionary assimilation into German culture—help pave the way for the Nazis? To what extent, asked the journalist Hans Lamm in the spring of 1940 (two years before the Nazis embarked on their campaign of wholesale genocide), did the "immeasurable arrogance" of German Jews contribute to the occupying Germans' brutal treatment of Polish Jews?[74] Was assimilation ever real in Germany, or just a construct in German Jews' heads?

A long *Aufbau* piece in 1946, "Tilting against Windmills in the U.S.: An Attack on German-speaking Jews," took on a writer in the Yiddish *Daily Forward* who contended that "the average Jewish immigrant from German-speaking countries is hardly a Jew. Most have, like all European Jews, gone through a lot and have lost many of their nearest. But Judaism has remained a side issue for them." In effect, said *Aufbau*'s writer, Michael Wurmbrand, the *Forward*'s piece rested on the thinnest evidence gleaned from a few overheard conversations taken out of context in a summer hotel and built up into the pretense of a sociological study. What did the *Forward*'s writer know about all the work that German-Jewish organizations, *Aufbau* paramount among them, had done in furthering the cause of Judaism all over the world? Apparently nothing. Does he know the statistics for the number of German Jews who have been active in Jewish organizations? Does he know . . . ?[75]

Nonetheless, the issue would never be put to rest. After the war, there were the fearful questions raised by people like Raoul Hilberg in his 1961 book, *The Destruction of the Jews*, by the psychoanalyst Bruno Bettelheim (more about whom to follow) and by Hannah Arendt in her writings on the Eichmann trial and the role of the Gestapo-imposed *Judenräte*, the Jewish Councils in the Eastern European ghettos, in facilitating the shipment of Jews to the death camps.[76] Without the help of Jewish leaders, Arendt maintained, the Nazis' whole dreadful program of genocide could never have been successfully carried out. Those writings generated an intense debate running through many issues in 1963 about the part of Jewish leaders, in the words of the powerful response from the Council of Jews From Germany "in the destruction of their own people" (more to follow). Some of those questions will probably continue to haunt Jews into the distant future.

The other question that haunted thousands of German Jews proud of their *Bildung*, as it has many others: How do you reconcile Bach, Beethoven,

Brahms, Schubert, Schiller, and Goethe—indeed the whole notion of German *Kultur*—with Hitler, the mobs on *Kristallnacht*, and the death camps? How could one square the power of Wagner's music with the virulent anti-Semitism of the composer? Were all Germans (excepting Jews and maybe a few others) Nazis?[77] In 2001, *Aufbau*, by then more a biweekly illustrated magazine than a weekly newspaper, ran an article pegged to a protest in Israel against Daniel Barenboim's decision to conduct Wagner there, headed, "Can Music Be Anti-Semitic?" The author's answer was no. Barenboim loved Israel and he loved Wagner's music. He was just trying to bring them together.[78]

And a related moral dilemma: Shortly after the end of the war, *Aufbau* ran a short piece headed "An Unmasking: The Shame of Richard Strauss" with the text of a "hymn" the composer had written in 1943 for Hans Frank, who, as the former Nazi Governor-General of Poland, oversaw the murder of thousands of Jews and was then a Nuremberg war crimes defendant. (Found guilty, he would be executed in October 1945.) Frank "kept us from harm," Strauss had written, "I shout praise and a thousand thanks/To the good friend, Minister Frank."[79] What no one knew at the time was that Frank, himself an amateur musician, had helped protect Strauss's Jewish daughter-in-law and Strauss's (by Nazi standards) Jewish grandchildren. But there was no question that Strauss, though refusing the Nazis' demands that he remove the name of the Jewish Stefan Zweig, the librettist for his opera "Die schweigsame Frau," from the credits at its premiere in 1935, continued to perform in Hitler's Germany. Strauss's dilemma became the subject of *Collaboration*, a trenchant one-act play by Ronald Harwood in 2009. "What," he asks his American de-Nazification interrogator, "would you have done in my shoes?" That, too, was a question that many in Europe could have asked. It was one of the questions that underlined the horror of the Holocaust.

More immediately, was America a haven of temporary exile or the place of permanent settlement? Was it possible ever to go back, even after the Nazis were gone? And what kind of place would—and should—it be? Should refugees engage themselves in Germany's reconstruction? Or was that a hopeless cause? Even before the end of the war, and with the coming Cold War, that became a complicated question. What about settlement in Palestine, which would become Israel in 1948? And, as always, there were the tensions with prior generations of American Jews (descendants of mostly Eastern European Yiddish-speaking Jews), just as those generations had made their predecessors, the fully assimilated German-Jewish immigrants of the 1850s and 1860s— the Seligmans, the Warburgs, the Loebs, the Goldmans, the Lehmans, the Sulzbergers—some of them refugees from the failed revolutions of 1848, more than a little uncomfortable with their loud voices and demonstrative behavior.

Again there was the fear that the new arrivals would fuel the old American undercurrents of xenophobia, nativism, and anti-Semitism.

To the refugees from Hitler, America was to be a place of liberty where you didn't have Nazi thugs beating up Jews on the street and the sudden knock on the door in the middle of the night. They fled, most of them, not for economic opportunity but to escape danger—for freedom. "We wanted to be sure to live in a country where we would not have to be afraid," one refugee told an interviewer, "but even in this country it takes time to lose this fear."[80] And some of the fears weren't unfounded. In 1938, a rumor was widely circulated that, in the words of one study, "New York department stores were hiring refugees and firing Americans. An embellishment of this story was to the effect that customers had to bring German dictionaries along when shopping."[81] The fear was reinforced by a piece by Milton Mayer, a Chicago-born Jew, in the then-widely read weekly magazine *Saturday Evening Post* (circulation close to three million) called "The Case Against the Jew," which was lambasted by *Aufbau* (and by many others) in April 1942—five months into the war—for "dreadful, shameful" lines like:

> In his unstinting effort to adjust, [the Jew] had moved away from the "kikes." . . . He changed his name in New York and his nose in Los Angeles. . . . He reformed his ancient ritual and then abandoned it altogether, just like the Gentiles, for the movies, the rumba and night clubs. . . . He changed his day of rest and contemplation from Saturday to Sunday and gave up the rest for golf and the contemplation for fried chicken, just like the Gentiles.
>
> The Jews of America are afraid that their number is up—if not today, then tomorrow or the next. They know that war breeds chauvinism and that chauvinism breeds bigotry . . . they know that the postwar collapse will remind a bitter and bewildered nation that "the Jews got us into the war."[82]

"If nothing else," wrote the young Irving Howe for a labor journal, the Mayer piece "has served to bring into the open a national discussion of the subterranean anti-Semitic currents swelling at the base of the American social structure."[83] It was still a country where Jews couldn't become partners in Wall Street law firms or sit on the boards of major corporations. It was a country where a lot of housing was restricted, and where the prestigious universities all had tight quotas in their admissions policies on all but male WASPs from upper-crust families and the right prep schools, something that seemed to surprise even immigrants from Nazi Germany. As late as 1939, the rabble-rousing radio priest Charles Coughlin, who had an enormous following and had been railing for years against the Warburgs, the Rothschilds, and other international Jewish bankers and (at the same time) blaming Jews for communism, was asking whether the entire world had to go to war "for six hundred thousand Jews in Germany who are neither American nor French, nor English citizens, but citizens of Germany."[84] And there was the old aviator-hero, Charles Lindbergh, a friend of Hermann Goering and other Nazi leaders, declaring that "Our civilization depends on a Western wall of race and arms which can hold back . . . the infiltration of inferior blood."[85]

Yet looking at it some seventy-five years later, one is also struck by how many private individuals and organizations (many listed earlier) extended aid: from direct financial assistance and loans to finding housing to job placement to counseling of every sort. At Selfhelp, the volunteer counselors would often contribute their old clothing and sometimes solicit garments from acquaintances to give to the refugees they were helping. Sometimes, according to Marion Lust-Cohen, who began working at Selfhelp in 1950, they would spot a friend or coworker wearing a coat or sweater that they thought a needy client could use and ask for it, almost literally taking the shirt off someone's back.[86] Here again, even as American nativists and anti-Semites vehemently resisted any increased inflow of refugees, thousands of other Americans were doing their utmost to help them. We are a nation of immigrants; but we have also been a nation of xenophobes and nativist immigration restrictionists.

The "Fourth Reich"

From the 1930s into the 1960s, the new German-Jewish arrivals clustered on the Upper West Side of Manhattan—as distant economically and socially from the Lower East Side, where so many poor immigrants had been crowded a half century before, as it was in name. For a time, so many lived in little apartments and furnished cold water flats or rooms rented from other refugees in the larger apartments in New York's Washington Heights, a stretch along the Hudson from roughly 139th Street to the top of Manhattan, that it became known as "the Fourth Reich" and "Frankfurt on the Hudson." Washington Heights was the boyhood home of the teenage Heinz Kissinger and *New York Times* editor Max Frankel. And one who lived there most of her life was (and is) Dr. Ruth Westheimer, born Karola Ruth Siegel near Frankfurt, the American sex therapist, whose parents, Orthodox Jews, died in a Nazi concentration camp. She fought with the Haganah during Israel's war of independence in 1948 and was badly wounded. She came to the United States (and to Washington Heights) in 1956.

The Washington Heights subway stop, a landmark to thousands of Hitler refugees and many more thousands from countless other places. (Creative Commons)

In 1940, there were at least eight kosher butcher shops owned by German Jews in Washington Heights, and many of its shops had signs in the window that read "Deutsch gesprochen." No embarrassment there. At the same time, there were German Jews in Brooklyn or Queens who bought their meat and sausage—mostly pork, probably—from Karl Ehmer's markets ("Meat and Sausage Products in the German Fashion") or from Merkel's thriving chain. On the streets in Washington Heights, German was as common as Spanish would be a half century later. There was the Prospect Unity Club and other German-Jewish social and athletic clubs and the soccer leagues, at that time a rarity elsewhere in America. By the end of the war, there were a dozen synagogues in Washington Heights founded by German Jews, most of them Orthodox. In addition, German Jews made up most of the congregations in several other temples in the area. Rabbi Alfred Gottschalk, who was beaten up as a schoolboy in his native Germany by Catholic kids avenging an alleged thirteenth-century crime and came to the United States with his mother in 1939 (and grew up in Brooklyn), would observe that, "There was an ethnic world in Washington

Heights, where, as the saying went, 'You could tell a Yankee from a Yekke (a German Jew).' On the Sabbath the men strolled in formal dress with hats, canes, and umbrellas."[87] There was also a joke about the two Jews who were shipwrecked and stranded on a desert island; having decided they'd be there for a long time and that they wished to lay a foundation for a Jewish community, they founded three congregations.

Washington Heights residents weren't typical of all German Jews in America, or even in New York, much less of those who settled in the Midwest or on the West Coast. Most of those who first settled there were not the upper-crust cosmopolitan *Deutschjuden* from Berlin, Vienna, and Munich. Nor was Washington Heights anything like Yorkville, the east-side neighborhood in the mid-eighties that was home mostly to German Aryans and the pro-Nazi German-American Bund. Though its shops often carried the same cuts of meat, the same bread and pastry, the same confections that they'd grown up with, most German Jews, needless to say, resented and sometimes feared Yorkville and wouldn't go near it. Just to reinforce the point, in July 1940, nine months after the Wehrmacht had swept through Poland, *Aufbau* ran a long piece on a Nazi propaganda movie called *Campaign in Poland* that had been showing in Yorkville. It was advertised as "the only authentic film on the eighteen-day campaign." The ghost of the Fifth Column, the piece said, "wafts through the place. The film should be shown to all American officials. Authorized by the propaganda ministry, there couldn't be a scarier film."[88]

Living in those small apartments or rented rooms with or without running water, often sharing bathrooms and kitchens with other residents, the refugees in Washington Heights tended to represent the lower end of the economic and social spectrum, among them a disproportionate number of Orthodox Jews from small towns in South Germany or Eastern Europe. Typically the average resident was "less intellectual, less wealthy, more 'Jewish' and less 'assimilated.'"[89] New York's cosmopolitan immigrant professionals from the urban centers, many of them Austrians, clustered further south along Broadway and West End Avenue on the West Side in the seventies and eighties, which, with exceptions like the very upscale Rumpelmayer's Café on Central Park South, was where most of the restaurants, cafés, bakeries, groceries, theaters, and social service clubs catering to the refugees were located.

In the 1940s and 1950s, the Thalia Theatre on Broadway at 95th Street was one of the few that regularly featured foreign film classics. It also showed Maurice Schwartz's Yiddish-language film *Tevya*, based on the Sholem Aleichem character (later Tevye in *Fiddler on the Roof*). Sentimental Viennese favorites such as Johan Strauss's *Der Zigeunerbaron* and *Die Fledermaus* (tickets from 77 cents to $2.20) played frequently at the Pythian Theater on Broadway and 70th Street.

The leading café was the Wiener Kaffeehaus Éclair established in 1939 by Alexander Selinger, the refugee son of a Czech father and an Italian mother, at 141 West 72nd Street, where the underemployed well-educated émigré waiters, intending no irony, called each other Doktor. It soon was a draw not only for the Viennese immigrants who came, some almost daily, for their pastries and their *Kaffee mit Schlag*, and maybe a slug of nostalgia, to sit schmoozing with their friends, or even for a full course dinner of *Wiener Schnitzel*, potatoes, and *Kopfsalat*. It was also an attraction for a long list of celebrities, many of them Jewish but few of them émigrés from the Nazi era—Aaron Copland, Burl Ives, Eddie Cantor, Melvyn Douglas, Jack Palance, Roberta Peters, Richard Tucker, Bruno Walter, and Barbra Streisand. "Thanks for the many, many calories," one wrote in the guest book. More tellingly, someone else wrote (in German), "He who can bake such cakes can also conjure up sweet memories of times past."[90]

Excepting only Isaac Bashevis Singer, who wrote only in Yiddish but may have been its most regular guest, the Éclair came as close as any place to be the Parnassus of the bourgeoisie of the German/Austrian-Jewish West Side. The historian Atina Grossmann, who said that as a child she lived on the Upper West Side "in a hermetically sealed refugee world" recalled that her father "had his *Stammtisch*," his regular table, at the Éclair, "and his regular Monday afternoon *Kaffee* with Frau B., who had red hair and was an old girl friend."[91] But there were many others in the neighborhood: the Wiener Café-Restaurant on West 71st Street; LaCoupole Café-Restaurant, also on 72nd Street; the Golden Fiddle ("European rendezvous spot") and the Café Vienna, both on West 77th Street; and the Johann Strauss Café-Restaurant on Broadway at 103rd. (For those who wanted cheaper fare than the Éclair's and distinctly less *gemütlichkeit*, there was a Horn and Hardart Automat across 72nd Street.) And like other economy-minded New Yorkers, the refugees on the Upper West Side had to go "downtown" for their department store shopping: to Macy's or Gimbel's or for bigger bargains further south to Klein's on Union Square, or even to the East Side to the then-midscale Bloomingdale's.

Some émigrés lived in the Bronx, in the Jewish parts of Brooklyn, or the Queens neighborhoods of Jackson Heights, Elmhurst (where the Trylon movie theater was a regular *Aufbau* advertiser), and Forest Hills (despite the fact that many apartments in Forest Hills were still restricted to Gentiles), and still later, as they could afford it, on Long Island and northern New Jersey. Some who lived in the working class Queens neighborhoods of Elmhurst or Jackson Heights told acquaintances they lived on "Longisland" (pronounced with a hard "g"), which was geologically correct, but still a little pretentious.[92] There was a cluster in San Francisco, and enough to form German-Jewish clubs, many

The Café Éclair and pages from its guest book, with the signatures of Max Reinhardt, Bruno Walter, and Franz Werfel. (café photo courtesy of Andra Moss, Landmark West, New York; guest book pages courtesy of the Leo Baeck Institute, New York)

of them renamed after the start of the war, in Chicago, Baltimore, Pittsburgh, Denver, and several other major—and some, like Newark, not-so-major—cities.

And there was Los Angeles, with its growing contingent of émigrés, many of them actors, writers, movie directors, and associated movie industry professionals, some of them living in a style so grand that they could hardly be recognized as refugees at all. The novelist Erich Maria Remarque, whose *All Quiet on the Western Front* had been condemned by the Nazis and led them to ban all his books, "had rented a handsome bungalow in the park of the Beverly Hills Hotel."[93] During most of the war, the writers Lion Feuchtwanger and Thomas Mann and their families, along with the social theorist Theodor Adorno, lived in the splendor of the oceanside bluffs of Pacific Palisades northwest of Los Angeles. Mann called it "German California" and called Feuchtwanger's house the "castle overlooking the sea." It must have been strange, someone later remarked, for Mann to write a dark, searching novel like *Doktor Faustus* in the sunshine of the Palisades. The playwright Carl Zuckmayer talked about having escaped the "golden cage" of Hollywood, where he had a fat contract to be one of the "serfs" of the studios, which he later described as a "sated living death." "Not for that had we escaped the Nazis' death camps."[94]

The biographer Emil Ludwig lived in Santa Barbara. Ludwig Marcuse, notwithstanding his poor-mouthing of American culture, lived for twenty years in Hollywood, Beverly Hills, and Santa Monica while he taught German literature at the University of Southern California. The Marxist Brecht, who, despite his even greater contempt for most things American, and especially for Los Angeles ("Tahiti in the form of a big city"), lived happily in Santa Monica until the Red hunts of the McCarthy era drove him to East Berlin. From Brecht's poem "Hollywood Elegies":

> The village of Hollywood was planned according to the idea
> People here have of heaven. In these parts
> They have come to the conclusion that God,
> requiring a heaven and a hell, didn't need to
> plan two establishments
> But just the one: heaven.
> It serves the un-prosperous, unsuccessful as hell.

Most, however, appeared to have little trouble with either the cultural or the climatic transformation to their new home in exile: Vienna-born Vicki Baum, whose German novel *People in a Hotel* became the great Broadway hit and the Oscar-winning movie *Grand Hotel*, lived and died in Hollywood. Baum

Alma Mahler and Franz Werfel in California. (courtesy of Marina Mahler)

told *Aufbau*'s women's page columnist Vera Craener that she emigrated even before Hitler became chancellor because she couldn't stand the early traces of the Nazis in Berlin.[95] Werfel, who, with his wife, Alma Mahler, had, like Feuchtwanger, been aided by Varian Fry to escape from Europe, died in Beverly Hills, as did Bruno Walter. Arnold Schoenberg lived and died in Brentwood.

After Werfel's death, Alma moved to New York, where she had lived many years before with her first husband, the composer Gustav Mahler, when he came to conduct the New York Philharmonic and the Metropolitan Opera. Once a famous Viennese beauty and a composer in her own right, she had been an anti-Semite, had been married to the architect Walter Gropius, had been the artist Oscar Kokoschka's lover, and had consulted Freud about her marital problems with Mahler. Werfel, her husband, was Jewish, as (at least in the Nazis' criteria) was Mahler, who had become a Catholic so he could become director of the Vienna State Opera. (Vienna, too, was worth a mass.) Alma was accustomed to change.

Among those now mostly forgotten, but for a time well-known after her arrival as a refugee, was the Berlin-born Thea Wittner, a prize-winning sculptor in Germany and later again in America. Changing her name to Madame Thea Tewi, she became a highly successful fashion designer in New York of a stylish (and for its time, somewhat risqué) line of women's lingerie in the 1940s. *Life* called her "the fireball of American designing."[96] Tewi linked her designs to the Gershwin songs in the recently released film *Rhapsody in Blue*, a decision Craener lauded as a brilliant piece of promotion (for which, Craener pointed out, there was not yet any German word) and proof that Tewi had been thoroughly Americanized.[97]

*

From time to time, various service organizations tried to disperse the Jews and get them out of the German-Jewish enclaves around New York and ease their assimilation into American society. They tried to attract them to the Midwest and the Pacific Northwest where, in the late 1930s, the Oregon Émigré Community, abetted by, among others, an *Aufbau* article headed "Go West Young Immigrant," was offering help and advice to those who wanted to start businesses there. (The article, published in 1939, acknowledged that there weren't many jobs lying around on the streets, but for anyone with a little capital there were great opportunities.)[98] *Aufbau* also ran pieces, one headed "New York Is Large—America Is Larger," about the work of the Resettlement Department of the National Refugee Service, which, despite the Depression, each week reportedly received some fifty-five hundred help wanted notices from around the country.[99]

In pieces headed "Should I go West?" *Aufbau* tried to advise readers hoping to relocate: A watchmaker in New York with an asthmatic child looking for a more favorable climate was told (in 1943) that while he should consult his doctor on the medical question, there were good income opportunities in Aberdeen, Olympia, Everett, and Vancouver, Washington. The wife of a former art publisher from Berlin, whose husband was now working as a dishwasher in New York, was told that while "few of us might be able to resume our old careers," there might well be more opportunities in San Francisco, Portland, or Seattle. (It appeared right next to the Carey McWilliams article "California—Land of the Future" cited earlier.) A bookkeeper with decent English who couldn't stand the climate in Texas was advised that he could immediately get jobs as an insurance agent in Portland or Seattle.[100] Some readers, like the man who had been a traveling salesman of women's shoes in Germany and had found nothing in New York but a meager income selling chocolate and cigarettes door to door, were advised to move to a smaller city. "You'll have to count on a little time to become acquainted," *Aufbau*'s unnamed help columnist advised the former shoe salesman. "But you'll have better prospects of finding a reliable job than you would in New York. Besides, you'll find it's easier to integrate yourself into the life of a smaller city than in the huge city of New York."[101]

In the years before Pearl Harbor, Roosevelt's Secretary of the Interior, Harold Ickes, proposed opening what was then the U.S. territory of Alaska as a "haven for *Jewish refugees* from Germany and other areas in Europe where the Jews are subjected to oppressive restrictions. . . . Nowhere in the world today will the immigrant find less racial or religious prejudice. Nowhere in the world is there a greater degree of liberty for the individual."[102] That prompted some serious discussion in *Aufbau*, including a glowing piece headed "Alaska—Land of the Future" and a bill in the House about admitting refugees above or outside the existing immigration quotas into the territory. Under one plan, they would then live there until their immigration quota number came up, at which point they could immigrate into the United States.[103] (A similar idea, though on a smaller scale, was also discussed about settling a few hundred refugees in the Virgin Islands.)

The belief that all of Alaska suffered from an arctic climate, said one of *Aufbau*'s contributors, was a fairytale.[104] In fact, said Sen. James M. Mead, a New York Democrat, in yet another *Aufbau* piece, Alaska had the same climate as Sweden, Norway, and Finland, it was sparsely settled, and its inhabitants, the most racially tolerant on earth, wanted more people to come. "This vast under-populated and freedom-loving territory," he wrote, "might easily and effectively assimilate many refugees and give them a country of liberty and justice such as they do not now enjoy."[105] (Whether he was also responding to the complaints of his own constituents about the foreign hordes besieging their state no one will ever know. But the idea only bore fruit some seventy years later in Michael Chabon's wonderfully imagined novel *The Jewish Policemen's Union*.)

HIAS induced some refugees who were barely off the boat to move to the Chicago suburb of Skokie, a place that then must have seemed almost as foreign as America itself, but where there were available factory jobs, and which, to this day, is one of the most Jewish communities in the country. (And which may long be remembered for a Supreme Court decision in 1978 in favor of the ACLU's argument that a group of uniformed American Nazis had a constitutional right to march through the town, roughly one sixth of whose inhabitants were then estimated to be Holocaust survivors.) Toward the end of the war, Roosevelt also established a small refugee colony at Fort Ontario on the shore of Lake Oswego in New York State. But its nine hundred inhabitants had no legal status, couldn't work or travel, even to visit relatives, and were expected to return to Europe after the war. After an *Aufbau* campaign ("Have the Refugees in Fort Ontario Been Forgotten?")[106] and appeals from various refugee advocacy groups and some big-name Americans—among them Eleanor Roosevelt and the philosopher and education theorist John Dewey—Truman, in 1946, granted them legal entry into the United States. As the last of them were leaving, *Aufbau*'s correspondent Richard Dyck, who likened Fort Ontario to the French internment camps he'd seen in the early 1940s, observed that they wouldn't be sorry to see the last of the place. But "as they were now able to live as free people in the freest land in the world, they may sometimes look back and be thankful to the little city on the shores of Lake Oswego which first provided them shelter on American soil."[107]

There were also attempts by the long-established Jewish Agricultural Society, among other groups, to get Hitler refugees into farming. It required a little capital, special skills, and for most, a willingness to plunge into an altogether unfamiliar life. In 1939, realtors ran ads in *Aufbau* offering, for example, a hundred-acre dairy and chicken farm with an eight-room house for $7,000, with $2,750 down. And, as if in answer, there were ads directed to anyone thinking of buying a farm to first consult the Agricultural Society at 301 East 14th Street. For a time in 1940, the society also ran a Refugee Farm Training School in Bound Brook, New Jersey ("a unique experiment") providing "an overview" and practical training "in all aspects of farming." The students included a salesman, an engineer, an expert in textiles, a journalist, and a former cattle dealer, all, the piece said, with a love of the land.[108]

And some did in fact buy farms both in the East and in California—and when the DPs arrived after the war, there would be many more.[109] In 1947,

Aufbau, as part of a larger report on refugee farmers, ran an item on Henry Schmikler, who had managed a German textile factory before the war, had been in a concentration camp, and was now running a turkey farm in Whitman, Massachusetts. Next to it was another about Mrs. Hugo Schwartz, formerly of Vienna, who had been growing produce on her Massachusetts farm since 1941 and said she liked farming much better than life in the big city. And below them, pictured on his tractor, was Eric Stang, until 1938 a "manufacturer" in Germany, now owner of three farms in New Jersey, and, next to that, a photo of three generations of the Leo Simon family, who had arrived in America in 1938, with their cows on their farm in Lebanon, Connecticut. All told, according to the annual report of the Jewish Agricultural Society (the source of these pictures), by 1946 the society had provided loans to help some five hundred refugee families buy farms in fourteen states.[110]

After the war, *Aufbau* editor Manfred George would occasionally try to introduce his New York–bound readers to "The Wild West Today," meaning, in one piece, "The Columbia River Empire"; in another, "states between today and tomorrow," such as Oregon and Washington; in a third "First Look at San Francisco"; and a fourth, "Insatiable Los Angeles."[111] Not quite the Wild West, but judging from *Aufbau*'s letters, refugees showed up in places as remote (and improbable) as Wyoming, where one unhappy accountant, then working for a cattle dealer, and his wife, a hair cutter, wanted desperately to move to the Pacific Northwest.

Many refugees also became orchardists and farmers, or resumed farming, in Palestine. And a few hundred became cooperative farmers in Sosua, the immigrant community in the Dominican Republic (then still Hispaniola), to which some Sephardic Jews were exiled during the Inquisition and which was the only country willing to take significant numbers of Hitler refugees after the Evian Conference that FDR had organized in 1938. Some of their descendants are still there. And some big city refugees, who had never done a day of farm work, learned, as did many other Americans, to stretch their wartime food rations growing produce—beans, tomatoes, lettuce, carrots, beets—in the victory gardens in empty neighborhood lots, or even in parks, and to can them for the winter.

Lengthening Shadows

But if many were torn between a powerful commitment to Americanize themselves as rapidly as possible and *Sehnsucht*, the intense longing for the old culture and ways, by the late 1930s they were even more anxious about immigration restrictions and naturalization regulations in America and the isolationists in

Congress who resisted any loosening of the national immigration quotas. And for nearly all there was intense concern about events in Europe: the *Anschluss*, the occupation of Czechoslovakia; the *Blitzkrieg* through Poland in 1939; then the invasion of Belgium, Luxemburg, and the Netherlands in 1940; the fall of France; the Battle of Britain; and later the war in North Africa; the battles of Leningrad and Stalingrad; and then, with increasing excitement, the march of the Allies up the boot of Italy; and, after D Day, over the same ground in France, Belgium, Czechoslovakia, and Germany through which the Wehrmacht and the Luftwaffe had so easily rolled four years before.

On Sunday nights there was Walter Winchell—"Good evening, Mr. and Mrs. America from border to border and coast to coast and all the ships at sea"—who, well before the war, was lambasting Lindbergh, Gerald L. K. Smith, and other alleged Nazi sympathizers. Later, like many others in America, little family groups huddled around the campaign maps in the *Times* every day and around the radio listening to Edward R. Murrow from London on CBS or to Richard C. Hottelet from the Normandy beaches and the Battle of the Bulge, and later to the reports from—and about—Palestine. Many, having first been rejected as enemy aliens when they tried to enlist, found themselves in uniform in those battles, first in the Pacific and North Africa, then in Italy and France, and then in Germany. Or in cases like that of Sargent Eric G. Newhouse, once Erich Neuhaus of Vienna, in American bombers over Germany, fighting for and regaining the same ground from which they had been driven a half dozen years before—something that some of them could hardly believe when they were taking part in those battles.[112]

And beyond the daily focus on the campaign maps and the broadcasts from abroad was the more intense, more immediate concern about the friends and relatives left behind. Some of those relatives—spouses, parents, brothers, sisters, aunts, uncles—had vanished before the war began, deported to what was often referred to as the generic "Poland," interned by the French or the Belgians once the European war began, or swallowed into the huge stream of refugees in the desperate flight from Hitler's armies—now maybe in Boulogne or Paris, or last seen in Bordeaux, Perpignan, or Casablanca, or rumored to be in . . . ? The worry about their fate, of course, immediately generated the sinking feeling about the closeness of one's own escape—that, but for grace of God, there go I.

And inevitably the desperate search for those people followed, through international agencies, the Red Cross, the international refugee relief agencies, and through the pages of *Aufbau*, which would play such a large part in that search. And if they found them, could they get the documents, often a string of three or four visas and the exit and residence permits and the money to get them out, money not just for ordinary passage but for bribes, smugglers, and forgers? And since those documents usually had tight termination deadlines, could the last be obtained before the first expired? What happened to people who had American visas if their sailing was delayed for lack of accommodations or if ships were held up? In her powerful novel *Transit*, written when she was an exile in Mexico and first published in 1944, Anna Seghers writes of a character, a physician held up in Marseille, who had a contract to work in Caracas, "and because of the contract, a visa, and because of the visa, a transit visa, but it took so long for the exit visa to be issued that the transit visa expired in the meantime, and after that the visa and after that the contract."[113] *Transit* reflected Segher's own experience. Born in Mainz, she had emigrated via Zurich to Paris and, when the Germans invaded France, fled to Marseille, from where, with Fry's help, she got to Mexico. A Marxist, after the war she would return to (East) Berlin, where she would win, among others, the Stalin Peace Prize.

The questions ran on: What organization could help? Could you get your brother or your father out of Dachau or Les Milles, or your aunt and your cousin out of Gurs? Was there a lawyer in Aix-en-Provence who could gather the documentation and write a letter to the commandant at Saint-Cyprien proving that your friend and former partner was not a German saboteur but a true friend of France?[114] Was your sixty-five-year-old father or mother well enough to make the trip? Could we get Oma into Switzerland? Who could write a letter assuring a nameless State Department official that your uncle would not become a public charge, as the immigration laws defined it, if he got his American visa? Who was able to provide the detailed notarized affidavits attesting that the visa applicant was a person of "high moral standing and personal qualities," who had absolutely no contact with "Nazi or Fascist organizations of any kind"?[115] Was there still space on a ship from Marseille (before the end of 1942, when the Germans officially took over) to almost any port not in Europe? In many émigré families, the correspondence was full of such questions. For a time in late 1940, *Aufbau* even ran an ad from "S. Frohman" at 55 West 42nd Street offering its services in processing and documenting applications for the release of dependents interned in the Gurs camp.[116]

The searches for people began before the war and became more intense in the years after, when the concentration camps were liberated and many of the survivors quickly found themselves in DP camps in Italy and Central Europe, where conditions were sometimes little better than they had been in the Nazi concentration camps. At the same time, American émigrés were sending care packages of coffee, tea, sugar, flour, canned meat, chocolate, cigarettes, and much else to those relatives—or even to strangers, not only in Europe but in Palestine and other places. That traffic had started before the war but became much heavier immediately after VE Day and in the years that followed. During the war, merchants such as Paula's Lebkuchen on St. Nicholas Avenue in Washington Heights would mail their merchandise (in this case gingerbread) "to your soldier in every part of the world." The commercial merchandizers who sold and shipped those packages often also provided what in effect were banking services, transferring cash and other assistance abroad.

One secondary indication of the anxieties was *Aufbau*'s regular pre–Pearl Harbor listings of ship sailings and Clipper flight departures with time and date for when the mail closed. Shortly after the start of the European war, Kurt Plaut of Plaut Travel, one of *Aufbau*'s regular advertisers, advised readers trying to send letters to Germany to route them through acquaintances in neutral European countries and have them relay them to Germany. Emigration from Germany as of that date, September 15, 1939, two weeks after the start of the European war, was still possible, Plaut said, if the traveler had a U.S. visa, a ticket for a ship from a neutral country, and a visa to the country from which that ship sailed—a lot of ifs. Passage could be arranged telegraphically, sometimes in no more than a day if the neutral-flag shipping line had an office in the United States. The line would then, to the extent possible, try to arrange a visa for the emigrant to the port of embarkation. Plaut said he'd just learned that the U.S. consulate in Berlin was still processing visa applications for eligible people, thus making it possible for refugees in America to arrange emigration for qualified relatives. But he warned that there could be changes daily in the situation and concluded, "There's not a minute to lose."[117]

And as late as the summer of 1942, one travel agent was still advertising "possibilities for trips to America for people currently in Spain, Portugal, Casablanca, Switzerland or in unoccupied France," all places, if they could get to them, where desperate refugees had collected and where, for most, the visa and the permit to stay would soon expire. And as many *Aufbau* readers knew well from their own experience, in the words of one letter from a travel agent to *Aufbau*, "the matter is quite complicated and the situation changes almost daily, so we can't be responsible for such information."[118] As always, among the biggest hardships for refugees on both sides of the Atlantic was the uncertainty, the not knowing—not knowing where one's parents were, not knowing who could be trusted and who was an informant, not knowing when the rules would change, not knowing what Roosevelt, Hitler, or the police chief would do tomorrow.

The "Second Wave"

What's striking—though hardly unprecedented—is the extent to which the children of this generation of immigrants, and often the immigrants themselves, took advantage of their opportunities—the public schools and the night schools, the public universities, the doors that, despite the barriers to Jews still

common well into the 1960s, were open to them. My elementary school class-
mate, the son of the lawyer from Munich who repaired typewriters, became a
dentist and probably would have been a doctor had the medical schools been
fairly open to Jews. But others who were brought here as immigrant children
and were mostly educated in the United States became major figures in their
respective fields.

A partial list follows of what Harvard's Gerald Holton and Gerhard Sonnert
called "the second wave,"[119] children brought here by immigrants who distinguished themselves: Kissinger; the financier Felix Rohatyn, who oversaw the
financial restructuring of New York City and later became U.S. ambassador
to France; *New York Times* editor Max Frankel; *Times* education editor Fred
Hechinger, who also grew up in Washington Heights; *Times* reporter Joseph
Berger, born in Russia, who immigrated with his parents as a boy from a German DP camp; *Time* magazine editor Henry Grunwald, born Heinz Anatol
Grünwald, later ambassador to his native Austria; the opera conductor Julius
Rudel; the composer and conductor Lukas Foss, born Lukas Fuchs in Berlin,
brought to the U.S. at the age of fifteen; the orchestra conductor George Cleve,
like Rudel born in Vienna and like Frankel a graduate of New York's High
School of Music and Art; and the jazz pianist, conductor, and arranger André
Previn, born Andreas Ludwig Priwin in Berlin. The announcement for a "Cabaret Evening" in June 1945 sponsored by the Los Angeles Jewish Club of 1933
listed Previn as the piano accompanist. He was a sixteen-year-old high school
student at the time.

Also included are the historian Fritz Stern, who grew up in Jackson Heights
and became a major influence in the postwar rehabilitation of Germany; the
cultural historian Peter Gay, born Peter Joachim Fröhlich (meaning "happy"
in German) in Berlin; the Renaissance scholar Werner Gundersheimer, long-
time director of the Folger Shakespeare Library; University of Chicago President Hanna Holborn Gray, born in Heidelberg, who was brought to this
country at the age of four; Gerda Lerner, born Gerda Hedwig Kronstein in
Vienna, who arrived in the U.S. at nineteen and became a leader in the field of
women's history; the art historian Peter Selz, born in Munich; the gallery director and art scholar Hildegard Bachert, who had been Selz's friend since they
met in a Zionist youth group in New York and like Kissinger (and the Israeli
cabinet minister Moshe Arens, a refugee born in Lithuania) had gone to
George Washington High School; the book publisher André Schiffrin, the son
of Jacques, who after having followed his father as editor at Pantheon was
pushed out there and then founded the pioneering nonprofit New Press; the
painter Wolf Kahn; the Polish-born Abe Foxman, who had been left behind by
his parents with a Catholic family when the Nazis arrived and was for many

George Washington High School with three of its more distinguished immigrant-graduates (*from left*): former U.S. Secretary of State Henry Kissinger, art scholar Hildegard Bachert, and former Israeli Defense Minister Moshe Arens. (Creative Commons)

years the national director of the Anti-Defamation League (ADL); the Holly-wood talent agent Sue Mengers, born in Hamburg; and the Berlin-born Harvard physicist Holton himself. One of the things the Second Wave did not assimilate out of, Holton and Sonnert concluded, was their parents' commitment to learning.

Beyond that list were many American-born children of Jewish refugees with distinguished careers, like the banker and diplomat Richard Holbrook. Given the era, it's not surprising that there are fewer women on the list. Still there are countless daughters of refugees, some American-born, some not, in academia, journalism, business, and other professions—Atina Grossman at Cooper Union, Renate Bridenthal at Brooklyn College, Marion Kaplan at New York University, Nina Totenberg at National Public Radio—for whom the glass ceiling in America was almost certainly higher than it would have been for them in Europe, even without Hitler. It has to include Vera Katz, the three-term mayor of Portland, Oregon, born Vera Pistrak in Düsseldorf, who was brought to the United States when she was seven and who, in the words of the *New York Times*, "presided over Portland's metamorphosis into a pedestrian-friendly city that embraced mass transit, environmentalism and other facets of progressive urban planning and that was regularly ranked among the nation's most livable metropolitan areas."[120] It should also include Madeleine Kunin, the three-term governor of Vermont, who, though born in Zurich, was brought to this country in 1940 at the age of seven by a widowed Jewish mother who feared the Nazi threat next door (and very possibly also distrusted the Swiss, who, for better or worse, were always more practical than principled). And then there was the rock concert promoter Bill Graham, born Wulf Wolodia Grajonca in Berlin, who was one of the Thousand Jewish Children who had been brought to the United States before the war. His mother and a sister died in the Holocaust.

As with past generations, the children and the teenagers assimilated much faster than their parents—learned in the schools, on the streets, from their peers, and at the movies on the occasions when they could scrape up a quarter for the Saturday matinee. They learned to play cops and robbers (or cowboys and Indians, the same game with a different name) and stoopball and stickball on the streets, and to hide the stick so that the cops wouldn't take it when the neighbors' complaints brought a patrol car around the corner. They learned about Spaldeens (made by Spalding), the lively red rubber balls that were the first choice for the stickball games; and, if they were lucky enough to have an empty lot to play on, how to wrap old baseballs and cracked Louisville Sluggers in black friction tape. One, Harry Ettlinger, who later became one of the Monuments Men, the military unit searching Germany and Austria for art looted by the Nazis, learned about American football by watching games at Columbia's Baker Field from a neighboring Washington Heights roof.[121]

They learned the language they heard and saw all around them: on the streets and from the headlines on the *Daily News* and the *Mirror* on the rack at the corner candy store, from the news on the radio and from Captain Midnight, the Green Hornet, and Jack Armstrong "the all-American boy," the radio serials that many must have thought were "cereals" for the brands—Wheaties,

Quaker Oats, and all the rest—that sponsored them. They listened to Mel Allen's broadcasts of Yankee games on WINS and, for a few years, the Giants, too, or maybe to Red Barber with the Dodgers. (None, of course, knew that Allen's full name was Melvin Allen Israel.) They learned to trade Topps bubble gum baseball cards—one Joe Gordon for two Carl Hubbells, or whatever. They became courant with the vocalists and the big bands—Glenn Miller, Tommy Dorsey, Sinatra, Crosby, and all the rest—by listening to Martin Block's *Make Believe Ballroom* on WNEW. They learned both the humor and the ethnic pecking order from Fred Allen, Bob Hope, and the Jack Benny show. And, of course, they often listened with their parents to the radio reports of the war news from Washington, London, the beaches in Normandy, and later from the front as it moved east into Germany. (Radio, come to think of it now, and later television, was one of the great tools of assimilation—and, for better or worse, maybe one of the great eviscerators of regional and indigenous dialects, languages, and cultures—that previous generations didn't have.) And they learned from the neighborhood kids who was a Wop, a Dago, a Mick, and a Spic, learned to mimic Japs and Nazis, learned how to avoid the blocks where the tough Irish kids lived, and told the same lame ethnic, misogynist, and lisping homophobic jokes: How many Poles does it take to screw in a light bulb? Four; one to hold the bulb and three to turn the ladder he's standing on. What do you call an Italian submarine captain? Chicken of the sea. And sometimes they heard the same kind of abuse that millions had heard before them: Why don't you go back where you came from. Or, simply, kike or dirty Jew.

If they could afford it, their mothers hired *Schwartzes* to come in once a week to clean their apartment, and they learned from them, too. Some of the refugee kids, those who didn't come from practicing Jewish homes, may also have learned a little from the American kids in the neighborhood about the Jewish rituals and holidays that they had never known—Passover, Rosh Hashanah, and Yom Kippur—and about the dietary rules. Who knew from meat dishes and milk dishes? They may have gone to their friends' Bar Mitzvahs and the feasts that followed—maybe their first time ever in a synagogue—and heard their first words of Yiddish in their homes. Some may also have been taken by their friends' parents on shopping trips to the Lower East Side, to Rivington Street or Delancey Street, where the friends' parents grew up and where, maybe, the grandparents from Poland or Romania still lived. From Hitler they knew they were Jews, but until they got to America some knew very little—and maybe nothing—about what that meant. (And even then, what they often remembered best were the stale Bar Mitzvah jokes: "Today I am a fountain pen.") In the war years in New York, and maybe in parts of Los Angeles, a

Aufbau front page of December 21, 1944. This tenth anniversary edition left no doubt about *Aufbau*'s loyalties. (courtesy of JM Jüdische Medien AG, Zurich)

Jewish identity was important; in the decades following, especially in the admissions process in the Ivy League, at the medical schools, and in the downtown law offices, it was downplayed.

Yet, given all the handicaps that the Hitler refugees came with, even the parents seem to have assimilated—learned English, established themselves economically and socially, settled into the wider community—more rapidly than prior immigrant generations. In part, no doubt, because they were better educated, more urbane, when they arrived; in part because America's wartime enemy embodied the terrifying consequences of anti-Semitism gone completely mad; and in part because the country itself was more mature and had more institutions to facilitate that process. In America, you celebrated equal treatment at least as an ideal if not a reality. (Among those who taught English to immigrants during the Depression was Bernard Malamud, later to be recognized as one of America's great novelists, who, as a Jew, had trouble getting a regular teaching job even in the New York schools.) In New York and some other cities, you learned about the balanced ticket—a WASP, a Pole, an Irishman, an Italian, and a Jew.

For the men and women who served in the military, which itself accelerated their path to naturalization, there would be the GI Bill. For all, there were the public schools and universities, New York's City College, paramount among them. For many others, thanks in part to the New Deal, there were the strong, vigorous labor unions, which were themselves training grounds in citizenship and democracy. Some American-born kids in refugee homes say they learned to speak English with a German accent, because the parents tried to speak English so that their children would learn it. But for the most part, it was the children who, like most prior generations of immigrants, tried to acculturate the parents.

Many of the children, knowing no English when they arrived, were put back a grade when they started school. But within a year or two, as they began to catch up, they skipped grades and, where the schools were accessible, passed admission tests with ease to selective high schools—Bronx Science, Stuyvesant, or Brooklyn Tech in New York, Boston Latin, or Lowell in San Francisco— within four or five years after they got off the ship. "The records of George Washington High School, on 190th Street," according to one report from 1951, "abound with the names of immigrant youngsters who after one or two years in the country reached the head of their class. In 1943, an immigrant boy set the all-time mark for scholastic achievement at this school."[122] (What many never learned were nursery rhymes, Mother Goose, the English names of trees and flowers, and the other things very young children are raised with.) Shortly after the war, among those who had already married, most of the boys had married immigrant Jewish girls, only a third had not, and very few had married Gentiles. But that would soon change.[123]

Most of that first generation—those born abroad and brought here as children by their immigrant parents—is now also gone. Those who are still left, all adolescents or young children at the time, recall little of *Aufbau* and, in many cases, little of the two worlds it reflected—rarely anything of the old and often not much of the new either. If they could read German, they didn't want to. Like most prior first generations of immigrants they wanted to shed all that and become American as fast possible. *Aufbau*'s stern semi-competitor, the *Jewish Way*, advertised itself as "the only exclusively Jewish newspaper in the German language in America," bringing "not cheap entertainment and sensation but rather a goal-oriented fight for Jewish faith, Jewish honor, Jewish rights and the Jewish future. Not superficial reminiscences of European big-city decadence but rather the eternal undying values of Judaism. . . . [It does not] bring Americanized Berlin reportage but rather essays on Jewish problems and issues of Jewish fate."[124]

But despite that—or, more accurately, partly because of it—*Aufbau* probably served, and reflected the story of, their parents' immigrant generation—and to some extent that of their time—as effectively as any medium could. In Denver, the eighteen-year-old Peter Gay, in America less than a year, had to drop out of high school in 1941 to help support the family, mostly as a shipping clerk packing military officers' caps in a factory at sixteen dollars a week. He later recalled that the German exiles there formed, "as refugees will, a kind of government in exile; they read the same refugee newspaper, the indispensable *Aufbau*; they discussed American politics and military events, and explored over and over again, helplessly, with almost total futility, strategies for rescuing relatives and friends left behind." But he also remembered that that was the summer that Joe DiMaggio had his record-setting fifty-six-game hitting streak, a record not likely ever to be broken, "and day after day I listened to the Yankee baseball broadcasts—rather vague about the game, nostalgic about the soccer games of my childhood, and hoping for a better life."[125] Five years later he graduated from the University of Denver and ten years later he had his PhD from Columbia. That, as much as anything, encapsulated the story of many in his generation of young men.

2

A Generation with Double Vision

1933–41

In the course of its seventy-year lifetime, *Aufbau* did indeed go through a great "many changes and circumstances," as George had said, adapting to events and to sometimes shattering developments both in this country and in the larger world, at the same time remaining both mindful of its readers' immigrant culture and championing their Americanization. Like them, it had a double vision, looking forward with hope and determination and nostalgically evoking a time now long lost. "In these barbaric days," wrote Hulse in a January 1940 commentary on the production (in German) in New York of popular Austrian plays by Anton Wildgans and Arthur Schnitzler, "the German language and German culture must find their home outside Germany. And in American eyes, in the eyes of the world, there is no more effective way to pillory the Hitler regime than through the cultural achievements of those who have been driven into exile [and] who put in the shadows everything that's offered as art in today's Germany."[1]

At the same time, as the publisher Peter Mayer, who was brought here as a boy, pointed out, some well-known European cultural figures — for example, Billy Wilder in Hollywood or Kurt Weill on Broadway — also made remarkable adaptations to American style and idioms. The "atonal experiments that made

Weill so famous in Germany," Mayer wrote in 2004, "more or less evaporated in his American reincarnation. Weill simply (or not so simply) became a genius at the expansion of the American idiom. This is just as true of Wilder if you compare his prewar German films with the 'American' genius of his films like *Some Like It Hot* or *The Apartment*."[2]

For at least a few immigrants, as for some *Aufbau* writers, there was always the familiar inner conflict: Forward to rapid Americanization at all costs? Determined retention of the old culture and language? Or some straddling of the two? In part, the emphasis depended on the age and circumstances of the individual. "Could one really renounce the language?" an *Aufbau* reader wrote in a letter to the editor a few years after the war. "Despite acquiring the English language, we would be poorer than before if we forgot the German language. We must not let anyone take the German language from us, not Hitler, and not any opponent of Hitler."[3] The person who alongside his newly acquired English continues to nurture his German, wrote another reader, "does not thereby become less of a patriot but a more erudite American."[4] And, in fact, there were determined efforts by many exiled writers to protect and nourish the language. Brecht, Feuchtwanger, the poet Ernst Waldinger, Heinrich Mann, Oscar Maria Graf, and others founded the Aurora Verlag in New York to publish exiles' works; there was L. B. Fischer, also in New York, which published the work of Americans and exiles as well as classic German literature. Notwithstanding fascism, Arendt would later say, "the language didn't go crazy."[5] That now sounds self-evident: That it was an issue, and that it needed saying then, tells a lot about how some refugees, particularly the young, felt about the nation and culture they'd been born into.

Hulse, who was among *Aufbau*'s most productive writers, was something of a polymath. He was one of the leaders of the Blue Card, Inc. (Die Blaue Beitragskarte), a major fund-raising organization originally founded in Germany, working through synagogues, the German-Jewish Club, and other groups to help victims of the Nazis, and later served as its American president. Quite conceivably, its regular advertisement in *Aufbau*, accompanied by a pledge form, was the *quid pro quo* for his column. Hulse served as an Army physician in World War II, was a prolific writer on a wide range of social and political issues, taught psychiatry at Albert Einstein Medical College, and sat on the boards of a number of Jewish medical and social service groups.

✳

When George became editor in chief in April 1939, he spelled out, in the words of one of his successors, "three major themes for the paper in its daily practice:

loyalty of America's new residents to their new homeland; to hold true to Jewish belief and remain aware of its majority Jewish readers and not to disown the link with the German culture, language and history."[6] Within a year, reinforcing that link, George would also appoint an "Advisory Board" of distinguished figures, not all émigrés or Jews, whose occasional pieces in the paper may have made them appear to be something more than mere window dressing, but not much more: Among them the Slovenian-born writer Louis Adamic, Roger Baldwin of the American Civil Liberties union, Albert Einstein, Lion Feuchtwanger, Freda Kirchwey, editor of the *Nation*, Emil Ludwig, and Thomas Mann. Tellingly, *Aufbau*'s offices eventually settled in at 2121 Broadway, near the corner of 74th Street, the very center of the neighborhood of the comfortable émigré bourgeoisie, not in the less-affluent neighborhood of Washington Heights. In November 1939, it published a statement of policy that reflected both its ambitions and the tensions and ambivalence in its mission:

> This paper is to serve the interests of all immigrants from Central Europe and their merging into the life and society of the American democracy. It is written and published in America; it is an American paper in which American problems and the future in America are given first consideration. It is a Jewish paper, intended to preserve the traditions of Judaism and to nurture the ties of the individual to his Jewish heritage, Jewish history, culture and religion, without, however, wishing to forget or neglect the interests of the non-Jewish immigrant and his problems.[7]

Aufbau had in fact been constantly transforming itself as the population of refugees increased, and as their needs—and *Aufbau*'s readership and revenues—increased with it. From the start, it sought to differentiate itself from America's ostensibly nonpartisan dailies, whose function, it said, was just to report the news. It declared in one of its first issues, then still mostly the German-Jewish Club newsletter, that it would be infused with a point of view: There was nothing more boring, it said, than an "unparteiische" paper—a word it set in self-conscious quotes and which could have meant anything from even-handed to dispassionate to nonpartisan.[8]

But in its early issues, when many of its advertisers (and probably some readers) were still in the alien precincts of Yorkville in the German-Aryan East Eighties of Manhattan, the paper devoted much of its space to the Club's agenda and on the related (sometimes very parochial) hometown concerns and activities of New York's German Jews: religious services and lectures (an eight hundredth anniversary talk on Maimonides; Jewish life in the Middle Ages; "The Destiny of Jews in Germany"; an essay on romantic piano music). In its third issue (February 1935), ten months before the promulgation of the Nazi Nuremberg laws, *Aufbau* published a front-page story about the Heinrich Heine fountain in New York, a memorial, the story pointed out, to another German-Jewish exile (in the France of the 1830s and 1840s) who admired the Germans but hated the Prussians. The fountain itself was a sort of exile. It was originally intended for the city of Düsseldorf on the centennial in 1897 of the poet's birth, but because its placement there was blocked by nationalist and anti-Semitic opposition it was erected in the Bronx two years later. The story reached for relevance by pointing out the things that, like Heine, *Aufbau*'s readers had in recent years lived through and been transformed by: first education in the German spirit of Goethe, Hölderlin, and Beethoven, then bitter disappointment, and then the way back to Judaism.[9]

In the same issue it ran a long essay headed "The Eternal Lie" tearing into *The Protocols of the Elders of Zion*, still a mainstay of hard-core anti-Semitism, which some publisher was reissuing. A few months later it ran a front-page obituary on the death in Berlin of Max Liebermann, the German-Jewish impressionist painter, and shortly after that a long excerpt from a paper delivered at the Jewish History Seminar of the Theodore Herzl Society about Herod the Great, the Roman king of Judea in the first century BCE, which was essentially a morality tale about war and peace,[10] and, later that summer, a front-page piece headed "Tolstoy and Judaism." Occasionally it ran a practical piece, an exploration of the American university system, for example—the entrance requirements, how long it would take for a degree, the cost, a little description of student life—which (at that time) found no anti-Semitism in the medical schools and, astonishingly, made no mention of Jewish quotas in college admission, except to the medical staffs of hospitals. (Later, it would find plenty.) One *Aufbau* writer (in 1941) pointed out that at New York's City College, about 75 percent of the twenty-one thousand students were Jewish, as were half of the fourteen thousand students at Hunter College, then all women. But because they had not been subject to much anti-Semitism, they felt no need to join Jewish organizations and seemed to care more, in the words of *Aufbau* writer Joseph Maier, later a distinguished sociologist, "about the theory and practice of baseball" than about the state of European Jewry.[11] What may have been more astonishing is that in the mid-thirties, two years into the Nazi era, travel agencies and shipping lines had still been running ads in *Aufbau* promoting summer vacation trips, not only to England and France but also to Germany.

In June of 1935 it published two pieces and a front-page "Warning Call" about the "march of anti-Semitism in America," focusing on pro-Nazi groups in Yorkville. But it still paid relatively little attention to the impending disaster in Europe, to the related issues of Jewish immigration, or the Americanization of the immigrants already here. The most cognizant of those issues in its pages appeared to be the investment banking firm of Kurt Werner and Co. on lower Broadway, which regularly advertised financial support services for relatives in Germany. Even the enactment in September 1935 of the Nuremberg laws ex-cluding Jews—meaning anyone with three or more Jewish grandparents—from German citizenship and forbidding Jews from marrying or sexual relations with persons of "German or related blood" brought only a "so what else is new" response from *Aufbau*. These laws, sanctioned with a lot of fanfare, it said, were merely the confirmation of a long-standing situation.[12]

Barely a month later, on November 1, 1935, the focus began to change and the tone to darken. A long article headed "Illegal Report from Germany," which *Aufbau*'s editors said had been smuggled out at great personal risk but had been received too late for the prior edition, outlined in considerable detail countless attacks on Jews in different German cities and towns that had begun even before the promulgation of the Nuremberg laws: the indiscriminate seizures by the Gestapo, now without any allegations of illegal acts or other pretext, of Jewish property; the signs on the streets urging people not to patronize shops owned by Jews; and, conversely, window signs on Aryan establishments that read "Jews not welcome" or "Jews not wanted"; a mob, accompanied by Nazi cops at a Jewish doctor's office accusing him, with no evidence, of indecent assault on a sixteen-year old girl. . . .

It was a long list, one incident after another in every part of the country—barbers refusing to cut Jews' hair, shoemakers refusing to resole the shoes of their long-time Jewish customers, young women who had associated with Jews being marched and jeered through the streets of little towns—all of which, said the article, had turned the prevailing air of nervousness into full-blown panic. "Despite the infatuation of some German Jews with Palestine, no one sees a way out of the situation in Germany. Everyone expects the worst." Immediately after the passage of the Nuremberg laws, *Aufbau* said, many Jews had hoped that there would be some attempt at a "bearable co-existence with the Jewish people" and that the anti-Semitic propaganda would let up. "But that hope has now vanished. . . . One has the impression that while the general population finds these tactics excessive," the article concluded, "the intensive propaganda campaign has begun to stick. . . . Many people say there must be something to it. It can't all be lies."[13]

Given the deportations, concentration camps, and the mass murder that would follow a few years later, this turned out to be only a prologue—barely a hint. But if *Aufbau* was any barometer of the German-Jewish community in America, it marked the beginning of a gradual change: from the house organ of the German-Jewish Club to an intense and broader soon-to-be-global concern with Europe's Jews, both overseas and in this country. "Forced Labor for Germany's Jews," was an *Aufbau* headline in October 1939, six weeks after the attack on Poland, about an order requiring all Jews, men and women, between the ages of sixteen and sixty-five to register for what had been said was for food rationing but was in fact to prepare lists of workers for slave labor.[14] "Nazis Must Pay," said a bold head, early in 1940. The cause then was the sweep by Nazi storm troops of Jewish homes and the deportation to concentration camps of their residents in cattle cars from the cities of Stettin in Pomerania and Königsberg in what was then East Prussia. Nine hundred, *Aufbau* later reported, had frozen to death on those trains.[15] In conquered Poland, all Jewish marriages were forbidden. In Mussolini's Italy, Jews were being excluded from many professions.

By late 1940, after the fall of France and the Nazi occupation of much of Europe, there were no more vacation journeys to Germany. The travel agencies now were mostly promoting vacation trips to Miami and Cuba and transatlantic passage from Spain or Portugal to Cuba and South America. Some issues were packed with ads from travel agents and lawyers for people seeking visas to Cuba, whose government in the prewar years had commercialized its issuance of visas, running from a low of $150, roughly $1,500 today, to extortionate amounts several times higher depending on the desperation of the applicants. Kurt Grossmann, a journalist and human rights activist in Germany and then, as an immigrant in America (and a frequent contributor to *Aufbau* and other publications) an influential advocate for refugee rights and restitution, wrote, "This exploitation of human needs is one of the most shameful chapters of the whole refugee tragedy."[16]

In his massive *The Abandonment of the Jews: America and the Holocaust, 1941–45,* first published in 1984, the historian David Wyman charged that even after the genocidal intentions of the Nazis filtered out in the summer of 1942, most Americans didn't hear of them until much later because, as he wrote "the mass media treated the systematic murder of millions of Jews as though it were minor news." The full scope and many details weren't known, and much was so horrendous that editors feared that they'd lose credibility if they gave it big play. Dorothy Schiff's *New York Post,* a strong backer of the New Deal, covered some parts of the story; as did the liberal *PM,* and sporadically the *Herald Tribune.* "The *Times,* Jewish owned but anxious not to be seen as Jewish-oriented," Wyman said, "printed a substantial amount of information on Holocaust-related events but almost always buried it on inner pages."[17]

Even the desperate battle of the Jews in the Warsaw Ghetto against the power of the German Army in the spring of 1943 ran on page 6 in one issue of the *Times* and on page 9 in another. That, too, may have had as much to do with the editors' incredulity—with the very enormity of it—as it did with their fear of being seen as Jewish oriented. Wyman makes a strong case that the governments of the United States and Great Britain made no greater effort to rescue the hundreds of thousands—ultimately millions—of endangered European Jews because of one insurmountable domestic political problem: They had no idea what to do with them if they did. The convenient, and not illogical, response was to concentrate all energies on beating Hitler. Until July 1944, the name of Auschwitz did not appear in the *Times*.

In June 1944, the month the Allies landed in Normandy and as two respected international committees confirmed reports of what *Aufbau* called the "mass extermination of the Jews" in the death camps during the prior two years, it reported them in an absolutely straightforward manner—they hardly required embellishment. According to one story, there were 150,000 victims from France; 50,000 from Belgium; 60,000 from Germany; 50,000 from Yugoslavia, Italy, and Norway; and 300,000 foreign Jews from various countries in Poland.[18] The numbers, of course, were very rough, early guesses and tragically incomplete. But the absence of any comment also seemed to indicate that even then, *Aufbau* couldn't believe the numbers.

To complicate matters, as Wyman and others have pointed out, the American-Jewish community was divided, again fearing domestic anti-Semitic backlash if demands and protests on behalf of Europe's Jews became too loud. The lawyer and speechwriter Sam Rosenman, who may have been FDR's closest Jewish advisor, urged the president to stay clear of any rescue effort.

Aufbau's editors had no worries about being perceived as Jewish, and relying on their own sources in Europe and the reports of organizations such as the Jewish Telegraph Agency (JTA) ran a great deal, probably as much as their readers could believe and/or—given their fears, guilt, anxiety and heartbreak—as much as they could stand: Reports that Vichy was preparing to intern all 170,000 French Jews by October 1, 1942; that it deported all foreign Jews to Nazi labor camps (with a commentary headed "Laval as Hitler's Lackey"); that the Nazis were shipping 7,000 Jews every day from Warsaw to concentration camps; that 300,000 Jews had been deported from Hungary. Such lists would later become horribly familiar.[19] But *Aufbau*'s readers were also in the compromising position of being beholden to the United States for their own safety and, loudly cheered on by *Aufbau*, trying to prove in every way that they were loyal Americans and not—as xenophobes sometimes charged—a Fifth Column forcefully promoting its own parochial interests abroad.

✳

Closer to home, both for *Aufbau* and, no doubt, many of its émigré readers, hung the question, in the common summary form of the time: Can it happen here? The question was triggered by the events in Europe—and most immediately both by the weak, submissive response of the French and British to Germany's remilitarization of the Rhineland in March 1936, a clear violation of the Versailles Treaty, and by the publication late in 1935 of Sinclair Lewis's political satire *It Can't Happen Here* about a fascist takeover in America in which "a president becomes a dictator to save the nation from welfare cheats, sex, crime, and a liberal press." How similar were conditions in America, at the time still sunk in the Depression, to what they had been in Germany in 1933? How widespread and intense was anti-Semitism in this country, now being spouted by a spectrum of groups, compared to Germany on the eve of the Nazis' electoral success? How effective was Dr. Goebbels's Nazi propaganda? And through much of it ran the frightening example of how in Germany Jews, socialists, liberals, and moderates had all underestimated Hitler until it was too late. Even now, said a long front-page piece in October 1936, the "overwhelming majority of American Jews have no idea of what the Nazi threat means."[20]

Along the way, and resonant with those questions, *Aufbau* published a series of occasional swipes at the far larger German-language *New Yorker Staats-Zeitung und Herold*. It never said outright that the *Staats-Zeitung* was a Nazi paper, but in pieces like "The 'neutral' *Staats-Zeitung*?" (in December 1935) and "Is the *Staats-Zeitung* Nazi?" (in February 1940), mostly quoting letters from readers, it insinuated as much.[21] In a piece in English attributed to a group of *Aufbau* readers who had been studying it, *Aufbau* accused it of, in effect, being a mouthpiece for German propaganda. When the Nazis throttled the democratic free press in 1933, the article said, many good moderate and liberal journalists became available but the *Staats-Zeitung* missed that opportunity. Instead, it found itself teetering between two stools—Jewish advertisers and pro-Nazi readers—and, in the effort to squirm between them, deploring blatant anti-Semitism while at the same time echoing German propaganda, including the German pitch against preparations by what would become the Western Allies—the French, British, and Americans—to resist the rapidly remilitarizing Germans. "For two years," the article said, "the *Staats-Zeitung* had described German re-armament, an open secret, as an invention of Germany's enemies." Along the way, the piece also referred to a ceremony during an excursion to Niagara Falls sponsored by the *Staats-Zeitung* in which a German government emissary offered a Siegheil to his country and to the Führer. "With the best will in the world, we can't imagine that Victor F. Ridder," the paper's publisher and a civic leader in New York, is "comfortable with its tendencies." It was he alone, it said, who battled against Heinz Spanknobel and his pro-Nazi friends of New Germany, a group that had been organized with the blessings of German Deputy Führer Rudolf Hess. How could he tolerate its retailing of Nazi propaganda?

Aufbau, having said that one shouldn't speak ill of the dead, marked the passing of the *Staats-Zeitung*'s editor by doing just that. It said the paper's articles were "a mixture of Hitler veneration and hackneyed clichés" (e.g., "Hitler has returned a shimmering defense to the German people" or "The re-occupation of the Rhineland was a dream come true for all Germans whose hearts had been seared by the diktat of the Versailles Treaty"). And then there was the *Staats-Zeitung* item headed "All Germans Like a Single Man for Hitler" and "Unanimity of the German People Buoys Hitler" (both of which may have been mostly correct).[22] Those *Aufbau* pieces, purportedly produced at arm's length by an independent group, simultaneously served two very obvious purposes — furthering the cause and beating the competition — but that was hardly an anomaly in journalism, either then or now.

In December 1938, it reprinted a whole *Staats-Zeitung* piece on the "Cold Terror" of *Kristallnacht* that sought to differentiate the Nazis from the German people, followed by *Aufbau*'s hope that the German-American community (*Deutschamericanertum*) "would, in self-interest, really wake up and march in the battle alongside the rest of the civilized world."[23] But, reflecting the painful ambiguities of its time and its readers, in February 1939 *Aufbau* published an article, "Germany in Its Lowest Depths," contending that the "blame of German society is not of today, but lies many years in the past."[24] As late as the summer of 1942, six months after Pearl Harbor, Alan Cranston, then an official with the Office of War Information (OWI), complained (the piece was in English) that "many editors of German-language newspapers (obviously with exceptions) have thus utterly failed to demonstrate their opposition to Nazism." The German-Americans, one editor told him, "don't like to run all that stuff about Hitler and Nazism. Every time you attack the Nazis, they think you mean them."[25] After the war, *Aufbau* went after the *Staats-Zeitung* again, tearing apart an article the paper had run echoing Nazi wartime propaganda about "the model ghetto" that the Theresienstadt concentration camp had been.[26]

Aufbau's broadening prewar concern showed itself in small items as well: Praise for Harvard President James B. Conant for "his manly stand in refusing the ten thousand dollar scholarship offered by Putzi Hanfstaengl," the idiosyncratic German-American businessman and Harvard alumnus, then a friend of Hitler; high marks for a column by Westbrook Pegler, hardly a bleeding heart liberal, in the *World Telegram* describing Germany's militaristic preparations for the 1936 Berlin Olympics; a note that the Germans had banned Charlie

Chaplin's newest film (no doubt, *The Great Dictator*) presumably because of the resemblance between Chaplin with his Hitler mustache and the original. Manfred George, reviewing it for *Aufbau*, loved it. "One can't say enough about it," he said. "Every minute is priceless."[27]

At the same time, writers in *Aufbau*, and no doubt their readers, were struggling with the identity question: refugees, exiles, émigrés, immigrants? "Merely, we fled," in the lines of the acerbic Bertolt Brecht. "We are driven out, banned. / Not a home, but an exile, shall the land be that took us in."[28] But that hardly put an end to the questions, much less answered them. Americanization yes, or maybe, and what did Americanization mean? An unsigned lead article late in 1936 cited the case of Carl Schurz, who it described as a *political* refugee. He'd fought against the Prussian Army in the Democratic Revolution of 1848 and, four years later, after the revolution was crushed, came to the United States. In 1860, he campaigned for the election of Lincoln, who named him ambassador to Spain and eventually made him a general in the Union Army, meaning, as *Aufbau* pointed out, that Schurz became a major political figure less than a decade after learning English. Immigrants from Nazi Germany, the piece contended, were not that kind of political refugees, something it never defined. But the Schurz story also demonstrated how easy it was for some immigrants to succeed in America.

"Let us forget what was," the article said. "We Jews should be grateful to Hitler for denying us the chance to stay and convert." But that didn't mean immigrants should plunge into unbounded Americanization. "That sort of apish mimicking is laughable. We'll never lose our German accent. . . . Let's be proud of the cultural heritage we brought with us from Germany." And then, even more ambiguously, "let us learn to look ahead!"[29]

But that was 1936. Beginning with *Kristallnacht* in 1938, the Nazis, and later the war, would help make things considerably clearer. By the 1940s, most reservations about the crudeness of American culture and the uncertainty between being Jewish and being American had evaporated. *Aufbau* and the immigrant community, George wrote in December 1944, when the Allies were on their way to victory in Europe, had found a double homeland in America: "The freedom of American society and its democratic world view, and the freedom to be what our forefathers were: sons and daughters of the Jewish people."[30] In America, more than anywhere else, you could be both.

Nevertheless, the question was always there, as it has been for nearly all generations of immigrants before and since. Yes, refugees should assimilate, one of *Aufbau*'s writers said in 1939, but the person who leaps into Americanization without thought, casting away everything he brought with him, will not make the best American. And for the newcomer who "the moment he leaves the pier is lost in the crowd" in this huge country, Thomas Mann, in a front-page *Aufbau* piece, advised "time and patience." In response to the refugees who disparaged their new country, Mann confessed that he was "enchanted" by it. "I've found a second home here," he wrote, "whose atmosphere of freedom allows me to pursue my work in peace." He allowed that he might be a special case (as he certainly was), but that didn't dampen his deep affection for Americans or reduce his belief that they "behaved wonderfully toward us."[31] Later, after the war, the rise of McCarthyism would greatly dampen his enthusiasm. But in a speech (in English) at a Nobel anniversary dinner in 1942, reprinted in its entirety by *Aufbau*, he declared that if "through the medium of the future peace . . . the clear and spiritually sound principles and the moral code of conduct upon which the Union was originally established by the Founding Fathers . . . should become the basic law of the world—the world would be the better for it."[32]

By November 1938, after Hitler's annexation of Austria, which the Nazis called the *Anschluss*, and after the Munich Conference, when the British and the French tried to appease Hitler by giving him the Sudetenland in Czechoslovakia (and soon all of Czechoslovakia), but just before *Kristallnacht*, *Aufbau*'s concerns had deepened. Those concerns, far beyond the narrow institutional agenda of the German-Jewish Club, would become its primary mission. In an angry boldface, front-page item headed "The Big Test," it lambasted the pusillanimity of the European leaders of the "so-called democracies" who had hurled "a brave and humane people [the Czechs] into the jaws of the insatiable swastika-barbarians," making visible "gaping holes in the fabric of civilization. . . . Will the endangered peoples who can still save themselves pull themselves together? If ever bold hearts, clear heads and strong fists are needed, then today [is the time], when nothing less than the future of mankind is in play!"[33] But this angry piece, the mournful "editorial" response in December 1938 to the depredations and brutality of *Kristallnacht*, a *cri de coeur* that was little more than a call to "bravely struggle through this anti-Semitic morass and the ruined lives to a brighter future"; the transcript of a radio talk by Manfred George, shortly before he became *Aufbau*'s editor, on the thousands of displaced and endangered Jews shut out by every civilized European nation; and an essay in March 1939, "Nazis and the Jewish Questions," parsing the supposed differences between the anti-Semitism of reactionaries and fascists, did little more than reflect the helplessness of the situation.[34]

Even in June 1939, after the ship *St. Louis* was not allowed to land its 908 Jewish refugee passengers either in Cuba or in the United States, *Aufbau*'s anguished articles hardly took note of the closed American doors, much less of the irony that its lead piece on the *St. Louis* ran under an article by Harold Ickes, Roosevelt's secretary of the interior, lauding the blessings of democracy as a bulwark against anti-Semitism and intolerance.[35] What George's radio talk did do was to call on those now in the safety of America to get engaged with whatever resources they had to make common cause with their fellow Jews trapped in a European no-man's-land or worse—with money if nothing else. It was their obligation to act. Nonetheless, all three post-*Kristallnacht* articles pointed to the paper's new direction and tone and gave the evolving, sometimes quarrelsome German-Jewish immigrant community a credible voice, a forum that, for all its ongoing internal divisions and differences, would bind it a little more closely together.

Not coincidentally, perhaps, the piece in the November 1, 1938, issue headed "Immigration into the United States" outlined a few, though hardly all, of the complex laws and regulations—and what it described as the lack of clarity—governing the process: the national origins quota laws based on place of birth, not citizenship (with Hitler's denaturalization of Jews itself a dicey definition), so that after borders were redrawn at Versailles, for example, a German born in the province of Posen was counted against the Polish quota. It outlined the provisions under which immigrants from Canada and other nations in the Western Hemisphere were not subject to quotas (probably a good thing because it encouraged some refugees, hoping to escape from Hitler and eventually immigrate to the United States, to obtain visas for Mexico, Chile, Bolivia, or Cuba) and the similar nonquota provisions for close relatives—spouses, unmarried children—of those already here. But it did not mention the affidavits and the guarantees from U.S. sponsors that the immigrant would not become "a public charge," which was one of the statutory provisions used by State Department bureaucrats in their exclusion of aliens they didn't like. Nor did it mention the other documents required even for a visa application, much less the fact that in the 1930s those State Department officials were filling less than half the already-low quotas the immigration law had set for visa applicants from the affected countries.[36]

For various reasons, Havana had become a sort of waiting room, a halfway house for thousands of refugees trying to get to the United States and whose need for support (at $4.50 per person per week, itself a meager sum) was straining the already over-stressed resources of agencies like the Joint, the American Jewish Joint Distribution Committee.[37] A few months later, *Aufbau* reproduced a piece from *Colliers*, a magazine which had once been a voice for anti-immigration

muckrakers, with "cold figures" showing that the supposed "alien horde," in
Colliers' words, was in fact "an alien trickle," a total of 457,000 immigrants in
the 1930s, the lowest number in a century.[38] And relative to population, the
lowest number in American history. What no one noted in the years following
is that the most progressive era in U.S. politics, the years of the New Deal and
the Great Society (roughly 1933 to 1965), were also the years of historically low
immigration.[39]

★

In New York, the "alien trickle" was nonetheless a substantial market and, in
some neighborhoods, a crowd. *Aufbau* beginning in the late 1930s and early
1940s was crammed with ads for sublets—mostly furnished single rooms (and
sometimes double rooms) in apartments on the Upper West Side, generally
going for four to six dollars a week (more for rooms with running water), some
with kitchen privileges, some offering board at additional cost. Pension Fischer
on West End Avenue offered eleven evening meals for $5.50 (Friday evenings
ten cents extra). There were seamstresses looking for work doing alteration and
repairs in their homes, pawnbrokers and other commercial buyers offering cash
for jewelry, furs, antiques, rugs, stamp collections, and other valuables. Miss
Suzanne was offering electrolysis and other depilation services; an unnamed
"American" about to travel to Germany was offering to contact relatives, get
affidavits, and perform various other personal services as well. And until Pearl
Harbor (and then again, of course, after the war) *Aufbau* still ran ads for merchandizers offering to send "the finest American foodstuffs"—cocoa, coffee,
chocolate—to Germany at seven dollars for a twelve-pound package.

    There were also ads offering instruction in basic or advanced English, in-
cluding "American English" at between twenty-five and fifty cents an hour,
sometimes in schools, sometimes in West Side apartments. Guttmann and
Mayer, the latter formerly of Mannheim, announced their new kosher meat,
sausage, and poultry store on West 184th Street "in the heart of Washington
Heights"; Mme. Caroline, formerly Frenzlau Fashions of Düsseldorf, announced
her new collection of elegant and sporty women's hats; Gustav Schulz, J.D.,
formerly attorney at law in Ludwigshafen-am-Rhein and in Mannheim, let it
be known that he was now located in a law office at 70 Pine Street (though with
no indication whether he had gone back to law school and now had a New
York State license or was just a rainmaker for some downtown corporate law
firm); H. Ely Goldsmith, "the only specialist in the field with his own office in
Havana," offered to help address immigration and naturalization problems;
Luis Rojas de la Torre, a Mexican lawyer on East 42nd Street, offered help

with immigration to Mexico. And there were ads (all in German) for tailors touting their skills in repairing or altering furs; for cold summer storage of furs; for pharmacies, attorneys, opticians, movers, translators, photocopying services, exterminators, funeral parlors ("simple or Orthodox Jewish funerals"), watch repairers, dating services ("New Friends"), and always for lessons and books that "teach you *how to speak and act American*."

And maybe as telling—about the times, *Aufbau*'s liberal politics, and the heavily Jewish labor force in the garment industry—were the Labor Day greetings (as in wartime 1942) from local union leaders in the industry and the celebratory Labor Day display ads: from the Amalgamated Clothing Workers, the New York Clothing Cutters Union, the Textile Workers Union ("For a Free Germany"), the Millinery Workers Union, the Millinery Blockers Union, the Dress and Waistmakers Union, and the Undergarment and Negligee Workers Union, Local 62 of the ILGWU, among others.[40] Here was the prior generation of (mostly) Eastern European Jews declaring its recognition of the newly arrived exile German Jews, a sort of rapprochement.

And there were dozens of personals in each issue announcing births, bar mitzvahs, engagements, weddings, and deaths, as well as ads for "matrimonial bureaus" and matchmakers like "Field's Introductions, 18 to 70," and many from people looking for marriage partners, more than a few of whom wanted to make certain that the putative spouse came with some financial resources: "Independent businessman, educated, good appearance, early forties, looking for a life partner; some capital desirable." Sometimes the ads were placed by widows or widowers, by mothers looking for spouses for their daughters, or from the friend of a "respected teacher, good income, pretty, charming personality, wide range of interests, swims, drives her own car [looking for] a cultured, marriage-minded man, under 45, with a good livelihood in New York." There were ads for fire, auto, and life insurance agents; for moth-free summer carpet storage; for Dr. Alfred Fleischner, an astrologer-fortune teller; and for realtors, some dealing in apartments and apartment houses, others in farms, gas stations, and boarding houses.

There were, in addition, columns headed "Wir bauen auf" ("We're building"), little business announcements that looked like news—maybe to show the nativists that immigrants weren't just taking jobs from Americans but were creating jobs and were thus good for the economy, but which obviously also served as unpaid ads: "Mr. Schanzer, the former owner and teacher of the Neudegger Driving School in Vienna, has opened a driving school at 1210 First Avenue under the name Autoschool Schanzer and offers readers of the *Aufbau* special rates" or "Charlotte Weissbarth, formerly Hats Rosenthal, Breslau, has moved her hat salon to 108 East 96th Street." Erwin Helfgott, former owner of beauty salons in Berlin and Vienna, was touting his twenty-five years' experience as a big-city ladies hairdresser at his new location at 201 West 95th Street.

What seemed clear was that in their first year or two in business in America, the émigré entrepreneurs mostly did business with other refugees. But that could hardly have been very different from the pattern of prior immigrant generations. Occasionally, *Aufbau* also got sarcastic swipes from readers in Palestine who didn't give a fig that Mayer had started a new sausage store in Washington Heights and who thought the paper was wasting space on it.

And as another indication that not all refugees came with nothing, there were display ads addressed to "immigrants" from stock and customs brokers and international movers and estate management firms; and, in a sign that others were already on the way up the economic ladder, private schools and kindergartens; and, in the spring and summer, even through the darker days of World War II, a growing number of hotels in the Adirondacks and the Catskills catering to German-speaking vacationers. Many of them were run by German-Jewish refugees like Walter and Irene Vogel and employed German-speaking clerks, waiters, and busboys (of whom during a couple of summers I was one) who could schmooze with the guests.

By the middle to late 1940s, there were many such resorts, where the *Sauerbraten* and the *Katoffelbrei* were done right and the entertainers played and sang the old songs: the Breezy Hill; the Mathes; the New Edgewood ("On Lake Switzerland"); the Lorraine; the Pinewood ("Not a Dull Minute"); the St. Regis ("German and Hungarian kitchen"); the Park Terrace; the Takanasee in Fleischmanns; the Grand Hungarian Hotel on the boardwalk in Belmar, New Jersey; the Colonial Inn in Pine Hill in "the heart of the Catskill Mountains" with "Our famous afternoon Kaffeeklatsch"; the St. Moritz in Lake Placid; the Hotel Adler in Sharon Springs; and the Ro-Ed Mansion in Saratoga Springs, both "Strictly Kosher"; and scores of others. And, almost as a measure of expanding prosperity after the war (and maybe assimilation as well), the geography of resorts, still advertising in German, expanded to Vermont, Pennsylvania, the coast of Maine, and Bermuda ("Spring all the Year Around!"). In the war years and early postwar years some guest farms such as Eilermann's Poultry Farm and Hede Altschuler's Hathaway Farm also advertised (in an echo of the old upscale German Kur-hotels, "rest and recovery"). The town of Saratoga Springs, New York, advertised itself as the "Carlsbad of America." And for those who were going to the Catskill resorts after the war, there was a wide choice of taxi services — Stern's, Bachenheimer's, Bloom's, Vollweiler's — that would take them door to door.

Among the many who didn't advertise was Blanche and Jimmy Cooney's Morning Star Farm in West Whately, Massachusetts, which became a very modest year-round rural retreat for a host of émigré artists and intellectuals. Among them the Austrian actress and writer Hertha Pauli, her friend the Austrian writer Karl (Carli) Frucht, and the German satirist and poet Walter Mehring (like Pauli an occasional *Aufbau* contributor)—who also had help escaping from Vichy France by Varian Fry and his Emergency Rescue Committee and had also hiked over the Pyrenees into Spain on their way out. It was at the Cooneys' where some German émigré authors first met their American translators, Richard and Clara Winston.[41]

Helpfully, as part of its summer "Resort Guide" (June 1943) and the tag line (in English) that "Vacations Are a War Need"—and, in promoting the natural wonders of the Catskills, probably part of a little mutual backscratching with its hotel advertisers—*Aufbau* also ran pieces on excursions in the Catskills and at Lake Placid; on "Ocean and Beach in New Jersey"; on "The Joys of Sea Food in Rhode Island"; and, alongside the ads, advice on how much to tip: ten to twenty-five cents for every service performed by a bellboy but more if he had to carry more than three heavy bags.[42] And, in the years just before Pearl Harbor, there were plenty of cars advertised, mostly used, but new as well, to get people there, from dealers like Lloyd Motors on Broadway or Auto Cappel (formerly of Düsseldorf, Aachen, and Krefeld, now in Queens). Plymouths, Hudsons, Packards, and Chevys were available for anyone who had $175 for a used 1936 Dodge or $195 for a 1937 Plymouth. Not everybody was poor even then.

Eyes Open, Hands Tied

By the end of the 1930s, coinciding with events in Europe, the reports in *Aufbau* became grimmer by the week. Even to read them nearly a century later, when so much about the Holocaust is familiar, they remain shocking. In July 1939, a "Report from Hell" detailed the story of a transport of German Jews, many of them elderly men, from an unnamed train station to camp "B," which began when the sadistic SS thug who guarded them introduced himself by saying that he'd begun the day by torching a synagogue, then smashing the jewelry and furnishings of Jews—just so they knew who they were dealing with—and ended twenty-three hours later when they were bloodied with beatings from rifle butts and steel rods in a march through a tunnel from the train, through a camp gate marked "My Country, Right or Wrong," then were ordered to stand while they were questioned about their occupations. When a man identified himself as a doctor, he was beaten until he said he was a rapist (in German, a "woman-shamer"); salespeople were beaten until they called themselves cheaters; and bankers had to name themselves counterfeiters. In between, they were further humiliated when many, having been fed some slop and suffering from diarrhea, weren't allowed to relieve themselves and so stood or sat with their pants full. The "Report from Hell" also included the story of a man already too demented to answer questions, whom the SS guards strung up on a tree by his arms, then cut down and kicked and beat to death. The piece ends with a description of how SS officials in the camp, in return for a spoon or a dish or even an old tin can (price three marks), extorted from the prisoners what little money they had managed to carry with them. Those who owned cars were forced into selling them for the absurd price of four hundred to six hundred marks, a price that, of course, was rarely paid.[43]

The article has a strange Kafkaesque quality. The source was said to be a decorated former officer with an Iron Cross, presumably from World War I, but was unidentified by name, as are the places—the city of origin and the camp. All this may have been to protect the source, perhaps another guard, who might still have been in Germany or may have had relatives there. Without any definite attribution, it would, in any case, never have passed muster under Anglo-American journalistic standards. Yet, despite the questions, given the many similar stories like it that emerged later, it's hard to question the story's essential accuracy. And it's certainly another marker in the growing awareness at *Aufbau* and among its readers of the nature of the Nazi regime—what the refugees had escaped from, what those they left behind faced, and the terrible things that lay ahead. But what may have been most revealing is that the article generated reader letters contending that "it would be better for us if everybody minded his own business and tried to forget a little and not try to stir up things that are of no use to anyone." (And those letters in turn generated an appropriately angry response from the philosopher Ludwig Marcuse: "Forget, they say to the abused victims, only don't remind the world of the monstrosities that occur every day. So be quiet, they say to the victims. Just don't be so noisy."[44]

In the same July 1939 issue as the "Report from Hell," under the heading "March of Time," one of many such columns that would appear in succeeding issues, it ran long lists of short items culled from other unattributed media, from almost everywhere of interest to Jews: the impressment by the Nazis in Vienna of Jewish men, ages eighteen to thirty-five, into forced labor on road construction gangs; the random beating of Jewish children in the public parks by roving gangs of Nazis; the reelection of Fritz Kuhn in New York as leader of the pro-Nazi German-American Bund, despite the criminal charges pending against him. . . .

Separately, it reported that Jews were no longer allowed in the Prater, Vienna's great public park; that the commanders of British warships off the Palestine coast were authorized to fire on any ship bringing in illegal immigrants; that in occupied Austria, Jews (as in Germany) were now forcibly given the middle name Israel and Sarah; that the authorities in Sofia had decided to drive all foreign Jews from Bulgaria; that the largest Italian mass-baptism since the time of the Inquisition had been recorded in Rome—more than forty-five hundred Jews, 10 percent of the Jewish population, had been baptized; that in Havana, the Cuban government outlawed the use of Yiddish on the radio; that in London, Colonial Secretary Macdonald told the House of Commons that for the coming six months all Jewish immigration (presumably to the colonies) would be blocked.

In August 1939, *Aufbau*'s "March of Time" reported that in the previous six months about one hundred thousand Jews had left Austria; that fifty Nazi storm troopers from nearby Memel trying to spark a pogrom in a Lithuanian town were driven off by Lithuanian border police; that in Geneva preparations were under way for the August Zionist conference—the opening address was to be delivered by Chaim Weizmann; that the police in the Italian protectorate of Albania ordered all foreign Jews to leave the country by September 3; that in Prague the German administration prohibited Jews from using the public baths; that in Zurich, Switzerland's Nazi leader, Alfred Zander, along with six others, was sentenced to six months in prison after his conviction on charges of espionage. In another column, it reported that a court in Berlin had found former Sturmführer Gustav Emminger, a friend of Goebbels, guilty of extorting 250,000 marks from Jews and had sentenced him to a token three weeks in prison: "Prize Question," the item concluded, "How much did his protectors get?"

Aufbau also reported that the Dominican Republic, pursuant to its agreement at the Evian Conference in France in 1938, had announced that it had admitted five hundred Jewish families, a vanguard, it was then thought, of further Jewish immigration, followed by a story on the first thirty-seven refugee settlers in Santo Domingo, which it described as a "land of hope."[45] Evian-les-Bains, the plush resort on the shore of Lake Geneva where the meetings took place in July 1938, was not a place likely to produce much empathy with the tens of thousands of desperate refugees whose plight the conferees were supposed to address.

In August 1940, two months after France capitulated, *Aufbau* reported that fifteen thousand Jews had been driven out of Alsace-Lorraine by the Nazis and were now wandering through Vichy France, many of whom would eventually end up in Gurs or one of the other concentration camps in Southern France. Some cafés in Paris, the article also reported, now posted signs "Jews and Negroes not admitted." (It was ironic, *Aufbau* later said, that it was now the Nazis who were filling those French concentration camps with German Jews.)[46] A week later, under the front-page head "World Crises and Judaism" it ran a

German translation of a powerful speech that Nahum Goldmann, the co-founder of the World Jewish Congress, had delivered to the Junior Hadassah in Chicago a few days before, attacking the dangerous divisions within the world's Jewish community, pointing out that five million Jews now lived under Nazi domination "in one vast concentration camp," five million others under Soviet dictatorship, and that only a few hundred thousand lived in free European societies. What that meant, he said, is that "There is no such thing as a special and privileged fate for one part of the Jewish people as compared with other parts. We are one people with the same past, and we must recognize the same future. We will all be free or all be enslaved; the destiny of one part will finally be the destiny of all." Nor could the world's Jews be "transported anywhere." Their yearning and dreams of centuries were directed to Palestine.[47] Although *Aufbau* carefully said it was publishing the text as the platform for all Jewish voices, there wasn't much doubt that Goldmann was speaking for the paper as well.

Closer to home, *Aufbau* ran the periodic Bulletin of the National Committee for Resettlement of Foreign Physicians, advising immigrant doctors where there were courses preparing them for U.S. certification and urging them to sign up with the Committee—the Committee also sought nurses for training and U.S. recertification. One issue also ran a plea asking American physicians not to prescribe pharmaceuticals made in Germany, where Jewish doctors had been driven out of non-Jewish hospitals. It published a brief declaration (in English) that it would not join the New York City Civil Liberties Committee's call to Jewish organizations to oppose a pending bill in the New York legislature that would make it illegal to incite or advocate "hatred, violence or hostility against any group or groups . . . by race, color, religion or manner of worship." *Aufbau*, it said, "shall support democracy to the utmost. Democracy, however, leaning backward to conform to democratic principles, is precisely what smoothened [*sic*] the way for the onmarching Nazi hordes in Germany. We have seen democracy committing suicide in Germany. . . . We would rather sacrifice a part of democracy than be forced to sacrifice all of it."[48]

It's hard to imagine that most of *Aufbau*'s readers in those years would have disagreed. (In 1985, it reported approvingly on a bill in the German Parliament that would outlaw denial of the Holocaust.)[49] One who clearly would have agreed with *Aufbau*, probably the leading defender of the idea that hate speech laws were not incompatible with democracy, was Karl Loewenstein, the émigré constitutional lawyer from Munich then teaching at Amherst who would later work with the U.S. Military Government in writing the postwar German Constitution: Based on his experience with the Nazi takeover in 1933, he held that democracies had an obligation to protect themselves, not only by banning hate speech but the symbols, uniforms, and other expressions of anti-democratic movements. He called it "militant democracy."[50] Aryeh Neier, another German-Jewish émigré, born in Berlin, would take a diametrically opposite course. As head of the American Civil Liberties Union in the 1970s, he stoutly defended (and took a lot of heat for) the ACLU's position in its defense in 1977 and 1978 of the right of the neo-Nazis to march in Skokie, where a lot of German Jews, and now some of their children, still lived.[51]

✱

For the historian of immigration in the Nazi era and the years after World War II, *Aufbau* in the late 1930s and early 1940s became, among other things, a chronicler of how, in the uncertain terms of self-definition of that era, all those who, as Arendt said, pretended they had left Europe "of their own free will" and were "newcomers" or maybe "émigrés" and looked down on the uncultured Americans, had become immigrants and, they hoped, future Americans. In 1891, at the height of the great wave of immigration from southern and eastern Europe, Henry Cabot Lodge, then still a member of the House of Representatives, later the Senate leader who was instrumental in blocking U.S. membership in the League of Nations, had impugned the thousands of Slavs, Greeks, and Italians who came to America with the intention of making some money and then returning to the country they came from. They were "mere birds of passage," Lodge said, "an element of the population which regards home as a foreign country, instead of that in which they live and earn money. They have no stake in the country and they never become American citizens."[52]

Not many refugees of the Hitler era came with such intentions, but in the first years there were no doubt some who hoped to return once the storm blew over and many more who were uncertain. In February 1940, *Aufbau* promoted a talk at the German-Jewish Club on "The Jewish Question after the Fall of Hitler" by the Zionist leader Kurt Blumenfeld (with the injunction that he who doesn't plan in the winter and sow in the spring won't reap in the fall). But, predictably, Blumenfeld's basic message was that Palestine made sense for the Jews not only socially and economically but as a chance for freedom, rebirth, and self-realization—the culmination, he said, quoting an unnamed French historian, of the Renaissance.[53]

The events of the late thirties and early forties clarified the issues. Exiles and expatriates became either immigrants or transients on short-term visas waiting to move to Palestine when the British opened the doors—or at times planning, when it became possible, to settle in Mexico, Cuba, Argentina, Chile, or some other country that would take them or where they had connections. But for most, all thoughts of going back had been forgotten. The pages of

Aufbau, which in its first years was itself ambivalent about Zionism, became a near-perfect indicator of the march of those events, their impact on the refugees, and of what, compared to prior generations of immigrants, would be an unusually rapid process of assimilation and Americanization.

And from the start, *Aufbau* devoted a great deal of space to help its readers get there: pieces explaining American political institutions, laws, and processes—for example, "Was ist New Deal"? or "Was ist ein Union Shop?," the latter quite pertinent to the employment circumstances of immigrants looking for work. In an open shop, *Aufbau* explained, anyone could take an available job, but the pay and working conditions were poor. In a closed or union shop, the pay was better, but you had to be a union member to get the job.[54]

In the summer of 1940, under the head "The Smoke-Filled Room," *Aufbau* explained how the presidential nominating conventions work and, in the fall, the convoluted Electoral College system, which must have seemed bizarre to any good European democrat. It noted that it was only in 1920 (twenty years before) that women got the right to vote.[55] As the campaigns progressed it published Hulse's celebration of American political democracy against Nazi dictatorship, which "propagates a return to the law of the jungle where force goes before rights."[56] And that fall, on the eve of the presidential election, it ran a long analysis of the contest, judging that FDR would probably win. Its pages were also dotted with political ads (in German) for both FDR ("The Man of the People") and Wendell Willkie, his Republican opponent, sometimes on facing pages. Willkie's ads deplored the failure of the administration, despite warnings from its emissaries abroad, to adequately prepare for national defense. And, as always, he lambasted FDR's run for an unprecedented third term, which Roosevelt's supporters claimed was necessitated by the crisis abroad. That kind of politics, Willkie's ad said, could lead to war. It was probably not the best way at that time for Willkie to get votes from German-born Jews.[57]

It also continued to publish detailed how-to articles on the sometimes-mutable immigration and naturalization requirements, including pointed periodic reminders for aliens to apply for their First Papers, which, it appears, many overlooked, either through ignorance or simple neglect.[58] There were items on "How do you get to know Americans" and a regular feature called "Say it in English": What does it mean to be "tight-fisted" or to say "his idea didn't pan out" or "to pull the wool over someone's eyes"? What's wrong with the statement "Let me explain you this" or "If it rains or not, I will make a walk"? Or "Please borrow me five dollars until Wednesday"? The column was authored by the owners of an English-language school at Broadway and 74th Street who in their regular ad warned that the column "should never be a substitute for a systematic and thorough study of English." There was also an occasional item called "1,000 Words—American" by a German émigré editor and publisher named Ernst Wallenberg, with common sentences in German-phonetic form. "Ai ämm inn AMERRike änd juh ahr in Ammerike." In the late 1930s, *Aufbau* sometimes also ran lists of immigration quota numbers with the dates when they were expected to come due—meaning the date when the applicant who had that number was eligible for an immigration visa, though sometimes the due date had come before the list was published. It published notice after notice for intensive English-language courses and instructions on where to register for the draft and how to get a driver's license.

But through it all, the paper never left much doubt that it was cheering on the Americanization and, in a number of pieces, made clear the presumably encouraging conclusion that because of its education and urbanity, this generation of immigrants—all its problems notwithstanding—was succeeding more quickly than any of its predecessors. As part of that effort, in 1941, the paper published an *Aufbau Almanac*, subtitled, "The Immigrant's Handbook," a 192-page volume, with an introduction by Einstein, elaborating on countless aspects of American life and society, everything, presumably, that an immigrant needed to know: the political system, the Constitution (in German) and its amendments, through the Twenty-First (the repeal of Prohibition); the text of "The Star Spangled Banner" (men, take off your hats), "God Bless America," the "American Creed"; the forty-eight states; the railroads, the education system; "the job of Congress," how bills become law; the legal system; sports (football is not fussball); centigrade and Fahrenheit; legal holidays; how to find an address in New York; New York's German-Jewish religious congregations and New York's points of interests; the telephone system and costs ($3.50 for a new connection and $4.35 per month); and sample questions from the citizenship test about the federal system, the Bill of Rights, and items such as:

> Q: Who is the ruler of the United States?
> A: The people

And a question, judging by the suggested response, no doubt regarded as reaching beyond the bounds of the possible:

> Q: Can a woman be elected President of the United States?
> A: The Constitution does not expressly prohibit it.[59]

The 192-page *Almanac* also had brief sections on America's "Rise to World Power"; about the contributions of German-Americans in the Midwest to

AUFBAU ALMANAC
THE IMMIGRANT'S HANDBOOK

1941   5701

Cover of the 1941 *Aufbau Almanac*, which tried to have information about virtually everything of interest to Hitler refugees and other recent immigrants. (courtesy of the Leo Baeck Institute, New York)

American Progressivism; about Greenwich Village, "The Montmartre of New York"; a list headed "What's Not in the Dictionary": big shot, hangout, trigger man, skirt, dame, babe, real McCoy, deadpan. And there was a lot of practical advice on dress, nutrition, and a warning (then too) that hospital charges were expensive, making it important to buy medical insurance before one got sick. In addition there was a short list headed "What to Read about America" that included Edna Ferber, Ole Rolvaag, and the Federal Writers Project Guides, accompanied by a full-page ad from the Book-of-the-Month Club for Hemingway's *For Whom the Bell Tolls*. At the front of the almanac was a photo of the immigrants' greatest hero, Franklin D. Roosevelt.[60]

The Future of Each One of Us

Aufbau's editors, like many émigré Jews, foresaw—all too correctly, as the world would slowly learn—that the stakes for Europe's Jews in the German invasion of Poland on September 1, 1939 (and, two years later, the invasion of Russia) and the broader war that shortly followed in Western Europe were immeasurably greater than for anyone else. Among George's first signed pieces as editor in September 1939, shortly after the Germans invaded Poland, was one that began, "Now the World Has its War," the war that the world had done so much to avoid and for which appeasement accomplished nothing. "Egotistical self-interest and an almost incomprehensible stupidity in grasping the situation on the one side," he wrote, "egomania, bloodlust and maniacal imperialism on the other have brought Europe to the point where it will now be transformed into a battle field." In this war, said George's angry editorial, the destiny of all Judaism is at risk. "The future of each one of us hangs on its outcome."[61]

In a companion piece, the paper cheered FDR's message to Congress that this was a war between peoples who cherished freedom and peace and "aggressor governments" that threatened the future of human civilization, and in calling on Americans and their government not only to recognize the danger but to be prepared to take all measures short of war to resist it. "There can be no doubt," said the accompanying piece, "on which side our sympathies, our hopes, our fears and our trust lie." It also reprinted a *New York Times* editorial urging caution and formal neutrality but emphasizing "that there is no point of honor and no scruple of neutrality [in denying] that the democracies of Europe are the outposts of our own kind of civilization. . . . Hitler has said that this is victory or death for him. But it is also victory or death for decent standards of international conduct and the democratic way of life."[62]

"FIVE MILLION Jews Are Under Fire in the German-Russian War," said a huge *Aufbau* headline in June 1941, a few days after the Germans, having collaborated with the Russians in carving up Poland, broke their treaty with Stalin and attacked their former ally.[63] At the same time, Hitler's attack relieved a lot of old Marxists from a terrible embarrassment, or maybe worse.

In an interview with *Aufbau*, the author Thomas Mann, a towering figure for all German émigrés and a frequent presence in *Aufbau*'s pages, touching on a related topic, condemned the bizarre claim by some on the right that it was Stalin who, in agreeing to the pact with Hitler, was responsible for the European war. "For six and half years I've been predicting that the Nazis were preparing for a world war. Now that it's here, I should suddenly say it was all Stalin's fault? Any comparison of fascism with communism on moral standards, will always fall unfavorably against fascism but when it comes to the denial of freedom, there's no difference between them."[64]

Paradoxically, for some German émigrés, the Hitler-Stalin Pact of August 1939, which confounded the anti-Semites' old argument linking Jews with communism, and the ensuing Nazi attack on Poland also seemed to bring a little assurance that Americans were at last beginning to get a clearer sense of what had driven many thousands out of Europe and the dangers they themselves would be facing. If the Russian communists were Jews, why had they sealed a pact with Hitler? As "Busdriver," an otherwise anonymous *Aufbau* writer, concluded after a ride through New England (and thus having listened to a sample of what he took to be ordinary Americans, most of them workers on their annual vacations), "Because of the war, the anti-Semitism whose relentless increase had been prophesized for years, has lost some of its support." It was headed "The Falling Veil."[65] In June 1941, when the Germans attacked the Soviet Union, thus making Stalin Hitler's enemy, no conspiracy theory seemed quite adequate. At the same time, Stalin's pact with Hitler, short-lived though it was, must have brought a little light to the European Jews who still admired the great Soviet experiment.

But for most *Aufbau* readers in the years that followed the invasion and swift destruction of Poland—the sweep of the Wehrmacht, beginning on May 10, 1940, through Holland, Belgium, and Luxemburg; the evacuation at Dunkirk later that month; the capitulation of France on June 22, supposedly the nation with the strongest army in Europe; and Britain's desperate battle to prevent the invasion that seemed almost imminent—little could have been reassuring. During the first days of the war, the paper reported, under the head "'Schm'a Yisroel'—in the Rain of Bombs," how the Jews in Warsaw, the observant ones rushing from holiday services into the lines, fought doggedly "to the last man" alongside Poles; and how students from various rabbinical schools organized in "children's battalions, took part in the battle." Among those who died in battle, according to *Aufbau*, was Bernard Mond, the only Jewish general in the Polish

Army, who, as commander of the garrison at Kattowitz (Katowice), was killed leading a desperate bayonet charge against the invading Germans.

Thousands, *Aufbau* reported, died in Poland in the Luftwaffe's terror-bombing raids. Invading German soldiers who had grown up under the influence of Nazi propaganda were randomly murdering Jews, sometimes on the pretext that they were partisans. Ten thousand Jewish refugees from Poland who had made it to Vilnius in Lithuania confirmed that German soldiers were conducting mass executions of Jews.[66] Thousands were in flight on choked roads; German pilots, using tactics they'd developed in Spain, were machine-gunning refugees on those roads. Twenty thousand people had been killed in the bombing of the then-Polish city of Lwów (Lemberg), *Aufbau* reported, of whom eighteen thousand were Jews. Some Jews in the Polish Army were committing suicide when their capture by the Germans seemed imminent. A month later, *Aufbau* cited a report in the *Manchester Guardian* that sixty thousand Jews had been killed in Poland.[67]

Some three million Jews, said W. M. Citron, one of *Aufbau*'s writers, also in the issue of October 1, 1939, had been living in Poland before the war; at least a million were under the control of the Germans (soon nearly all would be). There was little that could be done now for them. But between fifty thousand and two hundred thousand had fled to neighboring countries (where they weren't welcome either). The Allies have a double obligation, Citron said, to look after these desperate people, as Poles and as Jews. It would be a tragic error for the cause of the democracies if they dodged this responsibility. If it isn't possible to open Palestine to them, or to gain entrance to Turkey, then the French must find a solution in their colonies, Algeria in particular.[68]

On the same page, *Aufbau*'s generally prescient editor Manfred George, in one of his most ill-conceived pieces, concluded that for the Jews in America, the Russian occupation, pursuant to Stalin's pact with Hitler, of parts of eastern Poland would reduce Jewish emigration to the United States and thus stabilize the "melting-pot Zustandes" (the state of the melting pot) at the 1939 level. That would have "highly significant" consequences, presumably in lowering the heat of anti-Semitism in the United States. *Aufbau* would also report that month on what would become the last gasp of the Evian Conference that FDR had called the previous year but which had made hardly a dent in the willingness of the participating countries, notwithstanding their representatives' pious expressions of concern for Europe's tens of thousands of refugees, to open their borders to them.[69]

In the months that followed—well before the Wannsee Conference of January 1942, where the Nazis formally adopted their "Final Solution" of industrialized genocide—*Aufbau* became a chronicler, maybe the most consistent chronicler of its time, of the mounting progress of the Nazis' sadistic, and in those years, sometimes still random, brutality. *Aufbau* also reported the religious oppression of the one million Jews in the part of Poland that the Russians, pursuant to Stalin's pact with Hitler, had occupied between September 1939 and June 1941, when Hitler took it all. And again and again it recorded the pusillanimous shuffling of the leaders of the so-called democracies and of the bureaucratic callousness with which they treated the victims.

In Germany, the Nazis' forced labor program had been in full force since the end of 1937. By the start of the war, the Nazis had also imposed a curfew on all Jews. No one who was not required by his or her work could be on the streets after eight o'clock in the evening; ration cards issued to Jews were now stamped with a red "J"; and Jews could no longer make overseas telephone calls. German authorities were creating segregated air raid shelters for Jews and Aryans; Nazi publications in Germany also announced the establishment of a fourth institute for research into "Jewish Questions." And in order to get rid of "unnecessary mouths," according to a report from the Intergovernmental Refugee Committee, the Gestapo was said to be shipping unaccompanied young children of concentration camp prisoners to neighboring countries for them to feed. *Aufbau* called it "The Gestapo's Child Smuggling."

In German-occupied Poland, according to sources at the Polish government in exile in London, the Nazis were forcing rabbis and priests to clean the streets (which, of course, they'd been forcing Jews in Germany to do for years); they also grabbed men with long beards and cut half of them off. There were also unconfirmed reports of Jews—men, women, and children—being loaded into a boat in the middle of an icy river and then ordered to jump overboard; those who made it to shore were then shot down. In German-occupied Prague, Jews were now required to register for forced labor and to surrender their radios.[70]

In Vienna, according to the Jewish Telegraph Agency, the Nazi authorities had decided to deport Jews to Poland; reportedly the first transport had already left; as in Berlin, the Jews of Vienna were no longer permitted to leave their homes after 8 p.m. Possession of radios and telephones was forbidden. But for many Jews, little of that was news. It merely confirmed what they already believed. In Italy, the authorities had begun the mass arrest of foreign Jews, of whom many were taken to the German (formerly the Austrian) border. From France early in 1940, a few months before the fall of Paris, there came the *Aufbau* report that the Nazis had ordered all their foreign propaganda agents to cease their attacks on communists and to concentrate entirely on Jews.[71] In Romania, a new decree banned the country's eight hundred thousand Jews from membership in the governing (pro-Nazi) party which, in turn, excluded them from many jobs.

With the continuous iterations of such items came one of the leitmotifs of the era, often articulated by *Aufbau*'s editors, many of them without bylines: Hitler really meant what he said and did what he intended. If Europe's statesmen had read *Mein Kampf* more carefully, this war could have been prevented, and the "gravedigger of Europe would only be a memory on cheap prints in the backrooms of seedy taverns. Our politicians didn't have enough imagination for a Hitler. And our poor Jews even less. 'Nothing will be swallowed as hot as when it comes from the kitchen' was the accursed soothing phrase used to avoid everything. . . . We can't take the intentions of the Nazis seriously enough." *Aufbau*'s piece, based on reports and headed "Ghetto State—By the Grace of Hitler," described a grand Nazi plan for the "Solution of the Jewish Question" to herd three million German, Austrian, and Polish Jews into a region behind an "ethnic borderline" near Lublin, in eastern Poland. Ultimately, as the world would later learn, virtually all of Lublin's thirty thousand Jews were killed.[72]

By early 1940, some *Aufbau* readers couldn't bring themselves to believe all the paper's reports of the Nazi crimes. How was it possible? In answer to the doubters' observation that they hadn't read about all those crimes in other papers, *Aufbau*'s editors said that other papers didn't have the intense interest in the suffering of the Jews that *Aufbau* and its readers did. Moreover, it pointed out, of late, because of the leadership of the *New York Times*, various other papers have been running reports on the Nazi abominations in Poland that *Aufbau* (in a slightly self-congratulatory manner) had been reporting on for some weeks.[73] In a similar vein, *Aufbau* reported that twenty-five American students in a class in German at New York's City College wanted to replace the textbook with *Aufbau* so they wouldn't just learn the language but learn about the needs and problems of Jewish immigrants.

Not surprisingly, *Aufbau*'s tone in those early years of the European war, reflecting the anxieties of its readers, many of whom still had people in, or under the shadow of, Hitler's Germany, ranged between somber and near desperate. The decision by the British Colonial Office, as reported by the Jewish Telegraph Agency in a front-page *Aufbau* story in January 1940, that it would no longer issue visas for Palestine to German and Austrian Jews—they were now regarded as enemy aliens—was described as a heavy blow to thousands of Jews still in Germany, who regarded emigration to Palestine as their last hope—and no doubt a blow as well to many of their relatives in America.[74] But by then, the British, reacting to Arab riots, had already issued the notorious MacDonald White Paper reneging on the Balfour Declaration of 1917, which had promised the Jews a homeland in Palestine. The White Paper limited Jewish immigration to seventy-five thousand for five years and decreed that further immigration beyond that number was to be determined by the Arabs.

*

A month after the attack on Poland, *Aufbau*'s assessment of the situation was mixed at best. In what was a not altogether rhetorical question, Hulse asked whether the free world, then represented by Britain and France, could overcome the barbarians. "We may be hopeful," he said (with more hope than cool calculation), "but not before 1942."[75] And notwithstanding *Aufbau*'s skittishness about calling for more American help for the Allies in the two years of war in Europe before Pearl Harbor—lest this be seen, as the anti-Semites wanted it labeled, as a war for the Jews—Hulse wasn't hesitant in taking on the Lindberghs in their call for a European stand-down in the face of what they said was the greater threat from Soviet communism. In a long column in late December 1939, well after the Nazis had ravaged Poland and occupied Czechoslovakia, Hulse quoted an article Anne Morrow Lindbergh had published in *Readers Digest* calling Russia the "the potential invader of Europe, the real threat to European civilization." To exorcise the spirit of Hitlerism, she had written, "you must offer Germany and the world not war—but peace." Hulse savaged that argument: "Should additional millions of Poles, Czechs, Germans and Jews be sacrificed to the Moloch Hitler?"[76]

Ten weeks after the fall of France, an even year after the war began, Britain had not been invaded and seemed to be bravely holding its own in the air war, though very tough battles still lay ahead; FDR had just agreed to provide the Brits fifty old destroyers in return for landing rights at British bases, and most responsible political leaders, in that crucial election year, were doing everything possible to bolster the nation's will to fight. But Hitler had occupied eleven countries, from Norway to France and Czechoslovakia, with ninety-three million people, some of them without firing a shot, and had been joined by Mussolini's Italy. And there were mounting worries about Romania, the Balkans, and the Middle East.[77]

Inevitably, the European war also brought intense new questions for, and from, American residents, refugees, and others: about the formal, though evolving, American posture of neutrality; about anti-Semitism in the United States (How deep and widespread was it? Was Lindbergh a fascist?); about immigration and ways of getting extensions of visitors visas, which in turn often required the applicant to renew a passport issued by a government that had declared him a noncitizen; about ways to find and possibly help friends and relatives still thought to be somewhere overseas—refugees from Czechoslovakia now in England; the Czech and Polish refugees who had enlisted, or been drafted into, the French Army; and most of all, the Jews still in Germany, Austria, Poland, and Czechoslovakia; and about the hazards (and often the impossibility) of travel within or

from Europe. When, during the winter of 1939–40, the months of the so-called
phony war, the French began to release alien prisoners from their concentration camps, many on the condition that they would serve in the French Foreign
Legion (where they would be treated almost as badly as they had been in the
French camps), *Aufbau* ran lists of those it described as the best known.

Despite the war situation, for those (very few) with the proper documents,
emigration from Germany (in October 1940) was still possible, and anyone who
still had the opportunity, said an *Aufbau* item, probably written by a travel agent,
ought not delay. Refugees sailing from England to America were required to
sign a release declaring that "I am aware of the dangers of crossing the Atlantic
at the present moment and I also know that the Jewish Aid Committee, London,
would have maintained me if I had not left England. But not withstanding these
circumstances I wish to depart at my own risk on the Steamship —." Until the
American embassy resumed operations in Warsaw, now in the hands of the
Germans, *Aufbau* reported in October 1939, there was no way to send affidavits
or other documents in furtherance of visa applications; the same with money
transfers. It also advised senders of letters to Allied countries written in German
to so indicate on the envelope so that they would be directed more quickly to
the appropriate censor.

Six weeks after the Germans swept through Belgium, Holland, and Luxemburg, France, which not long before had represented asylum for tens of thousands of German refugees and then interned them as enemy aliens, capitulated
to the Germans and abjectly agreed to "surrender on demand" anyone the
Nazis wanted. In the chaos that followed, the searches for people and the questions became ever more intense and desperate, the uncertainty greater. How to
help, how to resist? In the summer of 1940, the weeks after the surrender, *Aufbau*
was so besieged by letters, phone calls, and in-person queries from people with
relatives and friends in France that it could no longer reply. Anyone wanting to
send money should get in touch with American Express, which had the forms
required to get clearance from the U.S. Treasury Department and be prepared
to wait for weeks for a response. To find people, get in touch with the Red
Cross. To find anyone abroad with an American visa, get in touch with the
Migration Service of the National Refugee Service on West 46th Street.

A year later, however, in the summer of 1941, before the U.S. entered the
war, Wall Street banks and travel agents were still advertising money transfers
to people in Germany and in Nazi-occupied France, Belgium, Holland, and
Poland. "We Are Again Sending Money to Your Relatives in Europe," said
Modern Tours, Inc., in bold type.[78] The changes in regulations and systems
must have driven some refugees to distraction.

When food packages could still be sent to individuals in Germany before Pearl Harbor but after the start of the European war and the imposition of an Allied blockade, an *Aufbau* reader, in a letter headed "I accuse," charged those who sent the packages with treason. "Hitler paid dearly (presumably for oil, or maybe grain) to break the blockade in his deal with Stalin," said the letter. "When Jews break the blockade it costs him nothing." The only way to help Jews or others in Germany was to defeat Hitler.[79] An unrelated letter in the same issue from another reader called such accusations false because the Nazis were doing everything they could to make it as hard as possible for Jews to get food. And a third said that in the face of the "refined brutality" of Hitler and his ilk it was hard to imagine all the consequences of one's acts. Nonetheless, he said, one can understand that Jews overseas will try everything they can to lighten the lives of relatives trying to exist in the Hitler regime. In March 1940, a group of Jewish organizations issued a warning that food parcels going to Germany were probably being used to feed German soldiers.[80] Exacerbated by the pervasive sense of helplessness among the American refugees in the face of the Nazi victories in Europe in 1939–41, this agonizing dilemma, too, was part of a wider debate in the refugee community.

At the same time, *Aufbau* continued to function as the immigrants' hometown paper—increasingly a sort of *global* hometown paper reporting on the activities of German-Jewish Clubs (some later renamed the New World Club, Central Club, or the Social Club) in Newark, Baltimore, Chicago, Pittsburgh, Philadelphia, San Francisco, Portland, and other U.S. cities, as well as other events in the hinterland. In Chicago there was an American Federation of Polish Jews. In Los Angeles there was the big Jewish Club of 1933 (no need to say German), which, with the coming of the war, transformed itself from what one writer described as "a primarily social and cultural support organization to becoming a political actor, negotiating and demanding an exemption from the enemy classification and its restrictions as it applied to the West."[81]

By 1940, there were also German-Jewish clubs or societies in Manila, New Zealand, and, according to *Aufbau*, in most South American countries, and *landsmanschaften*, hometown associations (of émigrés from Vienna, Munich, Frankfurt, and Baden) and other émigré associations in places like New York, where there were enough people eager to join and whose events were often listed in *Aufbau*. The Zionist Herzl Society in Shanghai was reported to have over a thousand members.[82] In addition, it ran occasional boxes on the job situation in various Western states, and a regular "Hollywood Calling" column written (in English, and often in showbiz vernacular—"Bert Brecht dickering with Elisabeth Bergner and Co. to have her produce and star in his adaptation of the play *The*

Duchess of Malfi") by the Vienna-born scriptwriter Hans (sometimes John) Kafka, who was not related to Franz.[83] It also had a periodic "Letter from London," later supplemented by its own correspondents in England, Palestine, and other places overseas, to which it was devoting increasing space.

The paper ran Vera Craener's regular women's section ("Housewives the world over meet one another in the *Aufbau*")—everything from recipes to the practical shoe for the working woman to the best way of keeping lemons fresh (put them in water in an airtight container) to translations of common culinary terms to a piece on the standardization of women's ready-made clothing made necessary by wartime shortages (fewer alterations needed, and thus less wasted cloth) to a passing item about the wartime shortage of butter and the increased demand for margarine (which, with a little food coloring, was made to look like butter). There was a piece on the culture of New York's Fifth Avenue (where, even in the middle of the war, women shoppers were so numerous that they seemed to dominate the image of the whole city) and a column headed (in English) "Blueberries or Huckleberries." And, as might be expected, there were columns with heads like, in December 1942, "What's with Rationing?" (Coffee, Coupon No. 27; Sugar, Coupon No. 10; meat, Coupon No. 2). Because of great military needs, rationing of silk was expected in the spring, but if buyers were mindful of shortages, there might be no rationing of wool or cotton.[84]

But Craener was also a strong voice of encouragement on the new demands put on immigrant women in America: The need to take jobs and earn an income, often so that the husbands could learn a new trade or get relicensed. The first question in America, she wrote in December 1944, wasn't "Do you work?" but "What kind of job do you have?" And of course, she said in commiseration with her immigrant readers, everything in the domestic economy—the currency, the weights and measures, the names for everything, the shops, and the available services—was strange. But, the always helpful Craener said, every adaptation was progress, and there were plenty of chances to discover America from the newspapers or from the novels of Sinclair Lewis, Sherwood Anderson, and Erskine Caldwell. From the moment we can buy our first book or theater ticket, she said, we sense that things are getting better, and that "physical labor can also lead to cultural joys."[85]

There was a periodic column called "Wall Street Telegram" with stock market news and leads (another sign that not all its readers were struggling paupers) and another called "Review of Labor." During the war there was also an occasional section called "Home Front Calling," with information on victory gardens—individual or "community plots"—and mini herb gardens in window boxes. There were occasional chess and bridge columns, a filler of advice (in English) from Consumers Union ("Your Dollar") on the best buys and the worst—"silk versus nylon versus Lisle stockings"—what to take to the beach in the hot New York summers, and whether or not one should buy things on the installment plan. After the war, in another indication of the growing prosperity of *Aufbau*'s readers, there were pieces, some with photos, on the latest women's fashions. And, as noted earlier, there was some poetry, old and new, in every issue—some, like Günther Bibo's "And Now the Deed," written in the French concentration camps.[86] Many, like Erich Kästner's "Railway Parable" of 1931, were eerily evocative of the lives of its refugee readers:

> We all sit in the same train
> And travel through time.
> We look outside. We saw enough.
> We ride in the same train
> And no one knows how far.
>
> A neighbor sleeps; another gripes;
> A third talks too much.
> Stations are announced.
> The train that chases through the years
> Never arrives at its end. . . .[87]

Or, for some, maybe many, whose nightmares would never cease, verses like Franzi Ascher's "The Refugee's Summer Night," in the voice of someone who has escaped but is still haunted by the terrors of the past. Even as the sound of the elevator door clangs and steps come nearer and nearer, and as the old fears return, the approaching steps don't stop at the door and the clinking glass turns out only to be the milkman:

> Don't allow yourself to be confused,
> Not every hand can reach across the sea . . .
> Outside the window there's the twilight,
> I know the day is no longer far away.[88]

✳

Consistent with the paper's self-appointed mission and that of the New World Club, it also carried the regular announcements and listings, columns of them in each issue, of religious services, lectures, concerts, art exhibitions, social events, and sports—tennis, swimming, soccer, gymnastics, and hiking particularly—that might appeal to German Jews, and often to all Jews. Manfred George also brought on Ludwig Wronkow as *Aufbau*'s regular (sometimes heavy handed) cartoonist, whose caricatures of the Japanese were as racist as those of most other cartoonists at the time. That, too, may have been a way to prove that one was a good American. There was a regular column (in English) called "Going Places in New York." There were wedding announcements and obits, its "Say It In English" column, and various columns of practical information—you buy milk by the pint (roughly one liter), meat by the pound (which in America is only 435 grams), and if you want to know how far you've gone in your car, you multiply the mileage by eight, then divide by five to get the equivalent in kilometers.

And it ran regular book, concert, opera, theater, and film reviews, as well as reviews of classical music records—far more than most mainstream daily papers run now—focusing particularly, though not exclusively, on plays, books, and films dealing with its primary subjects of interest and often with its own perspective. It reviewed—and remarked on—two translations of *Faust* into Hebrew that coincidentally appeared at the same time, one published in New York, one in Tel Aviv, when even one would have been rare.[89] It ran a series on "detective novels for the intelligent reader" on the stories of Ngaio Marsh, Craig Rice, and other authors of American who-dun-its. It ran pieces about concerts in Palestine, including a lot of chamber music in small towns and kibbutzes, as well as major events in New York. And since many of the major figures of the music world— Bruno Walter, Arturo Toscanini, Arnold Schoenberg, Rudolf Serkin, Emanuel Feuermann, Roman Totenberg, Arthur Rubinstein, and Fritz Kreisler—were European émigrés, the paper had a double reason to cover them. And it had Artur Holde, a German-born conductor and a knowledgeable and highly regarded music critic, to do it.

Like other publications, while *Aufbau* found the 1940 MGM film *The Mortal Storm*, the first Hollywood movie to deal with the ugliness of life in Nazi Germany, a "very gripping anti-Nazi film," the review also asked why it had taken Hollywood seven long years to get around to the topic.[90] But it didn't mention that even here the producers kept their heads down, not identifying the Jews as Jews, only as non-Aryans, and with stars like James Stewart and Margaret Sullavan, hardly even "non-Aryans." Nor, in the words of a recent appraisal, did MGM mention "the name of the country or the religion of origin of [the heroine] Freya's family because of the large German market for its films." But it was to no avail—the movie infuriated the Nazi government and it led to all MGM films being banned in Germany. But here the caution of both the producers and the review were indications of where the nation then was, and where Hitler's refugees stood within it.

It wasn't until America was at war that Hollywood, never known for its courage, would produce more openly anti-Nazi films. The greatest of them, Warner Brothers' *Casablanca*, would open in November 1942 — it was rushed to premiere right after the Allied landings in North Africa — and to open officially the following January. The cast, as *Aufbau* noted, was packed with German and Austrian actors, most of them refugees. Among them: Conrad Veidt who was the Nazi Major Strasser; Paul Henreid, born Paul Georg Julius Freiherr von Hernried Ritter von Wasel-Waldingau, who, like Veidt, was not Jewish, who played Victor Lazlo, the anti-Nazi resistance hero; Peter Lorre, born László Löwenstein in what was then Austro-Hungary, as the shady vaguely Levantine hustler Ugarte; and Helmut Dantine and Ilka Gruning. In considerable part, it was a story that many of the Hitler refugees had lived. *Aufbau*'s reviewer, needless to say, loved it, predicting that when uncensored films could again be shown in post-Nazi Germany, they'll be made in Hollywood.[91]

There were occasional listings of "where to get advice and help." There was its regular notice of the semimonthly meeting of the (Zionist) Theodor Herzl Society and announcements for countless other groups, among them the American Association of Former German Jurists, the Jewish War Veterans of America, and the Immigrant Jewish War Veterans. And it ran long lists of lectures and discussions resonant with the anxieties of the time: "The Jewish Woman in the Present Crisis," "What is the Future of the Jew in the Western Hemisphere?," "Need America Fear a Trojan Horse?," "The Jews Are Not Standing Alone!" And occasionally in the pre–Pearl Harbor years it ran double-page ads, probably unpaid, for the United Jewish Appeal on behalf of the Joint Distribution Committee, the United Palestine Appeal, and the National Refugee Service: "Six Million Brothers Wait for Your Help. Their Lives Lie in Your Hands."[92]

Meanwhile, despite the reduced flow of immigrants as the destruction overseas spread and the fog of war became thicker, "Looking For," the regular listing of short items for readers seeking friends or relatives, gradually grew longer. Listings were free for *Aufbau* subscribers and members of the German-Jewish Club, twenty-five cents for all others, with a limit of no more than two names for the persons being sought: Bertha Isler of 709 West 169th Street is looking for Mr. and Mrs. Moor, formerly of Nuremberg (most recently in Haiti); Kurt Schwerin of 205 West 87th Street is looking for Bruno Buchwald, formerly with the Berlin Stock Exchange; Herbert Lachmann of 35–45 81st Street, Jackson Heights, L.I., seeks Dr. Erich Cohn, formerly of Berlin; Alfred Weilheimer, formerly of Mannheim, being sought by Carola Rosenbaum, 514 West 184th Street; Fritz Berg, formerly of Frankfurt, a.m., sought by Ernest

Blum, 700 South 28th Street, Birmingham, Alabama. And as the lists grew longer, they also became global: Else Nathansohn of Chicago, formerly of Bremen, being sought by Federico Kauffmann, Casilla 9509, Santiago de Chile; Siegfried Bloch, formerly of Cernauti, Romania, being sought by Hansi Magnus, born Gruenberg, Bonaire, Dutch West Indies, Plantation Guatem. This was a new diaspora. After the war, the paper would occasionally run pictures, most from the refugee aid organization HIAS, of happy reunions of arriving displaced persons with American relatives they hadn't seen in many years.[93]

It reported on the formation of Hulse's "Immigrants Conference 1939" composed of two dozen mostly German-Jewish organizations (discussions with Italian, Spanish, Czech, and Polish groups were reported under way) and on the activities of the American Austrian League, the Austrian Jewish Council, the Austrian Artist Group, the American Council of Jews from Austria, Self-help, the German-Jewish Club, later the New World Club, the Association of Former German Jurists, the American Federation of German Jews, later the American Federation of Jews from Central Europe, Inc., the Immigrant Jewish War Veterans, the German-American Writers Association, and many others. In addition, there were countless other groups involved in the concerns of German-Jewish immigrants. The leadership of the Immigrants Conference, which, in addition to Hulse, included *Aufbau* editor Manfred George and several other people associated with the paper, indicated it was more than anything else a creature of *Aufbau* itself. Nonetheless, it was an impressive array. America was said to be a country of joiners, but these immigrants seemed to run a strong second in that category.

The paper ran a transcript of author Stefan Zweig's eulogy for Freud who had died In September 1939 in London. It ran a tribute to Walter Benjamin after his suicide in Spain by Theodor Adorno, his opponent in a once-famous series of philosophical debates. Both had been pillars of the Frankfurt School of social theory. It ran a story about the death in Berlin of conductor Bruno Walter's daughter Gretel. At a memorial ceremony in Zurich attended by Toscanini and other leading musicians, according to an *Aufbau* item, Walter went into an adjoining room and played the first movement of the Moonlight Sonata.[94] (The *Aufbau* story did not report that Gretel had been murdered by her husband, jealous over her affair with the Italian basso, Ezio Pinza, whom she'd met through her father, who had gone out of his way to engage Pinza to sing *Don Giovanni*.) Her husband then shot himself. A few weeks later, Walter, who'd left Germany in 1933 when the Nazis, threatening riots, stopped him from conducting, moved permanently to the United States.

Toward the end of the 1930s, *Aufbau*, by then published twice a month and soon to become a weekly (five cents a copy; later ten cents; subscription one dollar for twenty-four issues), began paying increasing attention to events in Congress and in Washington generally as they bore on the lives of refugees and their friends abroad.

Relying primarily on data from HIAS and other refugee agencies, it followed and reported the vicissitudes of the State Department's ever-changing and increasingly tight and cumbersome visa regulations, along with detailed information on how to fill out the forms and what affidavits and other supplementary documents were required. By July 1941, people with relatives in German-occupied countries were no longer eligible to receive visas, purportedly (in that Fifth Column–obsessed era) because they might be coerced into helping the Nazis. Like many of its refugee readers and many American liberals, *Aufbau* suspected (correctly, given the ill-concealed hostility to aliens at the State Department, and to Jews especially) "that the ruling represents a ruthless determination to bar as many victims of Hitler's terror as can possibly be covered by the least plausible excuse."[95] And with those changes came no end of questions: Would a visa holder, for example, who couldn't find a ship before his visa expired be able to get an extension?[96] And what were the government's requirements (in 1941) for reporting foreign assets, most of them by now probably seized by various governments?[97]

Aufbau tracked and then marked the demise of the Wagner-Rogers Bill, which would have allowed twenty thousand Jewish children into the country beyond the formal quotas. It ran pieces on how Congress could be persuaded to oppose the move in Britain to repudiate the Balfour Declaration. And beyond that it reflected the inchoate fear, in the words of one *Aufbau* commentary published in 1941, that "while everywhere [the Jew] stands shoulder to shoulder with those who are fighting to resist Nazi-fascist tyranny and, as in Palestine, he has offered to give the flower of Jewish youth in the preservation of human freedom, he is utterly in the dark as to the future of the Jew" once the Nazis are defeated.[98]

Aufbau supported as "a Needed Measure Against the Fifth Column," the Smith Act, to require all 3.6 million aliens in America to register with the government, to be fingerprinted and to carry their registration cards at all times (but which, in making it a crime to advocate the violent overthrow of the U.S. government, was directed more at communists than fascists). It cheered when FDR signed it in the summer of 1940 with his statement that it would not only enhance the nation's security but protect the loyal aliens who were the nation's guests.[99] It would help shield Jews particularly against charges that they were Fifth Columnists, and that spies had been planted among immigrants, a staple in the playbooks of Father Coughlin, William Dudley Pelley's Christian Party, and the other loud anti-Semites of the era.[100]

Friends of refugees (*clockwise from top left*): Harold Ickes, Francis Biddle, Earl G. Harrison, and Eleanor Roosevelt. (courtesy of the Library of Congress)

Shortly after, under the bold front-page head "NO HYSTERIA!" it ran Solicitor General Francis Biddle's letter to *Aufbau* and excerpts from Biddle's recent radio address about the fear of Fifth Column activities "in these terrible days." "One form that this hysteria has taken is the wholesale denunciations of all aliens living in America—a confession of fear and weakness that sees a spy behind every foreign accent," he said. But oddly, Biddle's only specific examples were recent mob attacks on—of all people—Jehovah's Witnesses.[101] Biddle was surely right that the hysteria was unfounded—it was an obsession at the time, and *Aufbau* ran countless articles (e.g., "Spies among Refugees?") to counter it.[102]

Anxiety among many refugees about the anti-immigrant hysteria, however, almost certainly was not unfounded. Nonetheless, in the midst of the war, *Aufbau*, like most Americans of that era, bought into FBI Director J. Edgar

Nativists and isolationists (*above*): Charles Lindbergh addressing an America First rally, Fort Wayne Indiana, October 3, 1941; (*below, left to right*): Breckinridge Long, Charles Coughlin, and Gerald L. K. Smith. (courtesy of the Library of Congress)

Hoover's warnings about the Nazi saboteurs being trained in Berlin who could land on American shores to disrupt the war effort, as they had clumsily tried, without success, earlier in the war. Americans must be alert and report anything that might look suspicious.[103]

But even after the Nazis invaded Poland and the British and French were officially at war with Hitler, *Aufbau* was chary of advocating anything that might be construed as a call for America to get into the war and was careful not to be too critical of the nation's tight immigration restrictions, restrictions that limited admissions of Hitler refugees in the 1930s to less than half of what even the shamefully tight national origins quota law allowed. When it published direct criticism of those policies, it usually used the voices of others—guest columnists or reprints of editorials in the *Nation* or the *New York Times*—or reported them in its own articles. But it did point out that there was no justification for the policy denying visas to anyone with relatives in German-occupied countries. And (in August of 1941, after Hitler had already been at war with Russia for two months) it pointed to a telling fact: Visa questionnaires asked whether the applicant was a communist but not whether he was a fascist or a Nazi. Both questions, of course, were naïve, no doubt included more to satisfy right-wing politicians than to elicit any information or screen out any enemy.[104]

Aufbau was often buffeted by ancillary issues in the immigrant community: when and where it was okay to speak German (especially after U.S. entry into the war); how to help relatives still abroad; as well as all the familiar problems of employment, housing, and social adjustment. The psychiatrist and *Aufbau* columnist Wilfred Hulse devoted a whole column to the pros and cons of name changes, citing Mencken's list of all the Levys who had become Levitt, Levoy, Levine, Lee, McLevy, or Lewis. America molds the immigrant not only into a new man, Hulse said, it changes his appearance, his wardrobe, his food, his name. It was an issue for all immigrants, he observed, with many consequences and something that should be carefully considered.[105] The German-Jewish Club, *Aufbau*'s parent, probably went through a similar process in 1940, when it changed its name to the New World Club because "the term 'German-Jewish' has become obsolete. The connection with the past has been broken. And this must be emphasized. One looks to the future and believes in the New World and the building of a new life in it."[106] (In 1941, a few days before Pearl Harbor, the Club also decided that all its executive officers had to be American citizens.) But another immigrant, at the time a young woman, later recalled that while today's visitor from Germany wears the same kind of clothes as Americans, "*we* looked different. We looked like refugees. We had clunky shoes and skirts that didn't fit the way American skirts did. Our stockings were made of heavy silk or cotton. American stockings were very sheer and had seams in the back. You could recognize a German refugee from behind ten feet away."[107]

In another column, Hulse concluded that it was imperative that immigrants learn English as rapidly as possible, but did German have to be abandoned altogether? No, of course not, he said, German is part of our culture; it was the language of Goethe, Heine, and Luther (a virulent Jew-hater and thus an odd choice for this list) before it was the language of Hitler. For many old people, it was all they had to connect them to anything. But it was foolish and pointless to use German on the street to prove that we're not all Nazis and want nothing to do with Hitler.[108] In November 1939, *Aufbau* polled its readers and reported that 20 percent wanted more English in the paper, 15 percent wanted less, and 65 percent wanted it unchanged. As a practical matter, often usage was already mixed ("Eine traurige Geschichte mit Happy End"); sometimes the head was in English and the body of the piece in German. Sometimes Fussball was soccer. The kindergarten of the German-Jewish Club offered the kids Milch und Crackers every afternoon. And as the demographics of the readership evolved over the years, there would be more English.

What Will America Do?

The German invasion of Belgium, Luxemburg, and the Netherlands on May 10, 1940, a date that many of the tens of thousands of refugees, who once thought themselves secure, would long remember; the entry of Mussolini's Italy on the German side not long after; and the fall of France on June 22, intensified everything, both for those in the shadow of the war and for the many thousands of their relatives and friends overseas. "WHAT WILL AMERICA DO?" was the huge headline on the *Aufbau* edition of May 17, the first after the invasion.

The paper, though still carefully avoiding any statement of its own that American nativists and anti-Semites could interpret as pressure from foreign Jews for U.S. engagement in the European war, cited the *Times* to make its own case. Hitler will keep looking for new worlds to ravage and conquer. The world "must take every step necessary to fend off that threat." And then quoting Walter Lippmann (in translation), "If the offensive succeeds that Hitler has now begun we'll not know peace again in our lifetime." As for those of us, *Aufbau* added, with the unbelievably good fortune to have escaped the hell of Europe and who now have taken an oath of loyalty and have their First Papers "we must now help our American fellow citizens with all our strength that the United States remains the land of Washington and Lincoln." And beneath that long unsigned front-page piece, and maybe of equal concern to its readers, *Aufbau* noted that there were 267,000 Jews in the countries under attack, 44,500 of them refugees.[109]

In the next issue, it again let Lippmann carry its message, running a column it headed in huge letters, "ZERO HOUR," calling for a great national effort to support the Allies. The people will support those leaders, he wrote, who don't treat them as children or as psychologically unbalanced and are not shaken up by the bitter truth. Six weeks before it happened, Lippmann predicted the collapse of France and the battle of Britain, which ensued, and warned that even

Aufbau front page of May 17, 1940, the first issue after the Germans invaded Belgium, the Netherlands, and Luxemburg, with the headline "What Will America Do?" (courtesy of JM Jüdische Medien AG, Zurich) the Atlantic was no longer a secure protector of the nation. It was not possible to send an army to help the Europeans—America, he said, had no army. "But what we can do is to immediately send word that we will do everything in our power to support the countries whose annihilation would so endanger our own security."[110] In the following years, Lippmann's column in translation became a regular *Aufbau* feature. The editors in May 1940 could not have known, or maybe even predicted, that shortly after Pearl Harbor Lippmann would write the column that immediately led to the presidential order authorizing the internment of the Japanese on the West Coast. "Nobody's constitutional rights," he would write, "include the right to reside and do business on a battlefield."[111] In April 1941, *Aufbau*, again letting Americans deliver its message, devoted four full pages to a German translation of *Time-Life* publisher Henry Luce's messianic screed "The American Century," which was not just an attack on isolationism but a call for America to "accept wholeheartedly our duty and our opportunity as the most powerful and vital nation in the world and in consequence to exert upon the world the full impact of our influence, for such purposes as we see fit and by such means as we see fit." It didn't call for U.S. involvement in the European war, but came close to it. *Aufbau*, in its introduction, said the effect of the Luce piece, which first ran in *Life* two months before, "had been extraordinary," going on to quote the liberal journalist Dorothy Thompson's prediction that it "will become one of the classics of American writing."[112] Luce was a Republican and *Life* was, at that time, a staple of the American middle class. *Aufbau* couldn't have picked a better messenger.

✶

Within days of the German attack in May 1940, thousands of refugees, German and Austrian Jews who had settled in Belgium, along with a few hundred self-styled "pure Germans" (Aryans), were packed without water in unventilated cattle cars and transported to internment camps in southern France. Tens of thousands of others found themselves desperately trying to escape the Wehrmacht—by train, by car, in oxcarts, on foot, or bicycle. Altogether, there were an estimated two million refugees in northern France in the first weeks after the German attack.

Aufbau ran personal accounts from survivors who had escaped the reach of the Nazis—or thought they had—stories of whole families struggling along country roads lined with broken-down cars and wagons, hoping to make it to Paris or the English channel, or wandering the streets and around the ports of France, and later going from consulate to consulate and café to café in so-called unoccupied France trying to get documents of varying legitimacy, looking for someone who might know someone, and learning the names of places hardly any of them had ever heard before—Hendaye, Portbou, Banyuls, Elne—and about French concentration camps named Les Milles, Le Barcarès, Vernet, Rieucros, Pithiviers, Gurs, Saint Cyprien, and a score of others. *Aufbau* ran whatever reports it could get from the camps themselves. It ran a piece headed "Unwanted Alsatians" about the thousands of people, including ten thousand Jews, driven by the Nazis from their homes into Vichy France (whose government would eventually imprison most of the foreign Jews at Gurs and, later, start many of them on the road to Drancy and then to Auschwitz).[113] It sometimes quoted from telegrams or letters that refugees in America received from elderly relatives in the French camps desperately pleading for help. It ran stories from refugee prisoners in the British internment camps. It published the long, first-person story of a woman who, after struggling along a slow torturous route, finally made it from Brussels to Paris, where, she says at the end of her account, she'll find work—not knowing that two-and-a-half weeks later the Germans will be there.[114] (In another little bit of irony, a small sidebar to her piece, published a week before the city fell, advises people wishing to contact Jewish refugees from Belgium to write the Federation of the Societé Juive in Paris.) In 1940, it also published the first installment of Hertha Pauli's story of her escape from France (also with the help of Fry, whom she doesn't mention, no doubt to protect him while he was still doing his work).[115]

And predictably, in the fog and rumors of war, *Aufbau* got some things wrong. Pierre Laval (at the time a minister in the Vichy government) did not release the prisoners in the French concentration camps, many of them Jews, in July 1940. But its huge headline "Chaos in France" was certainly correct.[116] By January 1943, when the Nazi program of genocide was in full gear and contrary to the reports of the releases from the French camps, it would publish list after list, presumably provided by the Red Cross and similar groups, of deportees, hundreds of them, from Gurs, Les Milles, and the other French camps to places then unspecified but which every refugee knew was to the Nazi concentration camps in the East. Most of the names on those lists were of German and Polish Jews. By the end of 1944, according to the most reliable estimates, the French had shipped seventy-five thousand Jews to the Nazi death camps. On arrival "most were gassed immediately."[117] But, had it been reported, no one would have believed that at the time.

In Italy, *Aufbau* reported in 1940, four thousand Central European refugees were desperately afraid that they would be shipped to what it called "Nazi-Poland." In Shanghai, where there were already some fifteen thousand middle-European refugees, the majority of them German and Austrian Jews, a massive

new influx of refugees from Nazi-occupied countries was expected.[118] (Predictably, the travel agencies now advertised "emigration from Europe via Russia
and Japan," which, judging from subsequent accounts, quite a few did.) In New
York, under a huge headline "STOP HITLER," *Aufbau* carried a story that
leaders of some major Jewish organizations called on all Jewish groups (in
English) to levy "a contribution of one day a week or its equivalent in earnings
from every Jewish adult to the Allied cause and American defense." There
should also be created "a huge fund to enable the Jewish community to buy five
hundred planes (in addition to tanks and other war materiel for the Allies) as a
specific contribution of American Jews to Allied victory" and a meatless day
each week "should be proclaimed throughout the country." (Which in fact did
occur after Pearl Harbor.)

Perhaps more compelling was the renewed call, in another front-page
Aufbau piece, by the militant Zionist leader Vladimir (Ze'ev) Jabotinsky, for the
creation of a Jewish Army. "It is high time," he wrote in a statement for the
paper (in English), "for us to stop being passive martyrs, and become instead
a nation which is actively participating in world events. This is the meaning of
a Jewish army. At one of the gravest moments in world history [we have a
chance] to prove we are worthy of self-respect and entitled to the respect of the
world. I hope we shall not miss it." It was published on June 21, 1940, coincidentally just as France surrendered. Six weeks later he had a fatal heart attack.
The American Zionist organization, almost certainly fearing nativist backlash,
summarily rejected Jabotinsky's plan, declaring that Jews were already strongly
committed to the Allied cause, that 130,000 Palestinian Jews had already regis-
tered for (British) military service, and that the Jewish Agency was prepared to
mobilize four divisions for the defense of Palestine.[119]

As Palestine became a war zone, *Aufbau* authors strove hard to make clear
that this was a battle of the whole free world against fascism and that Jews, of all
people, had a huge stake in it and much to contribute to it. It ran bold headlines like one over a piece from "our special correspondent" in Jerusalem: "A
Jewish Army Throughout the World."[120] It reprinted an article by David Ben
Gurion, who would later become Israel's first prime minister, deploring the
failure of the British to create a Jewish legion, as it had with Poles, Belgians,
Czechs, Frenchmen, and refugees from other conquered countries. "One
people," he wrote, "is conspicuous by its absence — the people that was the first
of all the victims of Nazi aggression, the people that more than any other in the
world has the strongest reasons . . . for fighting to the last man against the Nazi
monster."[121] And the next year, under the headline "The Jewish Army — the
Beginning of a Jewish Politics?," Hannah Arendt joined *Aufbau*'s call, declaring
(presciently) that a Jewish state will never be created in secret negotiations with

Hannah Arendt. (Creative Commons)

statesmen or with petitions from influential Jews, only when one hundred thousand Jews, "weapons in hand, are prepared to fight for their people's freedom
and their right to live. . . . A person attacked as a Jew cannot defend himself as
an Englishman or a Frenchman."[122] By then, *Aufbau,* while reporting on (and
running photos of) the Jewish units in the Palestinian (read British) armed
forces, had itself become firmly committed to the Zionist cause. In the ensuing
months, Arendt would return to the argument more than once: "We can only
fight anti-Semitism," she wrote in late December, shortly after the United States

had declared war on Germany, "when, with weapons in hand, we fight Hitler" and fight, not as Englishmen or Frenchmen, but as a "European people."[123]

And as *Aufbau* would through most of its existence, it took special note of the questions and anxieties of the newcomers, always tailored to their ever-changing needs and circumstances. In one long and revealing piece in May 1940, headed "New World—New Lives: A Roadmap Through the Problems Every Immigrant Must Solve"—it even called them "greenhorns"—it explained, among many other things, that a great deal in America—in religion, in business, in government, in social relations—is based on a deep belief in freedom and individual rights. It seemed implicitly to recognize that many of those German-Jewish refugees were still too German and telling them, in effect, that immigrants fleeing tyranny for freedom now have to get used to it.[124]

Newcomers have to learn that in America (presumably compared to the old Prussian Germany) men and women are treated equally: In the home, the wife has the same standing as the husband, and her authority doesn't suffer when she, as she often must, works outside the home. Children are accorded the same respect as individuals: "American schools teach children to think for themselves and to voice their thoughts freely. Even the parents draw them in that direction. The tug toward freedom in these child-rearing methods is natural and understandable in a people that treasures freedom above all else. Children say what they think and their parents freely discuss things with them." No one quiets or banishes children for such behavior. That creates an atmosphere in the home that Europeans erroneously deem as disrespect or even impudence. The same, the piece said, applied in other areas: men can't chafe if they have to work under a woman; European men had better get used to it. In making business contacts or applying for a job, learn to be open and friendly; fill out all questionnaires without grumbling, no matter how pointless they may seem. For a refugee who finds himself in a small city, all this may come easier; he will get to know Americans more quickly and they will quickly forget that he's a refugee.[125]

It was a recurring theme. Jewish immigrants from Central Europe, Manfred George wrote in 1941, may imagine that they lived in freedom before Hitler. But that wasn't freedom; it was only acceptance and tolerance. For Americans, the battle for freedom never ends. "Above all, one has to know why, at bottom, the American feels so self-reliant and so free to do anything, why he feels he is a *citizen* as opposed to the European *subject*." American freedom was born out of the pioneer experience; it was rooted in individualism as well as collective enterprise. That meant, among other things, that no one can count on help who doesn't help himself. And it meant that one man's freedom ends exactly where his neighbor's begins.[126] That it was not self-evident in that context was one measure of the things that, it appears, a lot of German refugees still had to learn: They were, at bottom, still too German.

At the same time, in what may never be as paradoxical in times of great stress as it seems, *Aufbau* ran frequent listings of moonlight cruises on the Hudson ("Mit Tanz und Broadway Show"). The back pages were full of ads for variety shows and other entertainment: the Continental Review "In Old Vienna" at Congregation Rodeph Sholom; the bill of Viennese comedians, the Robby Lewitsch Swing Band at the Variety Show and Dance at the Audubon Ballroom; the Hanukkah Ball with Ralph Hayes and His Famous Orchestra, the "Hamburger Evening" at the Prospect Unity Club, and the "Frankfurter Evening" at the Mecca Temple on West 55th Street (as hometowns, not foods); the New Year's Eve Celebration ("Cabaret—Dance—Surprises") at the Paramount Mansion on West 183rd Street; the 200 Cantors (!); and the world-famous star Molly Picon, with her brilliant repertoire in the great Gala Concert fund raiser for the Polish victims of the Nazi terror. And each week, the German-Jewish Club sponsored a Sunday evening tea dance at the Empire Hotel, admission twenty-five cents for members, forty cents for guests. The Empire, located (as it still is) at Broadway and 63rd Street, where many German-Jewish events were held, had by then become a center of refugee social events.

For that generation, at least, maybe for all generations of immigrants, acculturation seemed to be two sided: first to find a home and a get a decent job, to find your way through government regulations—or indeed to find your way anywhere—you had better learn the language and the rudiments of the culture. But in the music, in the cabaret acts—in all things one did for relaxation and entertainment or simply in the effort to retain the things one loved best about the old country—the old ways often lasted longer. Much later, talking about a very different generation of immigrants, Cesar Chavez's son Paul remarked that the "the first thing to go is language. The last is food."[127]

3

Friendly Enemy Aliens

1941–45

Notwithstanding the tensions and ambivalence between a whole-hearted commitment to Americanization and an ongoing attachment to the *Bildung* and enlightenment of pre-Hitler Germany and/or a broader European cosmopolitanism, *Aufbau* had never left any doubt on where it stood. But with Pearl Harbor and the ensuing U.S. entry into the war against the Axis, it edged very near the brink of outright jingoism, though perhaps no more so than the rest of the press—or Americans generally—did at the same time. "United We Stand," said the boldface, front-page headline on the December 12 issue, the first after Pearl Harbor. And then immediately under it, in bold type in English, with translations in French, Spanish, and Italian (the German version was relegated to the second page, which itself was telling): "At this moment, the immigrants who in recent years have found asylum and a new homeland under the Star Spangled Banner put forth but one desire and one pledge: to stand side by side with the American people and help them to the best of their abilities in the defense of our country and its ideals."[1] Those words were probably written before the formal declaration of war against Germany (on December 11), and so could be read as a passionate commitment of the Hitler refugee community to the

Aufbau front page of December 12, 1941, the first issue after Pearl Harbor. (courtesy of JM Jüdische Medien AG, Zurich)

American cause in the war against Japan, but by then everyone knew that war with Hitler was imminent.

In the months following, there would be similar headlines. In April 1942 one said: "Calling All Immigrants," and under that: "America's Enemies Are Our Enemies . . . We Were Their First Targets!" Immediately under it was an appeal for contributions to the "Loyalty Committee of Victims of Nazi-Fascist Oppression" sponsored by *Aufbau* and a host of Jewish organizations, including the New World Club, to raise funds to buy a fighter plane for the Army Air Corps (and later an ambulance for the new state of Israel).[2] "Make Yourself an Exemplar," said one of its pitches, "of fidelity and loyalty." Among the men who would fly the plane, a Curtis P-40 fighter (in the Mediterranean Theater), was Lt. Henry B. Perry, one of the black Tuskegee Airmen. A rabbi would later introduce Perry when he came to speak to a Jewish audience at an *Aufbau*-sponsored event in New York. Only in America. In Queens, the Kew-Forest Lodge of B'nai B'rith would also raise funds for an ambulance for the army— and there might have been others. The army officer who accepted the gift made note of the fact that many of the donors were not yet citizens, which almost surely was the point the donors hoped to make.

Aufbau, of course, had its own reasons for its unequivocal expressions of support in that struggle. The battle against Hitler had been the refugees' cause for nearly a decade, not only for all those who had been victims of the Nazis but for millions of others—Jews and Gentiles alike—who, like Thomas Mann, believed that the essence of European civilization was at stake. They wanted this war against Hitler, even though, as aliens and as Jews, they had been hesitant to call for it. So the cause of America was now also the cause of that European *Kultur*. What was hardly noticed at the time was that Operation Barbarossa, the invasion of Russia that Hitler had launched six months before Pearl Harbor, was not turning into the quick Blitzkrieg victory over the Slavic *Untermenschen* that Hitler had expected. Although the Germans came within a few miles of Moscow, the Soviet capital had not fallen and never would.

Nonetheless, *Aufbau*'s editors, like all German-speaking refugees, understood the difficulty of their position, especially in the face of—and even after— the unemployment of the 1930s and the undercurrent of nativism and anti-Semitism that had fed on it. America's welcome had never been unqualified. Still, it's not surprising that, as one study observed, *Aufbau* in the 1930s had been reluctant to challenge the open-door myth and make much of a fuss about the "anti-alienism" in American society "because that would have meant questioning the much-lauded American spirit of tolerance."[3] And while they might be Jewish refugees from Hitler and grateful to be in America, few would completely outlive the ingrained German sense of obedience and deference to authority that they had been trained for. "We [immigrants] are all still too much children of the authoritarian state," Hulse—sounding like a libertarian— wrote early in 1940, "sloughing off responsibility and happy for every organization, every committee, every law that lightens the work, but constrains freedom."[4]

And while the refugees' enemy was now America's enemy, technically German refugees were still German nationals, even though the Nazis had denaturalized all Jewish émigrés, making them stateless. Within hours of the attack on Pearl Harbor, the president formally proclaimed them "alien enemies" (or "aliens of enemy nationality"). Many had been in the same position in Belgium, France, and England before and had asked the same question: Why us? They had been ready to fight for their adopted countries and were rejected; they possessed badly needed skills. Why had thousands of Jewish refugees been interned in England and later deported to internment camps in Canada? Why were thousands rounded up in Belgium and France, packed without water or ventilation in stifling heat in cattle cars, the cars sometimes marked with large letters "Saboteurs" or "Fifth Columnists," and shipped to Saint-Cyprien, Les Milles, Vernet, and other French concentration camps?[5] The ultimate travesty (not known at the time, of course) is that within two years, the French, who had arrested these Jews as enemy aliens, would deliver tens thousands of them to the Nazis for shipment to the death camps in the East. "We were expelled from Germany because we were Jews," Arendt wrote later. "But having hardly crossed the French borderline, we were changed into 'Boches.' During seven years we played the ridiculous role of trying to be Frenchmen—at least prospective citizens; but at the beginning of the war we were interned as 'Boches' all the same. After the Germans invaded, the French government had only to change the name of the firm; having been jailed because we were Germans, we were not free because we were Jews."[6]

By December 1941, *Aufbau* reported that six thousand had been deported from France to "Poland," and that the total would soon reach ten thousand. (All numbers would later be exceeded many times over when the full dimensions of the Holocaust became known.) What sense did it make? And as Arendt would point out, both in *Aufbau* and more extensively in her classic *The Origins of Totalitarianism*, it was only the state that could guarantee enforceable rights. With no state, there were no rights.[7]

The émigré literary agent Felix Guggenheim, at the time a publisher of books by German writers in America and president of the Los Angeles Jewish Club of 1933, worried about another consequence of the label, a worry that may have been more an indicator of the anxieties of some émigrés than of a real threat. "It can only lead to confusion among our American friends," he said in a talk in 1942, "when we—refugees from Nazi Germany—are branded enemies of the American people, when the term 'Jewish refugee' is increasingly associated with 'enemy,' and when soon there will be those who behave anti-Semitically toward Jewish refugees without having their anti-Semitism put them at risk of identification as Nazis and fifth columnists. They will surely be instructed by their masters to agitate against us not as Jews, for a change, but as enemy aliens."[8]

"They Have No Rights at All"

Some Americans quickly complained about the "enemy alien" designation for the expatriated German Jews: "The present German law," wrote Walter R. Rothenberg in a letter to the *New York Times*, "denies the Jews (or rather, all those persons who, according to the Nuremberg laws are classified as such) the rights and duties of German nationals. They have no political rights; and, in fact, they have no rights at all, not even in economic life."[9] How could the United States classify them as enemy aliens? In February, a group of distinguished émigrés—Albert Einstein, Bruno Frank, Bruno Walter, Thomas Mann, and Arturo Toscanini—sent a letter to FDR pointing out that never before had there been such a situation. "It cannot be deemed just," they wrote, to classify them "under the discrediting denomination of 'Aliens of Enemy Nationality.' A clear and practical line should be drawn between the potential enemies of American democracy on the one hand, and the victims and sworn foes of totalitarian evil on the other."[10] At about the same time, Mann and Frank (among others) testified before a congressional committee, the Tolan Committee, named for its chairman, Rep. John H. Tolan of California, about the irrationality of a blanket "alien enemy" designation. Did Toscanini, whose benefit concerts would generate millions of dollars in the sale of war bonds and raise millions more for various other causes, including the March of Dimes (for which FDR himself was the equivalent of a poster boy), have to get special permission each time he traveled from New York to Philadelphia to conduct a benefit concert?[11] After the war started, the British quickly identified those it regarded as dangerous aliens and redesignated the great majority of refugees as "Refugees from Nazi Oppression" and took advantage of their skills and their military service.[12] But tellingly, Mann, in his testimony before the Tolan Committee, wasn't willing to defend the Japanese with the same certainty. "All of us know that the burning problem on the West Coast is the question of the Japanese," he said. "It would be a great misfortune if the regulations perhaps necessary in their case would be applied to the German and Italian refugees."[13] Many years later, Guggenheim would remark that it became clear early on that "one had made a

Albert Einstein and Thomas Mann in Princeton, 1938. (courtesy of the Leo Baeck Institute, New York)

terrible mistake with the Japanese." There was no attack on the West Coast and "no single Nisei in Hawaii [who were not interned] was caught working for the Japanese."[14]

The Tolan Committee members seemed sympathetic, and, beginning in the late spring of 1942, occasional announcements of modifications—some implemented, some only proposed—came through the fog from Washington. Spouses and parents of military personnel would no longer be classified as enemy aliens, nor would wives of U.S. citizens, people classified as bona fide refugees from political or religious persecution, or those who were over sixty years old and had been in the country continuously since 1924. Of the 300,000 aliens screened by the government, an estimated 150,000 would be eligible for reclassification.[15] Even as Mann was testifying, moreover, Congress was passing the Second War Powers Act, making any alien in the military eligible for naturalization after three months of honorable service, providing only his commanding officer approved.[16] In part because of it, between 1933 and 1945, according to *Aufbau*, more than 180,000 former "enemy aliens," many of them in uniform, became U.S. citizens, sworn in by some two thousand state and federal judges. (Baltimore District Judge William C. Coleman reportedly refused, maintaining that any German-born person who immigrated after January 1, 1933, meaning, in effect, Jews and anti-Nazis, could not be naturalized during the duration of the war. An appellate court overruled him.)[17]

The bigger worry, however, was the meaning of the "enemy alien" label itself. Would America, the land of the free, arrest and intern all those designated as enemy aliens—Germans, Austrians, Italians—as the Belgians and the French had in the first days of the war, and as the British at first started to do, and as the United States did with the Japanese on the West Coast (and not only aliens, but Japanese American citizens as well)? Had the Jews escaped the shadow of Dachau and Auschwitz only to fall under a similar shadow in America that could be nearly as dark? Before the end of the month, Francis Biddle, now the attorney general, issued another statement reassuring refugees that "they are aliens in the technical sense of the word only. As long as they conduct themselves in accordance with the law, they need fear no interference by the Department of Justice or any other agency of the federal government." *Aufbau* played that big on page one under the headline "Loyal Non-Citizens Safe."[18] A few days before Pearl Harbor, Eleanor Roosevelt, speaking at the Immigrants Conference in New York organized by the ubiquitous Wilfred Hulse, had similarly assured law-abiding aliens that they had nothing to fear. "We will never have concentration camps in this country," she said.[19]

In fact the president's executive orders of December 7 and 8 declaring all German (and Italian and Japanese) aliens to be "alien enemies" already imposed restrictions on travel in many places; prohibited all air travel without specific government authorization; banned them from designated areas around harbors, airports, and military installations; prohibited the possession of short-wave radios, cameras, maps, and other materials that could be used to damage the United States; prohibited membership in any organization (as well as attendance at any of their meetings or possession of any of their literature) listed by the attorney general as "opposed to the public interest of the United States"; and, more worrisome to any refugee, declared that all enemy aliens could be subject to removal, apprehension, detention, and interment.[20]

Reflecting what may well have been interagency disagreements about refugees and other "alien enemies" and the general governmental confusion and uncertainty in the early months of the war, Biddle issued a reassuring statement at the beginning of January, reinforced in later weeks by similar assurances from other federal officials, condemning the recent firing of alien employees by private employers, in some cases even because "they have foreign-sounding names." That, he said, was both wasteful and a violation of everything the

country stands for. Only in the case of secret, confidential, or restricted contracts and contracts for aircraft parts or accessories must the employer get
clearance from the concerned federal agency for the employment of aliens.[21]
There was now a severe shortage of skilled manpower, said Undersecretary of
War Robert Patterson; excluding loyal aliens was both "Un-American" and a
waste of crucial resources. Biddle, like Eleanor Roosevelt, was always supportive
of the refugees. But neither Biddle nor anyone else provided any further information. At that moment, three weeks after Pearl Harbor, probably no one in
Washington knew.

Through it all, *Aufbau* tried to be reassuring and urged its readers to co-
operate. In the view of a recent observer, it "presented a consistent message of
trust in the U.S. government and its efforts to prevent hardships for Jewish refugees."[22] Elow (Erich Lowinsky), a refugee writer and cabaret actor in Los
Angeles, who wasn't so sure, sent a little poem to *Aufbau*:

> We Aliens
> What do we have to do?
> We have to wait,
> Until we are called
> But then we have to be there.
>
> What do we have to do?
> We have to wait.
> But before we are called,
> We have to be ready.
>
> What do we have to do?
> We have to wait.
> But when we are called,
> We have to give everything.
> Our life too.
> THAT is what we have to do.[23]

Biddle's assurances to the contrary notwithstanding, the enemy alien designation generated no end of fear and confusion among refugees, not least because
the federal government, buffeted both by interagency disagreements and political and practical constraints, on the one hand, and influenced by the historic
racism on the West Coast, on the other, was itself conflicted, sending varying
signals about what it meant to be an alien enemy, a meaning that varied from

place to place and time to time. For weeks, Austrians, Czechs, and Poles didn't know whether they were "alien enemies" or not.

Within two months, thousands of people, not all of them Japanese, would find out. Things became clearer, though hardly more assuring, on February 19, 1942, just a week after *Aufbau* ran a large headline that there was "No Reason to Panic" when Roosevelt issued his now-infamous Executive Order 9066, which led to the internment of some 120,000 people of Japanese ancestry, including American citizens—the "dirty Japs" who had launched the sneak attack on Pearl Harbor, all standard phrases of the time—who had been living in California and other western states.[24] (But significantly enough, not those in Hawaii, where the Japanese had first attacked and which must still have been the biggest potential target, but where the growers, needing their labor, had enough political influence to get an exception.)

That immediately undercut the assurances that had been coming from Washington, including Biddle's, who, unknown to anyone on the outside, had vehemently opposed Roosevelt's evacuation and internment order. As applied to Japanese American citizens, he argued, it was almost certainly unconstitutional.[25] Contra Eleanor Roosevelt, there would indeed be concentration camps. Among the detainees would be some thirty thousand aliens who were not Japanese, members of the German-American Bund among others, who were suspected by the Justice Department to be Nazi loyalists, and not all of them German or Italian either (but very few Jews). There were over 1.2 million people in the country who had been born in Germany and an additional 5 million whose parents were German born. That made categorical internment of all Germans both politically and practically impossible. The Germans, moreover, were white and eligible for naturalization, as Japanese immigrants at that time were not. Further compounding the confusion was the fact that while aliens were not eligible for military service in the early months of the war, men were nonetheless required to register for the draft.

But beyond the internment of the Japanese, and despite the early assurances from the attorney general, Executive Order 9066 also empowered the military to impose other significant restrictions on those classified as enemy aliens. And this Gen. John DeWitt, the commander of the Western Defense Command, did: Enemy aliens on the West Coast were not allowed to leave their homes between 8 p.m. and 6 a.m. regardless of their occupations (meaning, for example, German émigré physicians could not answer night calls from patients) and were not to travel more than five miles from home at any time without authorization from the Justice Department. *Aufbau* headed the story "Sorrow Comes to the West Coast"; based in part on reports in the *Los Angeles*

Daily News, it was all in English, and so appeared to be directed as much to Americans as to *Aufbau*'s regular readers. "The reaction of the refugees themselves," it said, "can hardly be exaggerated. Those who until now have clung to the hope that only technically they may be regarded as 'enemies' of the American people have given it up now. Confidence in the future—so essential for people who have lost a great deal of their past—has shrunk overnight to the vanishing point."[26]

Beyond the demoralization—and the reminder of what many had so recently escaped—there also were practical issues: The curfew and five-mile limit prevented some from taking good jobs in industries that, with war-time labor shortages, especially needed their skills, others were kept from night courses for adults or just from commuting to their college classes. But it seems no one violated it, because, as Guggenheim said with an ironic laugh, "they were all Prussians, more or less."[27] But because there was no curfew in the East, refugees there, probably including *Aufbau*'s editors, were less likely to be troubled by the enemy alien label. And like the *New York Times* and most other mainstream papers (and most likely the great majority of Americans after Pearl Harbor), neither were they troubled by the internment of the Japanese, which one *Times* story described as "a new pioneering chapter in U.S. history."[28]

In response to complaints about the enemy alien categorization from groups like the Los Angeles Jewish Club of 1933, according to the most comprehensive study of the subject, War Department officials "referred the refugees to the Justice Department and Justice Department officials in turn pointed back to the War Department. The Justice Department eventually acknowledged the matter to be under its jurisdiction and began, in the summer of 1942, to consider the establishment of special hearing boards to determine the loyalty of individual refugees. These hearing boards were never created, however, probably because the government considered the administrative effort too onerous."[29] DeWitt's curfew and other restrictions on German and Italian aliens would be lifted in December 1942, roughly ten months after they were imposed. There was, of course, never any real military justification for a curfew that covered a strip of the West Coast from the beach to a line roughly one hundred miles inland. As with the racist internment of the Japanese, it only made sense as a political decision for domestic consumption.[30]

Nonetheless, even before Roosevelt signed Executive Order 9066 on February 19, a time when the news from the war in the Pacific was consistently bad, *Aufbau* reported that there was serious talk that the government, invoking the danger of a Japanese attack, would ban enemy aliens from living in some parts of the West Coast, with its great concentration of aircraft factories and shipyards. In New York, the *Daily News* ran a map of a coastal strip three hundred miles wide from Canada to Mexico where groups close to California Sen. Hiram Johnson—once a Progressive, now a leading isolationist, and always something of a racist—were said to be pushing for the removal of the Japanese. Among the places cited as particularly vulnerable were parts of Burbank, North Hollywood, and the San Fernando Valley, where some German refugees had bought little chicken farms. According to the *Aufbau* report, the Japanese fishermen and cannery workers who lived on Terminal Island in Los Angeles Harbor, which had a number of federal facilities (and which would later house a major federal prison), had already been relocated to the interior where their skills would be useful on farms desperately short of labor.[31] (In fact, nearly all had been interned, most at Manzanar in the Owens Valley on the eastern slope of the Sierra.)

By February 1942 there were also reports that some areas near defense-related installations on the East Coast might be closed to enemy aliens as well. Those reports again brought assurances from Earl G. Harrison in the attorney general's office (who, like Biddle, understood and supported the refugees' cause) that such a possibility never included plans for any general evacuation of enemy aliens, as was the case with the Japanese on the West Coast. But at the beginning of May, *Aufbau*'s huge headline, which, even discounting some journalistic excess, indicated considerable levels of anxiety among the German refugees, declared "No Measures against 'Loyal Aliens,'" with a following line: "No Mass Evacuation." The article even opened the possibility—never realized but intended to be reassuring—that there might be a process whereby the vaguely oxymoronic "loyal aliens of enemy nationality" might be reclassified. Those so designated would be treated the same as loyal American citizens.[32] But as late as June 1943, the army, the navy, and the Justice Department found it necessary to remind all defense contractors that discrimination against aliens believed to be loyal to the United States was a breach of their federal contracts.[33]

And, as might be expected in the face of such reports and, beyond them, the broader anxieties and uncertainties of the early months of the war spurred refugee organizations to sponsor events to demonstrate to Americans the loyalty of the aliens among them: a New Citizen Rally; a meeting of "Loyal Austrians" to counter their designation as enemy aliens; an "In Defense of Our Country" rally sponsored by the German American League for Culture, a largely non-Jewish organization in Yorkville that had even stronger reasons to prove its Americanism; and, among others, Hulse's three-year-old Immigrants' Conference, whose leaders included Manfred George, Paul Tillich, Max Ascoli (later the founder and editor of *The Reporter* magazine), and other major figures in the immigrant community. As Hulse indicated in an *Aufbau* piece, refugees now had a greater need than ever to show Americans their loyalty and commitment to the national defense. And in fact, *Aufbau* and its readers, who felt they had a lot to prove, would also do much more than their share.

Beginning with its first wartime issue, *Aufbau* ran a regular column of war-related information for civilians, including details on the government's ever-changing visa, travel, and residence regulations; and counsel for its readers, aliens particularly, beginning with an urgent reminder to every noncitizen to carry his alien registration card at all times — it's the best possible identification card, it said — and to make certain that changes of address are reported promptly. And any current German, Italian, or Japanese national or stateless person who was formerly a national of those countries must register as an enemy alien. Anyone who fails to do so is subject to severe penalties including internment for the duration of the war. (The detailed instructions in *Aufbau* were flanked by ads for photographers who would provide the three required ID photos for anywhere between twenty-five and fifty cents.)

Also: Do not speak German loudly on the street — doing so was likely to fan hostility to immigrants, especially during the war, and arouse suspicions about spies and saboteurs. (At least one reader challenged that admonition. Consider people, especially old people, he wrote, who have lost everything. The one comforting thing they have left is the language. Must they abandon that, too? *Aufbau*, itself, of course, constantly reminded its readers that it was dedicated to the preservation of the best in German culture.)[34] Conduct yourself quietly and learn from the Anglo-Saxons to be calm and even-tempered. Don't horse around in public — at times like this, Americans may not understand any silliness. The list also included reminders that the Civil Defense Authorities welcomed noncitizen volunteers — so would the Health Department — and the New York Police could use volunteer messengers, ages sixteen to twenty, and don't forget to give blood and buy U.S. Defense Bonds and Stamps. The best place to give blood (presumably so it would be credited to refugees) was at the League of Alien Blood Donors, 139 East 63rd Street. (Later *Aufbau* also ran the names of multiple blood donors: Willy Heymann and Hermann Goldmann of Buffalo each donated blood ten times; several others gave nine or eight times.)

Early in April 1943, *Aufbau* also ran a drawing inscribed "Blast Rommel," informing housewives (in English) that "Twelve tablespoons full of waste grease from your kitchen will make enough glycerin for powder to load a 37mm anti-tank shell. Save left-over fats in any clean can and rush it to your meat dealer when filled."[35] By the time the drawing ran, Gen. Erwin Rommel, Hitler's "Desert Fox," was on the brink of defeat in the pivotal battle at the end of the long contest for control of North Africa.

And another reminder: telegrams overseas may only be written in English. Along the way, *Aufbau* ran a list and a count of Jews (in early 1942) in important government positions: none in the Senate (one, Herbert H. Lehman of New York, would be elected to the Senate in 1949); eight in the House, four of them from New York; one, Treasury Secretary Henry Morgenthau Jr., in the Cabinet; one, Felix Frankfurter, on the Supreme Court; plus a host of others in various executive departments. Were their numbers proportional to the Jewish population at large? While no exact analysis was possible, *Aufbau* said, the answer in any case was no.[36] But probably many more Jews, immigrants among them, knew the names of the great Detroit Tigers slugger Hank (born Hyman) Greenberg; of Bess Myerson, daughter of Russian immigrants who in 1945 became the first and still the only Jewish Miss America (duly reported, under a chaste cheesecake photo, by *Aufbau*);[37] and those of comedians such as Jack Benny and Eddie Cantor, who as "a great American and Jew" was also the author of an *Aufbau* piece, in October 1940, headed "This Is America!"; or maybe even Fanny Brice (as Baby Snooks) than knew the names of Frankfurter or Morgenthau.

The war predictably brought increasing worries for the refugees. Could anyone still get out of what *Aufbau*'s piece called the European inferno? Again and again, the news from abroad was discouraging. In April 1942, *Aufbau* reported there were still two hundred thousand refugees in so-called unoccupied (Vichy) France, and the chances of getting them out were slim. Their situation, *Aufbau* said, was "unenviable."[38] Meanwhile, there were more arrests of Jews and dissidents, again in numbers and intensity that would seem mild when the final numbers were tallied after the war. Was there still transportation from Europe to America, and would Spain and Portugal, the countries on the way to Lisbon, now the last remaining neutral port in Western Europe, still allow refugees, even those with the rare U.S. visas, to cross their borders? Would emigration, as *Aufbau*'s headline put it, come to a complete standstill? Two of the old Portuguese ships, the *Nyassa* and the *Guinea*, which had once specialized in hauling refugees, were again the centers of the uncertainties: Could people who had booked passage get to them? And if they could, could the ships sail? That, too, was uncertain. Would *Nyassa* be allowed to pick up passengers in Morocco? At the last report, Spain had closed the border with France at Portbou and the Portuguese police would not allow anyone into the country until the sailing of the *Nyassa* was certain.[39]

As if in illustration of those doubts, immediately next to Biddle's statement about the employment of aliens was the story of the odyssey of the Portuguese ship *Serpa Pinto*, which had sailed from Lisbon with a load of refugees, had picked up more in Morocco, and after a stop in the Azores was scheduled to drop passengers in Havana, Santo Domingo, and Vera Cruz, before coming to New York. She was on the high seas when Hitler declared war on the United States a few days after Pearl Harbor, which generated all manner of rumors on

a ship crammed with people, some of them former inmates of the French internment camps, some who had been conscripted into slave labor battalions in North
Africa, some of them loyalist veterans of the Spanish Civil War, others who had
narrowly escaped the Nazis, all of whom were at wits' end—human ruins, in
the words of the story, two of whom died on the journey. Would the ship, although already in the Western Hemisphere, be recalled by the Salazar government in Lisbon, which was nervously trying to maintain good relations with
both sides? Would they all be interned in Santo Domingo or Havana?[40]

Nobody on board, according to *Aufbau*'s story, knew anything, not even the
ship's officers. And so they went from port to port, until they got to Vera Cruz,
Mexico, where they were all ordered off the ship, held for two days in a dock-
side warehouse while the ship was "disinfected," then allowed to continue. On
the way there were new rumors: We're again enemy aliens and will be held by
American authorities at Ellis Island. Then, in the words of the story, "came the
miracle. In New York harbor, US immigration officials came on board—
friendly people—to welcome these 'alien enemies.' At the pier stood waving
friends. Not alien enemies but free men were allowed to disembark. . . . The
handling of the passengers of the *Serpa Pinto* is shining proof that even in time of
war, American democracy takes in the victims of fascism and doesn't push
them away just because they were born in a country now overwhelmed by
Hitler."[41]

For refugees, like all other Americans, the war—and the preparations for
the war in the year leading up to it—opened thousands of new jobs. While
some jobs in the defense industry were still barred to enemy aliens, and sometimes to all aliens, many were now open in work for the military build-up and
to fill the vacancies left in civilian industry by the hundreds of thousands of men
going into military service—jobs for men, and increasingly for women, too.
Aufbau's labor column pointed out that, while initially there were uncertainties
and delays as industry retooled, there would soon be more jobs—and after
Pearl Harbor still more. That was both assurance for its readers and a deter-
rent to the nativists complaining about refugees taking jobs from Americans.
By April 1943, *Aufbau* would be running front-page stories like the one about
War Manpower Commission Chairman Paul V. McNutt's demand that the
defense industry hire more aliens.[42] Rabbi Gottschalk recalled that his observant Orthodox father worked on the Sabbath "because he was employed in a
defense plant. The salary for the day's work went to charity. To work on the
Sabbath to help defat Hitler was a necessity but not one from which he chose to
profit."[43]

And, as predicted, soon there were plenty more. By 1943, in the midst of the
wartime labor shortage, *Aufbau*'s pages, though constrained by paper rationing,

were crammed with help-wanted ads, especially for cutters, finishers, and machine operators in the garment industry, but also for stenographers, tailors, seamstresses, shipping clerks, billing clerks, bakery workers ($33.80 for forty-eight hours for men, $26 for forty-eight hours for women), "soda girls," bus boys, and dishwashers, none of them dream jobs, but still jobs. Yet even at the height of the war, when there was a labor shortage and when millions of women for the first time took factory jobs that had always been done by men—when "Rosie the Riveter" became an icon of the war effort—there were still anti-Semitic incidents. In the Boston neighborhood of Dorchester, then still nearly all Irish, according to the left-wing New York newspaper *PM*, there were reports over a period of months of attacks on Jews—adults and children. Massachusetts governor Leverett Saltonstall first said they were exaggerated, then ordered them investigated.[44]

In December 1944, the government lifted its order closing much of the West Coast to the Japanese, allowing the return of the internees, though in many places nativism and racism—reinforced by stories about the Bataan Death March and other Japanese atrocities, some true, some not—made return nearly impossible. The last of the internment camps was closed in 1945. But the categorical "alien enemy" label for former German nationals wasn't lifted until well after the end of the European war, leaving the travel restrictions on enemy aliens in effect and prompting a volley of criticism from *Aufbau*.[45] As some individuals were reclassified, however, and the designation's practical effects for Germans and Italians eroded under the war's demands for manpower (both in the military and in defense production), and as the war progressed, it became less of an issue. Meanwhile, like most of the German Jews bearing that bureaucratic label, *Aufbau* became more red-white-and-blue, more super-American, than the average American, cheering on the war effort, promoting bond drives—it sponsored its own "Buy War Bonds" campaign—and blood drives. It solicited maps for military intelligence from the émigrés of the places they'd come from, and probably much other information as well, and, apparently, got plenty.[46]

A disproportionately large number of refugees appear to have enlisted in the military even before Pearl Harbor. Many more volunteered, or were drafted, as the enemy alien designation gave way to the need for more manpower. Some wrote pieces for *Aufbau* declaring how proud—even honored—they were to be accepted for military service in their adopted country and to serve on an equal basis with its native sons.[47] When most of those "alien enemies" became officially eligible for army service in September 1942, the paper urged émigrés to enlist. And by the war's end, roughly thirty thousand aliens from the "principal enemy countries"—Germany, Austria, and Italy—had done so.[48]

Predictably, the demands of the war created all manner of shortages—in raw materials, industrial capacity, and manpower. Perhaps the most unusual shortage was in the documentation for the nurses who were desperately needed both by the military and in civilian hospitals and clinics that lost people to the war effort. For many of the refugee nurses who wanted to serve but had been trained in Europe or had worked there—and who fled without their papers— obtaining such documentation was nearly impossible. So the Labor Division of the New World Club, working with the National Council of Jewish Women, produced a list of one hundred fifty otherwise eligible nurses and made arrangements with the New York State Nursing Board to use affidavits from former coworkers or others to certify their claims. Finding those former coworkers wasn't easy either, but apparently it was successful enough that the American Nurses Association urged its affiliates in other states to adopt it. It probably made a very small dent in the greater shortage, but it was yet another demonstration to the nation of the efforts that the Hitler refugees were making.[49]

"Our Boys in the Army"

For *Aufbau*'s Jewish editors, some of whom had served in the German Army in World War I, military service in the war against the Axis was especially important as a shield against the anti-Semitic libel, like that after the World War I in Germany, that Jews had been draft dodgers and war profiteers. And so *Aufbau* paid particular attention to the Jews in the U.S. military. Under the ongoing head "Our Boys in the Army" it ran photos of young soldiers in almost every issue (occasionally there was also an item headed "Our Girls," though it stretched to include Jewish women in the British Army). It ran stories of their exploits in columns called "This Is the Army" (an echo of the Irving Berlin song) and "Jews in Uniform," obituaries—often with photos—of those who had lost their lives, and pieces encouraging people to send packages and mail to men in the service, especially to the single men who had no families. During the holiday season, it sometimes ran letters from soldiers asking readers to send cards or gifts to comrades: "Regarding your call to leave no-one out, I'm sending you the address of a soldier who has no one here. His father was a victim of Hitler, his brother died with the French Foreign Legion."[50] (The Foreign Legion was itself a means, some desperate German refugees in France believed, of escaping internment or deportation. Many later regretted it.) But the story of the soldier with "no one here" was not unusual.

"Yesterday Refugees, Today Soldiers," said one headline in 1944, telling the stories of a half-dozen refugees, now enlisted men who had distinguished themselves in combat zones in Italy, France, Holland, and Germany. One,

Aufbau, April 13, 1945, with one of many items headed "This Is the Army" or "Our Boys in the Army." (courtesy of JM Jüdische Medien AG, Zurich)

forty-five-year-old Sgt. Richard F. Stern, a veteran of the Kaiser's Army in World War I, overwhelmed a German machinegun nest and forced it to surrender; one Julius Brunner, formerly Heilbrunner, from Freiburg in Baden, a radio operator, though under heavy enemy fire, maintained contact between army units in France; another, Pfc. Theodore Bachenheimer, who had been parachuted in, organized a group of Dutch civilians in what was still German-occupied Holland into a resistance unit; a fourth, Corp. Erich Liebenstein from Wurzburg, in company of two others, one of them also a refugee, had captured thirty-two "Nazis" in a French wood.[51] The story also cited the praise that both Roosevelt and Thomas E. Dewey, his opponent in the just-concluded 1944 election, had heaped on the thousands of refugees who were serving with the U.S. Armed Forces.

It ran lists of Jewish military personnel who had been promoted or won medals and other honors, complete with current hometown in the United States and German birthplace: "M/Sgt. Harry Jacobs, previously Mannheim, now Washington, DC." There were extensive laudatory stories about defense contractors such as the Eagle Precision Tool and Die Company of Long Island City, most of whose employees were refugees from Hamburg, Ulm, Vienna, Munich, Prague, and Budapest, who were honored with an Army-Navy "E" award for "your fine record in the production of war materiel."[52] It published first-person accounts by soldiers and airmen (in the true *Reader's Digest*-fashion of that era) like "My Toughest Air Combat" by Staff Sgt. Schiller Cohen, who won the Distinguished Flying Cross for his bravery in one of the fifty-two missions he had flown to that point in the fall of 1943 as a tail gunner on a Flying Fortress over North Africa and Italy.[53]

It ran a short piece by Hulse, who had been a frequent contributor as a civilian, about his return to Germany, now as Captain Hulse, an army doctor. He described a short break from his medical duties when he was invited to a dance attended by nurses from Mississippi and pilots and artillerymen from Boston and New York. "After a couple of hours of fun on German soil," he wrote, "the pilots went back to their planes, the artillerymen to their cannon, and the nurses and I to the wounded and the mutilated, each to his own place, to win the war against the Nazis. But no one whispered any of this in my ear when I was on the Berlin-Paris express (escaping the Nazis) in 1933. Life is strange."[54] Several thousand became members of a special intelligence unit named the Ritchie Boys, for the base in Maryland where they trained, which relied in considerable part on the cultural background of German-speaking refugees— among them familiar émigré names like Hans Habe, Guy Stern, and Klaus Mann, son of Thomas, who served as interrogators of prisoners and later as translators at the Nuremberg war crimes trials. During the war Mann served with the army in Italy and, later, as a correspondent for the army newspaper, *Stars and Stripes*, in France.

For the soldiers interrogating POWs, the reversal of roles must have been at least a little strange. According to a recent study, by all accounts many— trying to show the prisoners, and later the Germans they questioned in the de-Nazification process, the behavior that the Germans failed to show Jews— "were guided by a moral ideal of a decent soldier and human being, which was inspired by the motivation to be morally superior to the Germans."[55] But almost certainly others were less proper.

And more than a few were among the liberators at the camps. One, Morris Eisenstein, who had won two Silver Stars and three Bronze Stars for bravery, later said that the star he most prized was the yellow Jewish Star with the word "Jude" that he got from a prisoner at Dachau.[56] Ernest (born Ernst) Michel, a survivor of Auschwitz who immigrated in 1946 under President Harry Truman's Displaced Persons Act and eventually became executive vice-president of the United Jewish Appeal in New York, recalled that right after his liberation, when he covered the Nuremberg trials for a German newspaper, his stories carried the byline "Ernest Michel, Former Auschwitz Inmate #104995 Now Special Correspondent at the Nuremberg War Crimes Trial." He also recalled that during a brief association with the American Military Government, "some non-Jews learned that a Jew from Mannheim was working with the Military Government. Some came to see me at the office [and] everyone had a story about how they and their families had tried to help Jews. I methodically threw every one of them out of the office."[57] As the honorary chairman of the American Gathering of Holocaust Survivors in 2008, Michel had been among the many people demanding that the Mormon Church honor its promise to stop the macabre practice of posthumously baptizing Jewish Holocaust victims, among whom were his mother, father, and grandmother.

More somberly, as the camps were liberated, soldiers like Staff Sgt. Fred Levy went looking for relatives in the human wreckage—Levy was searching for his uncle David Jungermann, who had been deported to Buchenwald in 1942—usually without success. And like other papers during the war, *Aufbau* occasionally ran lists of its "hometown" soldiers who had been killed in the service—one list with seventy names of former *Aufbau* readers ran in December 1944. It also published a list provided by Sen. James Mead of New York of scores of Jewish soldiers, Marines, and sailors who were the first in their state or their town to lose their lives in the war: Fineman, Schleifer, Rosenberg, Leopold, . . . "Wherever the American flag has gone," *Aufbau* (again making its case) quoted Meade, "Jewish soldiers on every battlefield have followed." For many young immigrants, it may have been a risk even more worth taking than it was for the average American. For them, military service had an attraction in addition to the chance to fight Hitler: It put them on a fast track to citizenship and helped prove their devotion to a country some of whose citizens had met them with something less than a warm welcome when they and their parents arrived just a few years before.

And it helped them deal with the sense of helplessness that they and their parents had felt in the face of the abuse from the Nazis. "I had first-hand experiences with the Germans," recollected Bernard Fridberg, born in Hanover, who was a gunner on a B-17 bomber, "so I was anxious to get even with them a little bit."[58] Some worked hard to get a posting in the European theater, which, for obvious reasons, they regarded as their own particular cause. Many joined because they wanted some measure of revenge, though apparently they rarely took it out on the individual Germans they met when they got there.[59]

One who got particular satisfaction in the service was Harry Ettlinger, born Heinz Ludwig Chaim Ettlinger in Karlsruhe in 1926, whose family was dirt poor when they arrived in America in 1938. As soon as he graduated from high school in Newark, he was called up and, because of his knowledge of German and his high test scores, became one of the Army Monuments Men who were assigned to recover the thousands of pieces of art looted by the Nazis. In the course of that assignment he found the rare prints and bookplates that had been hidden in a German warehouse by his grandfather a decade before.[60]

Henry Kissinger would later say how, working with men in the army from many backgrounds, "real Americans" made him feel "like a real American."[61] Similar words came from others. It is "a pleasure," wrote a man from Fort Campbell, Kentucky, who had been teaching German in the Army's Armored Force, "to watch the boys of all nationalities, that is Puerto Ricans, Filipinos, Chinese, Italians, Germans, Norwegians, Danish and what not work together and try to profit from each other's experience and knowledge."[62]

A few months after the end of the war, *Aufbau* ran a long interview with Col. Julius Klein, a native of Chicago, who had served in the South Pacific, where he was honored for heroism, and who lauded the "outstanding" immigrant soldiers he'd known—many of them, he said, were readers of *Aufbau*.[63] But since he was, among other things, the author of something called "Combat Public Relations," a combination of psychological warfare and propaganda, he may also have been practicing his skills in the interview. After the war, he became commander of the Jewish War Veterans of the United States of America and campaigned strenuously—among other things he led a parade down Fifth Avenue—for the creation of what became the state of Israel.

✳

Even for those who were never in the service, as for millions of other first- and second-generation immigrants—Italian, Slav, Greek, Jewish—the war pulled Americans together as nothing ever had before. That immigration levels since the late 1920s, when the National Origins Quota Immigration Act went into effect, were the lowest in American history probably didn't hurt, no matter how deplorable they were on other grounds. But there was no doubt that the war, bolstered by the Office of War Information and other official government propaganda as well as by Hollywood, fostered an ongoing celebration of American unity. In the movies, every B-17 and every submarine had a crew that included at least one Irishman, one Italian, one Slav, one Jew, and a few WASPs; and, in the case of the submarine, one or two black mess boys, who were, as always, patronized to varying degrees.[64] For German Jews of that era, the disadvantage of the cruelly low immigration rates thus had one small silver lining: It made assimilation a little easier for those who got to America.

In an *Aufbau* piece titled "My Son in the U.S. Army" in June 1943, the pacifist-socialist Leo Lania remarked on how fast and how radically young Europeans Americanize themselves—and not just on the surface. In a few months, "the young Europeans become American heart and soul." And in fact, it seemed that the percentage of Hitler exiles participating in the war effort—in the military, in volunteer work, and as blood donors—was greater than the national average. At the same time, especially in the first years of the war, *Aufbau*'s pages occasionally reflected concerns that Jewish soldiers who were taken prisoner, German refugees especially, would be treated more harshly than their non-Jewish comrades.[65]

As the war progressed, *Aufbau* paid increasing attention to events in Palestine: to the beginning of the political maneuvering and the diplomacy over the possible establishment of a Jewish state, the violent resistance by the Arabs to the increasing presence of Jewish immigrants, and the mounting Jewish militancy that accompanied it. Late in 1943, it reported that shortly before of the start of the European war, 250 "secret emissaries" had been carefully selected and trained in the bigger cities of Palestine and in the kibbutzes to return to Poland, France, Belgium, and Holland to help European Jews resist and survive in the face of the Nazi terror that would soon come.[66] How much of that was exaggerated and what it accomplished probably will never be known. But it was surely a morale booster for *Aufbau*'s refugee readers. The paper also urged the British to form a Jewish brigade with its own officers to fight the Germans in North Africa in defense of Palestine, not quite the separate Jewish Army that Jabotinsky wanted, but close. In 1944, the British, who correctly feared that such a group might become the core of the battle against British control of Palestine, as Jabotinsky hoped, finally consented to form one such brigade.

Before the end of the war, it would also be a source of hope and self-confidence for many demoralized Jewish refugees from the Nazis. They badly needed it.

There was still a residue of uncertainty about Palestine among émigré Germans, voiced with uncanny accuracy in one unsent letter that *Aufbau* published in 1942 by Arthur Schnitzler, the fin-de-siècle Austrian-Jewish playwright and Herzl friend who had died a dozen years before, expressing his doubts about the Zionist cause. Show me anyone, he wrote, who, unaware that he is a Jew and "grew up in some other country—Germany, France, England—who if he landed accidentally in Palestine, would feel at home there."[67] *Aufbau*, like many of its readers, was by then earnestly following the issue and supporting the cause and by the time Schnitzler's letter appeared *Aufbau*'s views on Zionism had changed. In May 1942, a week after it ran the Schnitzler letter, it published the text of a speech by the Zionist leader Chaim Weizmann at a major conference in New York on "The Present and Future of the Jewish People," in which he argued that the future of Europe hinged in many respects on the future of the Jews, three million of whom, he said, were homeless. (He could not then know that four months before, the Nazis had decided on the extermination program that would lead to the murder of most of Europe's Jews in the death camps.) Because the major Allied powers had a vital interest in the stability of the Middle East, which was the bridge between East and West, guarded the route from Europe to India, then, of course, still ruled by the British (and which was the source much of Europe's oil), Weizmann said, Palestine could have an important role in the rebuilding of the postwar world. He doubted that a two-hundred-thousand-man Jewish Army could be created, as some had imagined, but he would be content with a few Jewish regiments, which he hoped could be organized.[68]

At the same conference, David Ben Gurion, who would proclaim Israel's Independence in 1948, lead the new nation in its War of Independence against the Arabs, and become its first prime minister, declared that there was no inherent economic conflict between Jews and Arabs; the only problem was the unwavering Arab political opposition. The immediate task was to get official agreement among major Jewish groups in the United States, England, the dominions, and, if possible, Russia to gain a Zionist solution to the Jewish problem based on three (actually five or six) principles: an unequivocal restatement of the Balfour Declaration and the development of Palestine as a Jewish Commonwealth; the immediate recognition of the Jewish Agency (for Palestine) as the authority controlling immigration into, and the development of, the country; full equality for all Palestinian residents; home rule for all municipalities and other local jurisdictions; and autonomy of all religious and educational institutions. Coincidentally, *Aufbau*'s report on the conference appeared an even six years to the day before Israel declared its independence. It marked the beginning of the passing of the torch from the old European Zionists to the new militants on the ground.

More generally, with the turning of the tide of the European war—first in North Africa, then in Italy, then, after D Day in Western Europe, but most of all, perhaps, in Russia—*Aufbau*, like all German émigrés, also began to look more closely at what the world, and Germany especially, would, and should, look like after Hitler:

- It cheered the "historic" passage of the resolution sponsored by Rep. William J. Fulbright, then a young Congressman and former Rhodes Scholar from Arkansas, putting the Congress on record as supporting the creation of an international organization with the authority to maintain "a just and lasting peace among the peoples of the world"—what would become the United Nations. In the House, the vote in favor was 360 to 29.[69]

- It began to discuss the question of restitution of property and rights of the victims of the Nazis. In early 1943, it repeated a bold headline it had run three years before, when it was only wishful thinking—"The Nazis Must Pay"—over a report of a seventeen-nation conference in London in which the major Allies and a host of other countries at war with Hitler warned all concerned, including people in neutral countries, that the Allies reserved their right to "declare invalid any transfers of, or dealings with, property, rights and interests of any description whatsoever," in the countries controlled by the Nazis, whether by "looting or plunder" or purportedly legal means.[70]

- It began to push hard on a matter that was also on the agenda among Allied leaders, but was then still an unprecedented idea: the punishment of Nazi leaders for what became known as war crimes, the full monstrosity of which was then still unknown. By late 1942, it was running Gallup Poll results showing that only 6 percent of Americans blamed the German people, 74 percent blamed the government. Under bold front-page headlines such as "President Roosevelt Promises: No One Who Is Guilty Will Escape," it ran stories about the assurances FDR had given a delegation of Jewish leaders that the "authors of the crimes against the Jews will be brought to account."[71] And under a front-page headline asking "Who Are the Guilty Ones?" it started its list, some obvious—Hitler, Streicher, Goebbels, Goering, Rosenberg, and Frick—and some long since forgotten: SS Obergruppenführer Herbert Backe, who devised the plan to starve millions of Slavs and Jews in the Nazi-occupied parts of Russia; the Nazi theoretician Rudolf Jung, said to have been a big influence on Hitler; among others.

- Even before the formal Nazi surrender on VE Day, under the headline "Help with the Punishment of War Criminals," it appealed to readers who were victims of or witnesses to war crimes to report details to the

paper—names of prison officials and guards, the camps, dates, and times—
which would immediately forward them to the appropriate authorities.[72]
And once the war ended, it covered the major war crimes trials in depth. It
also reported on the demands coming from all over America directed to
John J. McCloy, the U.S. High Commissioner for Germany, that there be
no amnesty for war criminals. The story included the conclusion of its
unnamed "special correspondent" about the lame excuses some ex-Nazis
filed in their appeals for exoneration; few expressed any regrets for what
they had done. Just to make clear where the paper stood, it listed McCloy's
Army Post Office address.[73]

But George and *Aufbau* were always chary about anything that smacked of
pure revenge against the German nation. "Hatred," he wrote immediately
after VE Day, "never can be the basis for a future, which we all want to improve.
Firmness and justice are the surest support of a democratic world." It was a
tricky prescription, probably reflecting both the sharp divisions among many of
its émigré readers and the ambivalence that others probably felt. The Germans,
he said, had first to acknowledge that their situation was self-inflicted. Then
they had to find a "form of inner and outer freedom that allows them to gradually regain their human rights. Until then the world must act as guardian, which
it will happily relinquish when it no longer has to do that."[74]

Ultimately, of course, the list of war criminals grew much longer. *Aufbau*
warned that Berchtesgaden couldn't be allowed to become a monument after
the war.[75] At the beginning of 1945 (and indeed through much of that year)
when the outcome in Europe was all but assured, George remarked approvingly
on the prospect that "England, the USA and Russia are united [on] the necessity of total German disarmament and the destruction of all German industry
that could lead to a new war."[76] On that matter, as the world would soon learn,
Stalin, whose "War on Ukraine" led to the starvation of an estimated four million people, was far more cold-blooded than his wartime allies. But George,
remarking on the ongoing unwillingness of many Germans to face the reality of
their defeat, continued to cling to his fears—not entirely unjustified at the
time—of a remilitarized fascist Germany. He would for some time put the
blame on the Truman administration—which was much more realistic about
the shape of the postwar world than many American liberals believed—for the
fraying of the wartime alliance. All the Russians wanted, George believed in
the year after the war, was secure borders.[77]

But by early 1947, following a trip to Europe and Russia, he had begun to
have doubts. He approvingly quoted a *St. Louis Post-Dispatch* editorial declaring
that "the battle for world power between the United States and Russia had

finally begun." The chance for fundamental discussions about diplomatic possibilities for peace was past, George said. "We have to face reality." The clincher was the Soviet veto at the United Nations of a U.S. proposal, drafted by the financier, philanthropist, and presidential adviser Bernard Baruch, then also a hero to American Jews, that atomic weapons be eliminated from all nations' arsenals and proposing the creation of an international inspection system to make certain that atomic energy is used for peaceful purposes only.[78] The proposal had probably always been a propaganda ploy based on the near-certainty of a Russian rejection.

At the same time, George worried that America, in stiffening its resistance to communism, was tilting too much toward reactionary regimes such as Franco's Spain and handing too much of its Marshall Plan money to help the big European industrialists and not ordinary people, thereby driving the masses into the hands of the Comintern. At *Aufbau*, and probably among many of its readers, the liberal ghost of Weimar died only slowly. George sought a "third way" between Stalinism and unfettered capitalism.[79] And on the matter of punishment of war criminals, even corporate executives, *Aufbau* seemed to be having its way. Just a few months earlier, Gen. Telford Taylor, one of the military prosecutors in Germany, had unsealed the government's war crimes indictment of twenty-four directors of the chemical industry giant I.G. Farben in the planning and support of "aggressive war": the plundering and robbery of Nazi-occupied nations and the enslavement and mass murder of their populations as well as membership in the SS, a criminal organization.[80]

By the end of the 1940s, after the communists, with Soviet backing, overthrew the democratic government in Czechoslovakia and after the start of the Berlin blockade a few months later, and in the face of the Soviets' unvarnished anti-Semitic rhetoric, there was no longer any doubt about Soviet intentions, and hopes for a "third way" were gone. As it began to report regularly on the repression in East Germany and the anti-Semitism in Russia, hardly news to the *Ostjuden*, it became increasingly clear that *Aufbau* was moving ever closer to the U.S. Cold War position. In 1949, *Aufbau* ran a three-part excerpt from *Prisoner of Stalin and Hitler* by Margarate Buber-Neumann, a German-Jewish communist who had moved to the Soviet Union to escape the Nazis. There she would be arrested by the NKVD (Stalin's secret police) and sent to slave labor camps in Kazakhstan and Siberia. Then, in 1940, during the brief time the Germans and Russian were allies, the Russians delivered her to the Gestapo, who sent her to the Ravensbruck concentration camp. She was liberated in 1946. Stories like hers helped put an end to the liberal illusion that Stalin was less of a monster than Hitler.[81] By 1953, *Aufbau* would praise Chancellor Konrad Adenauer, then visiting the United States, for his commitment, notwithstanding the terrible legacy he was burdened with, to offer restitution, to "find a way to expiation," and for leading Germany into a firm alliance with the West.[82]

Predictably, *Aufbau* ran debates among its readers about broader issues of guilt. Was it all of Germany or only the Nazi leadership (or maybe just Prussia) that was culpable? Other articles asked related questions such as "Which is the real German people?," in the course of which some readers said they had been proud to be Germans in the Weimar years but now were ashamed.[83]

Even after Hitler's defeat, would it ever be possible, as one writer had asked in 1943, to conclude a lasting peace with the German people? What moral and political guarantees could the German people provide after Hitler was gone?[84] The émigré biographer Emil Ludwig (née Emil Cohn) warned a Congressional committee before the end of the war that even if the Prussian Junkers, certain of defeat, deposed Hitler, as he thought likely, it would be a bad mistake to make peace with them. They were no better than Hitler.[85] That followed a sharp debate in *Aufbau*'s pages between Ludwig and the Protestant theologian Paul Tillich about how much latitude the Germans should have after the war to govern themselves: Ludwig would have allowed very little. He even proposed that every German school have a foreign expert to supervise instruction.[86]

Hans Kafka, *Aufbau*'s Hollywood columnist, lambasted the Jews who had joined a conciliatory Council for a Democratic Germany, founded in May 1944, a month, as it turned out, before D Day, which was headed by Tillich but whose members nearly all came from the left, among them at least two communists. Their statement that "When Germany goes through with its revolution it should not be hampered by any force from outside," Kafka wrote, sounded almost like a quotation of an early speech by Hitler, who, Kafka said, would no doubt endorse its statement that "Germany should not be partitioned either economically or politically." The members of the Council, Kafka said, were overcompensating for their guilt or appeared to be people who feared they would have no better place to go after the war than Germany.[87] Manfred George called them "Luftmenschen, who never knew they were Jews."[88] Some on the Council's list, like Brecht, did go back.

Ten days after Germany surrendered, on May 18, 1945, *Aufbau* ran a front-page piece headed "Never Again Krupp." (And then it pivoted. At the top of the same page, it ran the pictures of the seven senior U.S. admirals and generals. The bold-face line under them, "Every War Bond You Buy Is a Weapon against the Japanese," seemed as much as anything else a belated declaration that *Aufbau* and its refugee readers hadn't just been fighting as anti-Nazi exiles but as Americans. Nonetheless, another article in the same issue, "Land War against Japan," much of it on the strategic choices in beating the Japanese, was striking: rarely before had *Aufbau* focused on anything but the war against Germany.)[89]

In December 1945, as the war crimes trials were getting under way in Nuremberg, George rhetorically asked, "Is Nuremberg Necessary?," followed by what he regarded as a series of straw man moral questions: Is murder morally justified to punish murder? Wouldn't the Nazis have done the same if they'd won? And of course he answered affirmatively—the recent arrests of German industrialists, he said, was a good omen. He hoped that the dictators Franco in Spain and Juan Perón in Argentina were paying close attention.[90] A week later, under the head "*Aufbau* as Witness in Nuremberg," it ran a photocopy of a cable declaring that a recent issue of *Aufbau* was "introduced to the court as evidence by U.S. prosecutor [later Senator] Thomas Dodd, showing that persons all over the world search for relatives which [*sic*] disappeared in concentration camps."

Aufbau reported without comment the resolution of the American Federation of Labor, the crafts union that was the older and more conservative of the two major labor organizations, supporting the creation of a Jewish homeland in Palestine but, in light of an expected labor surplus after demobilization, opposing any increase in immigration.[91] It was a position that would remain fundamentally unchanged in the labor movement until the 1980s, well after the merger of the American Federation of Labor (AFL) with the younger and more progressive Congress of Industrial Organizations (CIO), when membership was in decline and they needed Latinos and other immigrants, most of them in lower-paying jobs, to bolster the ranks.

★

Despite the nation's residual xenophobia and its historical push-pull ambivalence about immigration, *Aufbau* was steadfast in its embrace of its unequivocal Americanism, making clear that it regarded German Jews in America not as exiles but as immigrants. It urged its readers to attend "I Am an American Day" celebrations and sponsored "I Am an American Day" contests on topics like "The Road to America" (first prize, a one hundred dollar war bond). In 1944, and perhaps in other years, the full text of the winning essay appeared on page one next to a story about a petition signed by leading academics urging Roosevelt to press the British to open Palestine to increased Jewish immigration. The second-prize winning essay ran inside. Even with its global perspective and ambitions, part of *Aufbau* was still a small-town weekly.

And despite wartime shortages and rationing, which to many refugees seemed absurdly mild compared to the shortages they'd known in Europe, next to the help-wanted notices for garment industry cutters, sewing machine operators, and low-level jobs as dishwashers and stock clerks, *Aufbau*'s back pages carried ads for upscale luxury goods and services: single family homes in Forest Hills and Kew Gardens (prices ranging from $11,800 to $28,000), higher in Scarsdale; for fur coats and hats, jewelry, winter vacations in Miami; and listings of recitals by some of the greatest artists of any era, many of them also refugees (Lotte Lehmann, Arthur Rubinstein, and Vladimir Horowitz). Meanwhile, Bruno Walter was introducing, and sometimes broadcasting, the music of Gustav Mahler to American audiences.

In a similar vein, in his Galerie St. Etienne on 57th Street, the Viennese refugee Otto Kallir (born Otto Nirenstein) introduced German Expressionists and Vienna Secession artists—among them Oscar Kokoschka, Lovis Corinth, Gustav Klimt, and Egon Schiele—to America, some of whose works, in the words of one of his first exhibitions, he had "Saved from Europe." He was among *Aufbau*'s earliest advertisers.[92] Later his gallery also introduced great folk artists like Grandma Moses to Americans. As chair of the Austrian-American League in the 1940s, he was also a hub of the Austrian-Jewish émigré community in New York, working simultaneously to help Austrians obtain U.S. visas, sponsor Austrian cultural activities, and convince Washington that Austria was a victim—not a collaborator—of the Nazis.[93] (For a time there was a joke that Austrians tried to persuade the world that Beethoven was an Austrian and Hitler a German.) In 2016, Galerie St. Etienne was co-owned by his former partner Hildegard Bachert (born in Mannheim in 1920), who came to the United States as a teenage refugee in 1936 and is among the world's leading authorities on the great German graphic artist Käthe Kollwitz. Bachert joined Kallir in 1940 as a young assistant and, at the age of ninety-four in 2015, celebrated her seventy-fifth anniversary with the gallery. The other co-owner is Kallir's granddaughter, the Schiele scholar Jane Kallir. In 2016, it was still on West 57th Street, a few doors from where it was in the 1940s. Otto Kallir, Bachert would later say, did a lot of business with émigrés, Lotte Lenya among them. "We sold to people who had more money than we had and bought from refugees who had less."[94] By war's end, *Aufbau* was also running ads for bookstores featuring books in German.

And alongside the luxuries, as if to underline even then (January 1943) the excessive domestic consumption and waste of resources, Consolidated Edison regularly ran large ads (all in German) pleading with the paper's readers to "use less gas in your home for cooking, home heating, cooling and heating." Cook as many meals as possible in a single pot, use the oven as little as possible, fix dripping faucets, let warm food cool before putting it in the refrigerator, and don't heat the kitchen with the oven burners. "Your government beseeches you to use less gas."[95] Apparently some of the émigrés who had been offended by America's superfluity and wastefulness when they first got off the ship were now taking on the same wasteful habits. After the war, of course, the list of advertised luxuries grew exponentially, along with the success of the émigrés who could afford them.

Familiar Ground, Unbelievable Horrors

By late November 1942, information had begun to emerge about the mass murder of European Jews in what Rabbi Stephen Wise, chairman of the World Jewish Congress and probably the most influential American rabbi of his time, called the Nazi "extermination campaign" (which, the world would later learn, had been approved and codenamed "The Final Solution" at the Wannsee Conference of leading Nazis outside Berlin the previous January). Half of Europe's four million Jews, Wise said at a press conference in Washington, had already been killed. Poland, which had 3.3 million Jews in September 1939, now had two million; in Germany, where two hundred thousand lived in 1939, forty thousand remained. But as discussed earlier, even the *New York Times*, fearful that it would be attacked as a special pleader for its Jewish owners, wasn't confident enough of the report to run more than a short wire story on an inside page and a longer follow-up on the following day attributed to sources in the Polish government in exile in London.[96] Through 1942 other American papers were still counting the victims by the hundreds, not the millions, if they were paying attention at all.

At the same time, however, *Aufbau*'s editors, who had been reporting on Nazi atrocities from the late 1930s on and always focused on the plight of Europe's Jews, had also begun to pay increasing attention to the progress of the war in North Africa and, soon, in Europe, though much less so in the Pacific. The Pacific was not their place or their first cause. Among the less obvious reasons for the neglect was that the war in the Pacific was largely the war of the navy and the marine corps, and for a variety of reasons never fully explored, few aliens got into the more conservative, buttoned-down (and possibly more anti-Semitic) navy. The photos and names of those listed under *Aufbau*'s small "Our Boys" heads were almost entirely army (occasionally including the air corps, then still part of the army), the vast majority of them enlisted men (and women). There were no items called "Our Boys in the Navy" or "Our Boys in the Marine Corps," which was in the vanguard of the fighting in the Pacific.

Inevitably, the track of the war ran through places that were familiar to many of *Aufbau*'s readers—from the North African landings at Algiers, Casablanca, and Oran in November 1942, through Sicily to Salerno, the landings at Anzio and up the boot of Italy beginning in 1943. It reported as much as it could about the heroic uprising, following the murder or deportation of some three hundred thousand Jews from the Warsaw Ghetto in November, of the remaining Jews as the Nazis were preparing to murder them in the spring of 1943.[97] The Warsaw Ghetto uprising was probably the most dramatic and certifying act of Jewish resistance to date. On the same page that it reported on the Warsaw Ghetto, *Aufbau* also carried a story about a German Afrika Korps general surrendering to a twenty-three-year-old Jewish Army lieutenant named Klein from Waukegan, Illinois: "Nazi General Surrenders to a Jew."

Aufbau, like other papers, recorded the fall of Mussolini and the capitulation of Italy in September 1943. And then, after D Day in June 1944, it followed the Allied drive from Caen and Saint-Lô through Paris, across the Rhine, through the Ardennes and the Battle of the Bulge to Brussels and then into Germany. Those battles ran through a Baedeker of old hometowns and familiar places, now illuminated by the letters home from soldiers who only a few years before had been refugees—Trier, Metz, Aachen, Saarbrucken, Strasburg, Karlsruhe, Heidelberg, Frankfurt, Freiburg, Munich. And in the background the bloody Russian victories—Leningrad, Stalingrad, Smolensk—in the East and the Red Army's march through, for some, another set of familiar places—Warsaw, Cracow, Prague, Vienna, Berlin, and scores of others. Some, when the Red Army tanks arrived, were no more than streets of rubble.

Aufbau had its special reasons to mourn the death of Franklin Roosevelt at Warm Springs on April 12, 1945. "We can die," wrote Thomas Mann in his moving eulogy in *Aufbau*, "in the secure knowledge that we have seen a great man."[98] And only eighteen days later came Hitler's suicide in his Berlin bunker. And with the military victories came the death notices of young men who, not many years before, had arrived with their parents as child refugees, such as Cpl. Heinz Maas of Cleveland, formerly of Karlsruhe, and Pfc. Gerhard Sachs of Jeannette, Pennsylvania, formerly of Münsterberg, and many others, who had died in the service of their country on the same soil on which they had been born some twenty years before.

At almost the same time came the first of the terrifying lists of liberated concentration camps and the photos of their spectral survivors: Auschwitz-Birkenau, Bergen-Belsen, Buchenwald, Dachau, Mauthausen, Sachsenhausen, Sobibor, Theresienstadt (Terezin), Treblinka, all agonizingly familiar names to many refugees. And with the liberation of the camps came the heart-rending black-bordered death notices, scores of them of loved ones who had died in the camps, sometimes many years before:

> We have just learned that our dear mother, sister, grandmother and
> mother-in-law Hanna Guttman, born Meschelsohn, on January 9, 1943,
> and eleven days later her daughter, our dear mother, sister, niece and

mother-in-law Martha Wertheim, born Guttman, died in Theresienstadt. In deepest sorrow, Hildegard Traube, born Guttman, Forest Hills, N.Y.; Käte Wiener, born Guttman, Jerusalem; Martha Wertheim, born Meschelsohn, Bath, England; Werner Wertheim, Santiago de Chile; Ernest Wertheim, 1st Lieutenant, U.S. Army, Pacific."[99]

There, in just a few lines, was the whole dreadful story.

★

Almost everyone in America, but the refugees more than anyone, had followed the war in the daily newspapers and on the nightly newscasts, and sometimes, as during the Normandy landings, all day with the outcome still in doubt. For the refugees on New York's West Side there was the Embassy Newsreel Theater on 46th Street, and for most others there was the Movietone news, the March of Time, and other newsreels between the features at the Thalia and the Trylon Theater on Queens Boulevard in Elmhurst or in the other neighborhood movie houses. Through it all, there were journalistic footnotes that would have been major stories in other circumstances.

One was *Aufbau*'s story of the plight of the thousands of Jewish refugees who had been driven into Vichy France by the Nazis when they seized Alsace and resettled it with Germans. In November 1942, after the Allied landings in North Africa prompted the Germans to occupy all of so-called unoccupied France, some tried to flee into Spain. When Franco's Falangists interned most of them, the New York–based American Jewish Joint Distribution Committee was, in essence, paying a ransom to Franco's government to feed and house them.[100]

Another was the story, almost coincident with Italy's capitulation to the Allies in June 1943, that according to "Underground" sources, fifty-two thousand Jews had been deported from Belgium to concentration camps in Poland. Those numbers turned out to be too high—the best estimate was about twenty-five thousand by war's end—but the basic facts were correct. Of the twenty-five thousand who were deported, just over twelve hundred survived.[101] What wasn't known in the last months of the war is that even as German cities were being pulverized by Allied bombings and the Wehrmacht was being battered on both fronts, the Nazis intensified the pace of the genocide, giving the murder of additional tens of thousands of innocents what appeared to be a higher priority than the war itself, driving prisoners in forced marches from one camp to another as the Russians were approaching. Thousands more died on those marches.

And as countries were liberated, and then the concentration camps, *Aufbau* ran list after list of those who had been freed as the names became available (as ever, the first names to become public were those of prominent people).[102] There would be lists of former residents of Vienna who had been prisoners at Theresienstadt and had returned home; there was a list of Jews living in the American sector of West Berlin (actually, *Aufbau* pointed out, most of them were not full Jews but *mischlings*, part Jews, who may have had Aryan relatives to protect them); there was a list collected by the Joint of former inmates of Bergen-Belsen and the Salzwedel concentration camp, some with their barracks numbers, looking for friends and relatives in America. And as the camps were liberated, the "Looking For" lists in the paper and the appeals for help—food, clothing, medicine—grew longer even as every new set of pictures and the stories of yet another group of emaciated, hollow-eyed surviving prisoners seemed more dreadful than the last. It also ran lists headed "First Signs of Life" of recently liberated concentration camp inmates seeking people whose where-abouts were unknown.[103] The "Search for the Missing," in the words of an *Aufbau* headline, was "a monstrous task that requires patience."[104]

Toward the end of the war, and in the weeks after, its pages were also crammed with ads from people desperately seeking information from anyone about a relative who had been deported, often many years before: "Who can provide information on my parents Simon and Etka Wassermann and sister Friedl Wassermann, last living in Nuremberg, reportedly deported November 1941 to Stuthoff. I pray for news. Lea Wassermann, 289 Clinton Place, Newark, N.J."[105] Or the plea from Elsbet Jordan, for information about her mother, Jenny Haas, who would have been sixty-three in 1942 when she was deported to "an unknown place." Some listed the former residence of the lost person in terms bordering on the macabre: "Helene Foerster, from Vienna, last stopping place Prague, then Theresienstadt." Some were placed by people in Australia, Brazil, Canada, and South Africa, in some cases looking for information about parents that, given their ages, were almost certainly dead. It's impossible to know how many of those ads were heartfelt searches for loved ones and how many came from people who were already certain that there was no chance of finding the loved one alive and just wanted closure or maybe to settle an estate or get information on long-lost possessions. But whatever the reason, the pain was real.

When *Aufbau* ran a page of pictures from Bergen-Belsen, it headed them with the plaintive line: "They wouldn't believe us." In the early months after the camps' liberation, its back pages were jammed with columns of names in small type under heads like "Jews in Buchenwald," "Jews in Theresienstadt," "Jews in Thüringen," "Jews in Berlin," even "Jews in Stockholm, Seeking." Separately, the "Looking For" lists included items like: "Samuel Friedman of New York being sought by Ethel Friedman of Bergen-Belsen" and "Eugen

Kopstein of New York, being sought by Ludwig Schmidt, Buchenwald," hundreds and hundreds of them, an inventory of survival, sadness, hope, and despair. There is no way to know how many refugees in America, Palestine, South Africa, Cuba, Shanghai, and elsewhere, many of whom had narrowly escaped the same fate, had close connections with the faces in the photos from the camps, much less with those who were no longer there behind the barbed wire or the many more who had been murdered by the Nazis in the fields and woods and in the towns and were never sent to the camps. The world remembers the number six million, but no number will ever exist for those who narrowly escaped or for the loved ones they left behind. How many of *them* were there?

The bombing of Hiroshima and Nagasaki in August 1945 left *Aufbau*, like most other American publications, scrambling for the right words for what its front-page headline (probably like a thousand others) called the beginning of the atomic age. A new epoch had begun for mankind, Manfred George said in his lead editorial. "Since August 6, 1945, the world holds the power of life and death in its hands." As elsewhere in the America of that time, the terrible moral questions about the incineration of the population of two whole cities — or the nearly forgotten incineration of hundreds of thousands of other civilians in the fire-bombing of Tokyo and other Japanese cities in the months before — that would be debated in later generations were just beginning to be touched on. Few bothered to ask whether the United States, even then, would have dropped the atomic bomb on German cities.

Still, George understood the stakes. Never in all the previous centuries put together, he wrote, was the need greater for human brotherhood. And because the underlying moral question was largely overlooked, so was the question about how many American lives were saved at Hiroshima and what other alternatives might have been available to induce Japan to surrender without resort to the atomic bomb. Less than two months after Hiroshima, it ran a lengthy translation of *Saturday Review* editor Norman Cousins's powerful essay "Modern Man Is Obsolete," warning about the "ultimate self-destruction . . . extinction" attendant on atomic warfare as the "best articulation of the issue to date."[106] In 1950, with an introduction that the debates of whether something "as gruesome as the hydrogen bomb should be developed" had just skimmed the surface, *Aufbau* ran a piece by the polymath Protestant theologian-physician-organist Albert Schweitzer called "Reverence for Life," with the conclusion that no man is truly ethical who does not shy from any destruction of life.[107]

As ever, *Aufbau*, notwithstanding its uncompromising opposition to any use of the bomb, also played its equivalent of the local angle, in this case the role of Jews in the research that led to the development of the bomb: the Jewish nuclear physicist Lise Meitner, born in Vienna, who probably would have shared the

Aufbau front page of September 20, 1946, with Einstein's article "The World Must Learn to Think Differently," about the dangers of atomic warfare. (courtesy of JM Jüdische Medien AG, Zurich)

Nobel Prize that was awarded to her collaborator Otto Hahn for the discovery of nuclear fission (thus probably a victim of two forms of discrimination); her nephew Otto Frisch, who did the theoretical work first in England and later the actual work at Los Alamos on the triggering of the bomb; and his collaborator, the Berlin-born British physicist Rudolf Ernst Peierls, later Sir Rudolf. "Three Jewish names," *Aufbau*'s unsigned piece said, "who Hitler in his stupidity drove out of Germany."[108] It could have mentioned countless other refugees from fascism who were trained in Europe and contributed both to the building of the bomb and to the science that led to it, but for unknown reasons it did not.

There was, coincidentally, another future Sir Rudolf—Rudolf Bing, a Jew born in Vienna—who also fled to England and later became the influential general manager of the Metropolitan Opera for some two decades beginning in 1950 and who oversaw its move from its old home on 39th Street, where many of *Aufbau*'s readers first saw it, to the grand hall that anchors Lincoln Center today. He, in the words of the *New York Times*' James Oestreich, "ruled much of the operatic universe in autocratic fashion."[109] In 1950, *Aufbau* lambasted Bing for engaging the great Wagnerian soprano Kirsten Flagstad, who had returned to her native Norway during the Nazi occupation and whose husband got rich profiteering under the collaborationist Quisling regime.[110]

4

In the Shadow of the Holocaust

1945–65

For Hitler's refugees, of all the events that occurred in a great rush, one after another, at the end of the war, probably none was as agonizing as the fate of Europe's remaining Jews, the 250,000 who survived the Holocaust, among them those who called themselves Sh'erit ha-Pletah, the "surviving remnant," from the liberated Nazi concentration camps. (And who soon organized themselves under that name in the DP camps in which many soon found themselves.) In addition, tens of thousands who had lived underground in Germany and other Nazi-occupied countries and still others refugees from Eastern Europe also ended in the displaced persons camps in West Germany, Austria, and Italy that were set up and initially run by the military.

After the intolerable conditions in some camps, where the DPs were no more than prisoners, became impossible to ignore and the tensions between the DPs and the army too great, the camps were taken over by the United Nations Relief and Rehabilitation Administration (UNRRA), which was dominated by the United States, the Joint, and by the inmates themselves. In a piece for *Aufbau* in April 1946, Simon H. Rifkind, a Lithuanian-born federal judge who had been on leave to serve as counselor to the U.S. occupying forces in Germany on Jewish issues, described their miserable conditions. Surrounded

Albert Einstein, his secretary Helen Dukas, and his daughter Margot taking the citizenship oath, October 1, 1940, in Trenton, New Jersey. (courtesy of the Leo Baeck Institute, New York)

by a hostile population that hated them, they were suffering both in body and in spirit: "Their whole civilization, built with love and hard work over a thousand years, lay in ruins. Everything they knew as a normal life is missing in the lives of these people. On liberation, they'd expected a welcome from repentant mankind. Instead they found themselves in the chill of a DP camp."[1] In December 1945, after Gen. George S. Patton was killed, *Aufbau* ran an editorial lauding him as "A Great General," which in the military context indeed he was. But *Aufbau* was not then aware that he was also a racist and a frothing anti-Semite, nor did it seem to know that he had been in charge of those camps. The people who complain about the conditions in the camps, Patton wrote in his diary, "believe that the Displaced Person is a human being, which he is not, and this applies particularly to the Jews who are lower than animals. . . . I have seen them since the beginning and marveled that beings alleged to be made in the form of God can look the way they do or act the way they act."[2] He seethed when he read Earl Harrison's report to Truman on the miserable conditions in the camps he was supposed to be in charge of.

Some six million European DPs had been returned to their old countries soon after those countries were liberated. But the roughly one million who either could not or would not go back—among them Jews running from the pogroms and virulent postwar anti-Semitism in Russia, the Baltics, Hungary, Poland, and Romania as well as the non-Jews running from the Russians—became a major concern not only for Jews in America but major factors in the debates about immigration both to America and Palestine. The fact that the DP camps in which they were housed, sometimes behind barbed wire, were almost as awful as the Nazi camps from which they'd been liberated, excepting only that their prisoners weren't being systematically murdered, made the immigration and Zionism issues all the more urgent.

That the DP problem overwhelmed the relief organizations came clear in a letter from two angry Jewish U.S. Army officers charging the Joint with having "failed in every way to aid in restoring to these people the hope and love of democracy, that we soldiers of the United Nations have fought, worked and died for. . . . In not one instance have these people benefitted from the generosity of World Jewry who support you."[3] But because most nations still refused to admit them, UNRRA and the International Refugee Organization (created in 1946 and later charged with the issue) confronted a nearly unsolvable problem. Again, George wrote a few months after VE Day, the doors were closed to European Jews. The coming months would determine not only whether in this war the Jewish people were the perpetual sacrifice but whether they would again become the perpetual loser.[4]

In early December 1945, *Aufbau*, in combination with Selfhelp, other Jewish groups, and the urgent pleas of the refugees, the lucky ones who had escaped, mounted an intense campaign to impress on the world—and on the president particularly—the need for action to alleviate the suffering of their fellow Jews still in the DP camps. Six months after the end of hostilities, it pointed out, the Jews who became the first victims were still waiting for the hour when their misery would end. It also highlighted part of a piece Eleanor Roosevelt had written for the paper the previous week: "We cannot look with a clear conscience at the pictures of these emaciated, suffering people in Europe while we sit comfortably in our easy chairs and allow fifty of them to die each day."[5] Two months later, it quoted a column she'd written after a visit to the camps: "The misery in these camps is terrible . . . the misery of the Jews is something I will never, never, forget." In the same issue, there was a front-page story about Nazis telling soldiers in the American occupation forces that Jewish Holocaust survivors crammed into houses that had been requisitioned to handle the overflow from the camps were thieves who had stored their loot in the basements of those houses.[6] In response, *Aufbau* contributed regular full-page ads through the early postwar years to a campaign by the United Jewish Appeal to raise $100 million in 1946, $147 million in 1947, and $250 million in 1948 for the relief of Jews in Europe and Palestine—large sums at the time—to which its refugee readers were almost certainly regular contributors.

In June 1945, President Truman sent Earl Harrison, who earlier had been the U.S. Commissioner of Immigration and was now the Dean of the University of Pennsylvania Law School, to Europe to look at conditions in the camps. In August Harrison reported back: "Three months after V-E Day and even longer after the liberation of individual groups, many Jewish displaced persons and other possibly non-repatriables are living under guard behind barbed-wire fences, in camps of several descriptions (built by the Germans for slave-laborers and Jews), including some of the most notorious of the concentration camps, amidst crowded, frequently unsanitary and generally grim conditions, in complete idleness, with no opportunity, except surreptitiously, to communicate with the outside world, waiting, hoping for some word of encouragement and action in their behalf."[7]

Now Truman, responding to reports by Harrison and others on the dismal conditions of the DP camps, the most recent from Gen. Dwight Eisenhower, who had followed up on Harrison's report and personally inspected a few, as well as the mounting complaints from *Aufbau* and Jewish welfare organizations, tried to do what he could. Truman faced stiff opposition in the Senate, led by Sen. Chapman Revercomb of West Virginia, who chaired the key committee, to any revision of the tight immigration quotas in the blatantly racist U.S. Immigration Act passed in 1924 or to any modification of the law that would allow new immigration visas to be counted against the thousands of places that had been left unfilled in the quotas for prior years. Some of that opposition was almost blatantly anti-Semitic; for example, a call by North Dakota Sen. William Langer to give preference to the ethnic (Aryan) Germans evicted from Eastern Europe after the war since they were "much worse off than the so-called displaced persons," most of whom, he pointedly said, "are related to residents of New York."[8]

In view of his inability to get the quotas liberalized, Truman directed the government agencies involved—the State Department, the Justice Department, the Public Health Service, the War Department—to take the small steps available to them to focus on the immigration of displaced persons, without exceeding existing quota limits, and thus "do something to relieve human misery and set an example to the other countries of the world which are able to receive some of these war sufferers. . . . Most of these persons are natives of central and eastern Europe and the Balkans," Truman said. "The immigration quotas for all these countries for one-year total approximately thirty-nine thousand, two-thirds of which are allotted to Germany. Under the law, in any single month the number of visas issued cannot exceed 10 per cent of the annual quota. This means that from now on only about thirty-nine hundred visas can be issued each month to persons who are natives of these countries."[9] Those measures didn't increase overall immigration, but they opened the doors to some twenty-two thousand DPs in the succeeding year or two, two-thirds of whom were Jewish.

Inevitably Sh'erit ha-Pletah and the tens of thousands still in the DP camps also brought new urgency to the portentous question about the creation of a new homeland — some regarded it as the restoration of an ancient homeland — for Jews in Palestine. It brought new names to the headlines, among them Rabbi Leo Baeck, who had headed the official organization of German Jews in the early years of the Nazi era, declining a number of offers from American institutions of help to immigrate to the United States, choosing instead to stay with his community. In 1943, he was deported to the concentration camp at Theresienstadt, where he spent the rest of the war working with the prison authorities in his efforts to alleviate the despair of his fellow prisoners for whom "living in the expectation of death by gassing would only be harder," a nearly impossible moral choice for which he was later attacked as a collaborator by Hannah Arendt, among others.[10]

When he was interviewed during a visit to New York a few months after he was found alive at Theresienstadt, Baeck, who would later be honored by New York's émigré organizations as a hero, told *Aufbau* that under no circumstances should émigré Jews return to Germany, nor should those who had survived the war in Germany stay there. "The history of Judaism in Germany," he said, "has come to an end. The clock can't be turned back. I knew that when I was still in Germany [presumably before he was deported]. When I advised Jews at the time to first send the young out, you older people can stand it until you can follow, I was called a defeatist. And I was correct. I could have saved a lot of lives [if people had listened]. I don't see any possibility that Jews can return to Germany. The period 1933–1945 has seen too much murder, too much plunder. So much blood, so many tears, so many graves can't be extinguished." As to the anti-Semitism in Germany: Is it set so deep that it can no longer be uprooted? "The older generation has more than a few times behaved decently. As to the younger generation, namely the Hitler youth, they've been so thoroughly corrupted and perverted that I don't see how even re-education can help."[11]

At the time, he was no doubt speaking for the thousands of Jewish émigrés everywhere who shuddered at the thought of ever going back. Such doubts seemed to be confirmed by *Aufbau*'s stories, such as one in the summer of 1947 headed "The Pogrom Mentality in Germany," which reported on, among other incidents, the showing of a newsreel about the reopening of a synagogue in Munich. The voiceover statement that only five percent of Jews had returned was met by catcalls and a shout that "they should all have been exterminated."[12]

Nor, as *Aufbau* reported, was the evil confined to Germany or Eastern Europe. In a piece headed "Poisoned Europe: Anti-Semitism Has Bitten Deep," *Aufbau* writer Richard Dyck reported on indigenous anti-Semitism in France, Luxemburg, and Prague. For the foreseeable future, he said, citing a "businessman," who was not Jewish, who had just returned from Paris, "life for Jews in Paris will be completely impossible." Anyone thinking of returning should be aware that "the bacillus of hatred for Jews has bitten deep into the French people."[13] At the same time, *Aufbau*, beseeched by questions from readers asking how—as people who knew Germany and spoke German—they could be helpful to the military or to civilian organizations in the first years of the occupation, provided a list of possible jobs. Citizenship was required for nearly all civil service jobs, but there was UNRRA; there were "war jobs" with the Office of War Information that employed some noncitizens, but not overseas; there was the Foreign Economic Administration that would be looking for accountants and bankers to examine German stocks, but they wanted only people who had been U.S. citizens for at least fifteen years, meaning no Hitler refugees and probably no Jews; and of course, *Aufbau* said, there were hundreds of noncitizens with the army in Germany, some in highly important jobs.[14] But the picture would change quickly.

By 1951, six years after the end of the war, *Aufbau* editor Manfred George, after one of his European trips, was reporting that young Germans under a certain age had not been infected by Nazism. "What they'd seen of it had oriented them powerfully against it. They listened willingly to Allied radio broadcasts and to talks about freedom."[15] Nor would many refugees have predicted that, by 1951, Home Lines and other shipping companies would be advertising regular voyages to Hamburg, $170 for tourist class, $280 first class; or that by 1950, Pan Am would be advertising direct flights in *Aufbau* to Frankfurt ("Only $442.70 to Germany and Back"); that KLM would offer flights to Frankfurt, Hamburg, Nuremberg, Düsseldorf, and Munich; or that not long after, all the major airlines, Lufthansa among them, would advertise flights to German cities in *Aufbau*; or that there would be ads for some of the major European summer music festivals; that the Bellevue Hotel in Baden Baden and others in Wiesbaden and Badgastein in Austria would promise rest and recovery to *Aufbau*'s readers; or that by the mid-1970s, *Aufbau* would be carrying large ads (in English) for Mercedes-Benz.

Maybe it wasn't surprising that eventually teachers from Germany would be coming to America to learn how U.S. schools taught about the Holocaust. Nor was it entirely surprising that by the mid-1980s, German textbooks weren't dodging the subject: They named those responsible and asked questions about the responsibility of people who watched their neighbors being deported and did nothing.[16] But few could have imagined that by 1970 the Berlin Senate

would have taken the suggestion of Hans Steinitz (George's successor as *Aufbau*'s
editor) for a visitor program for former Berliners, or that by 2010 an estimated
thirty-five thousand of them, now American citizens, would have participated
in it (or that thousands more had participated in similar programs in other
German cities).[17] Also unimaginably, in 1969, a Dr. Block would be advertising
his German-style Kur Sanatorium in the salubrious Luftkurort Lenggries in
Bavaria. This was not just going back to Germany; it was a return to the old
culture of the haut-bourgeoisie.[18] Or that a half century after the war there
would be a Leo Baeck Institute with offices in New York, Jerusalem, London,
and Berlin; and that the American Jewish Committee, which calls itself America's "oldest human relations organization," would likewise open a Berlin office
and "in an unprecedented step establish itself as a permanent player on the
German scene."[19]

*

Probably the best known of the new names in that sad era was that of the fifteen-
year-old Anne Frank, who died at Bergen-Belsen just a few weeks before it was
liberated and whose diary, published in English in 1952, would become a classic
of Western literature. But the world would also hear eloquent voices for human
rights like Elie Wiesel and become acquainted with the Nazi hunters Simon
Wiesenthal (like Wiesel, a camp survivor) and Serge and Beate Klarsfeld. Another former inmate of Dachau and Buchenwald—he was released before the
war—was the controversial Viennese refugee psychoanalyst Bruno Bettelheim,
who became director of the Orthogenic School for emotionally disturbed children at the University of Chicago (and much of whose European vita was later
exposed as a complete fraud). Bettelheim's contention that millions of people,
"like lemmings, marched themselves to their own death" because of the Jews'
"ghetto mentality" and their "unwillingness to fight for themselves" added yet
more fuel to the ongoing debate about the alleged failure of Jewish leaders to
resist fascism before it was too late.[20]

The decades after the war also brought reminders of the long and as yet
still-incomplete list of the war criminals who organized and managed the Nazis'
mass murder: from Adolf Eichmann and Josef Mengele, "the angel of death of
Auschwitz," whose medical experiments on prisoners still shock the conscience;
to Martin Bormann, Rudolf Höss, and Ilse Koch, "the Beast of Buchenwald,"
who was said to have made lampshades from the skin of murdered death camp
inmates (for whose trial *Aufbau* said it could provide the names of 120 witnesses).[21]

For a paper of its size and limited resources, *Aufbau* probably was more
consistent—and often tougher—than any publication in America in its coverage

of the European war criminals, and it had some well-connected, knowledgeable people for much of it. Among them: the émigré journalist and human rights activist Kurt Grossmann, who pursued the issue doggedly, with pieces like "Justice in the Twilight," about the ability of lower-level Nazi court officials not only to escape punishment but to get similar jobs in postwar Germany and the foot-dragging of some of the bureaucrats in some of the German states in settling restitution claims.[22]

It also got first-class background pieces on former Nazis still in official positions from the émigré lawyer and Weimar-era Prussian prosecutor Robert Kempner, who was a member of the prosecutorial team at Nuremberg (and who was an occasional contributor to *Aufbau*). In an article in 1964 for the weekly *Der Spiegel*, which got generous coverage in *Aufbau*, Kempner had been among the first to remind the Germans that there were hundreds of war criminals whose names were never widely known who escaped justice in the courts of the individual German states. "They're letting the big ones go," said *Aufbau*'s head on the Kempner story. "Nazi death sentences remain un-redressed."[23] In 1969, Kempner would write several *Aufbau* reports on a clandestine, well-financed German lobby in the late 1960s working to create a statute of limitations for, or to entirely exonerate, Nazi white-collar murderers, an effort, according to Kempner, that was at least partially successful.[24] (Still later *Aufbau* would run a piece by Kempner, headed "Goering Was the Incendiary," about how Kempner had recently learned from a former Luftwaffe general that it was Goering who had organized the Reichstag Fire in February 1933 that the Nazis blamed on a Dutch communist and that became the pretext for Hitler, who had become chancellor just a month before, to assume total control.)[25]

Aufbau had no end of terrible people to write about, some notorious, some obscure. Among the latter were the two Austrians who headed one of *Aufbau*'s postwar lists of surviving war criminals. One was Anton Burger, former aide to Eichmann and once the notoriously cruel commandant at Theresienstadt, who twice escaped from prison after the war, assumed the name of a prisoner he'd murdered there, and died in his bed in 1991. The other was Alois Brunner, an officer of the SS, also an aide to Eichmann, who sent thousands of Jews from Vienna, Salonika, and Paris to ghettos and concentration camps. He also escaped after the war, eventually ending up in Syria under the protection of the brutal Hafez al-Assad, father of the country's strongman in the first decades of the twenty-first century, where he was useful, it was reported, in advising the ruling Ba'ath Party on Nazi torture techniques.[26]

There was Klaus Barbie, the "butcher of Lyon." There were new names like that of the retired Ukrainian-born Cleveland autoworker John Demjanjuk, who may or may not have been a notorious guard at Treblinka, Majdanek, and

Sobibor. In 1986, as another late reminder of the unfathomable depths of the war crimes issue (and of *Aufbau*'s journalistic persistence), Henry Marx, then *Aufbau*'s coeditor, echoing Grossmann's piece of some twenty years before, reported that, forty years after the war's end, not a single Nazi judge or prosecutor in the people's (lower) courts had been convicted, meaning they could claim their pensions and other benefits. Under the notorious Nazi Roland Freisler (who was killed in an Allied air raid early in 1945), that court had summarily sentenced thousands to death. "To speak here of a scandal," Marx wrote, "is to use too weak a word."[27]

And reflecting the concerns of some other Hitler refugees of that era, *Aufbau*'s attention was also uniquely drawn to overseas "drill fields," as in Chile, where unreconstructed Nazis were dreaming of a comeback.[28] It noted, as did many others, that in light of the revelations of his suspicious past as a Nazi officer and as a possible war criminal in the Balkans in World War II, the election of Kurt Waldheim as president of Austria in 1986 (endorsed, *Aufbau* noted in passing, by the Kremlin and by Saudi newspapers) was more evidence that that country had still not yet confronted its Nazi past. The following year, the U.S. Justice Department barred Waldheim from entering the country because he "participated in activities amounting to persecution" of Jews and others in Greece and Yugoslavia during World War II.[29] In 1987, after the French finally put Barbie on trial, *Aufbau* ran a long piece on Elie Wiesel's testimony, delivered in fluent French, a trial, Wiesel said, that was "important for the survivors, important for Lyon, and important against not forgetting." The story ended with the reporter's observation that the last eleven rows in the court in Lyon had been filled by students and young workers who sat there day after day and, during the breaks, tried to engage the survivor-witnesses in conversation.[30]

It was sheer coincidence that on the day in August 1945, after the great celebrations of VJ Day in America, a French court convicted Marshal Philippe Petain of treason and sentenced him to death. A national hero for his military leadership at Verdun in World War I, Petain became a defeatist under whom the Vichy French government delivered thousands of Jews to the Nazi extermination machine. Petain, said *Aufbau*, was not a traitor in the ordinary sense of the word, no Benedict Arnold; his guilt lay in his destruction of the ideals of the French Revolution: He was a fascist. The death sentence was soon commuted to life in prison, by which time he had become a demented, pathetic figure.[31]

But probably the paradigmatic figure of the decades after the war—and the spur for hot controversy among Jews—was Adolf Eichmann, one of the planners and then an executor of what the Nazis called the Final Solution. When the Israelis kidnaped Eichmann in Argentina and brought him to trial, it raised more sharply than ever the questions about how to encompass the monstrosity of the Holocaust and the related issues of guilt. In that context, Hannah Arendt's controversial *New Yorker* series on the Eichmann trial and her book, *Eichmann in Jerusalem: A Report on the Banality of Evil*, first published in 1963, sparked a searching—and sometimes soul-searching—"journalistic symposium" in *Aufbau* about her allegations of Jewish complicity in the Holocaust that ran in the paper's pages through several issues that year. Part of the Nazi system, said the Council of Jews from Germany in its response to Arendt, was to "force leaders and officials of Jewish communities by the most brutal means to give technical assistance in the execution of orders given to those communities." Nonetheless, many "tried countermeasures or secret resistance" for which they, too, were murdered. Who had any right to place blame?

The series also included pieces by the New York Rabbi Hugo Hahn, a refugee whose synagogue in Essen had been destroyed in the Nazi rampages of *Kristallnacht* in 1938; by Kempner, who, in addition to aiding in the prosecution of Nazi war criminals at Nuremberg, had testified as an expert witness at the Eichmann trial; by the Israeli philosopher Gershon Sholem, who told his former friend Arendt that not having been there, she had no right to make such a judgment and accused her of a "demagogic will-to-overstatement"; and a response to Sholem by Arendt herself. As she and many later observers pointed out, much of the criticism was based on misreadings and distortions of the book—some of them almost certainly intentional.[32] But the book and the attendant controversy touched a nerve in the refugee and survivor community that had been raw long before Arendt's *New Yorker* pieces about Eichmann appeared and took a long time to heal. It's not likely there were many camp survivors who didn't ask themselves dreadful questions about their right to survive when so many others who had been close to them—children, spouses, parents, friends—had not.

There was a similar *Aufbau* symposium in 1964 on Rolf Hochhuth's controversial play *The Deputy*, then being performed in New York, about the failure of Pope Pius XII to speak out against Nazi crimes, including a piece by Schweitzer. Schweitzer, speaking as "a witness to mankind's denial," broadened the accusation to all churches, including Protestant churches, and concluded that the play wasn't just history's indictment but a warning call to "our time" that was again hardening into "thoughtless inhumanity."[33] In the same issue, *Aufbau* reported that New York's Cardinal Francis Spellman, who it identified (correctly) as a conservative, had attacked the play. But while indicating that it didn't want to get into a dispute with him, it recorded its surprise that Spellman, in taking on the play, had said that he'd neither seen nor read it.

By then, the question of guilt for the crimes of the war, debated in the pages of *Aufbau* and by thousands of people elsewhere through much of the war, had become increasingly difficult and contentious. There was no doubt about the identity of the leading war criminals or the need to impose whatever justice was possible under the circumstances—a familiar list headed by those who, unlike Hitler, Himmler, and Goebbels, hadn't already committed suicide: Goering, Hans Frank, Joachim von Ribbentrop, Alfred Rosenberg, Rudolf Hess, Ernst Kaltenbrunner, and the dozens of others who were the first to be tried at Nuremberg. A few, like Hjalmar Schacht, Hitler's economics and finance minister, who an *Aufbau* headline had called a Nazi war criminal, were acquitted; most were not. Goering, who was sentenced to death, committed suicide the night before he was to be hanged.

The list would only get longer in the following years: judges and lawyers; prison guards; doctors; the looters of art, silverware, and every other kind of valuable, and the dealers who profited from it; the perpetrators of the insurance and banking frauds not only in Germany and Austria but in Switzerland and other neutral countries. During the war, every refugee had his own list, in many cases a list based on personal experience. For more than a half-century, they'd continue to turn up.

And increasingly, the issue of guilt brought terrible moral and philosophical problems: Where was the line? If all were guilty, then no one was. If, as Bettelheim and Arendt argued, Jews were themselves culpable for failing to resist, then was the guilt of the Eichmanns and the Himmlers proportionately diminished? As the war crimes investigators and the de-Nazification interrogators, many of them German-speaking refugees, quickly discovered, nobody in Germany claimed he knew anything about the death camps, nobody had ever heard of them. And of course, many Jews did resist—in the Warsaw Ghetto, as guerrillas fighting alongside Polish and Russian partisans in the East, with the underground in Norway, France and Belgium, or simply by smuggling out children or not collaborating with butchers in uniforms. And if, as the defenders of the Judenräte asked, one could save some by collaborating in the inevitable murder of others, what was the morally correct choice?

Neither *Aufbau*'s editors nor most others could have had any clear sense during the war of the conditions that would color and constrain the issue of Nazi guilt after the war ended: Stalin's hard line and the postwar partition of Germany into four zones—American, British, French, and Russian—which would soon lead to the creation of two separate German states and the ongoing Soviet domination of Eastern Europe and the Cold War that soon followed. All these hard, unpleasant facts affected the question of who would govern West Germany and under what rules, as well as who would run the waterworks and the railroads, who would rebuild the electric utilities, repair the roads, teach in the schools, staff the hospitals and the police, sit as judges in the courts. . . . Would every judge, engineer, policeman, government bureaucrat and school principal have to be cleared of every hint of a Nazi background? What, as one researcher put it, of the "significant continuity of personnel in the West German Foreign Office from the Third Reich to the Bundesrepublik"?[34] If, as *Aufbau's* headline had said not long before, "Never Again Krupp," would there be no steel production? No automobile manufacturing, no I.G. Farben, and no chemical industry?

And then, as Stalin's crimes came to light—or more accurately, maybe, when the propagandists' rosy haze of Allied unity began to lift and the Russian crimes were recognized—the picture changed dramatically: the forced starvation of some seven million Ukrainian peasants in the 1930s; the Katyn Forest Massacre of Polish officers and political leaders that the Russians first tried to pin on the Germans; the so-called doctors' plot in Russia, most of them Jews, of the early 1950s; the stratum of anti-Semitism that lay as deep across Russia, Czarist, Stalinist, whatever, as the black soil. Within a few years, and clearly after the Russians blocked access to Berlin, divided into four sectors—American, British, French and Russian—within East Germany, was West Germany now needed as a buffer or even an ally in the Cold War? The victors did not prosecute Wernher von Braun, who designed the V-2 rockets as terror weapons and oversaw their construction in a plant that relied heavily on slave labor. Von Braun and several of his fellow V-2 engineers were brought to the United States to work on, and eventually head, the army's ballistic missile program.

Nor, during those early postwar years, did the victors do nearly as much toward the reconstitution of Germany as a demilitarized, de-Nazified German democratic state as *Aufbau's* editors and most of its readers wanted. In the spring of 1947, it ran a series of pieces by the Hungarian-born refugee journalist Hans Habe headed "America's Defeat in Germany" on the failures of the AMG in everything from rooting out old Nazis to its failure to reduce industrial production capacity of basic materials like iron and steel that could be used for rearmament to eliminating Nazi-era textbooks in the schools. Habe, who had by then returned to Germany as part of a military propaganda team and had launched eighteen newspapers in the American zone, deplored America's fading prestige, caused, in part, he said, by the loutish behavior of off-duty American soldiers, their involvement in the black market, even the reverse influence of deeply entrenched Nazism on the occupying troops.[35] Maybe the most noteworthy example, though not known at the time, may have been "Old Blood and Guts" George Patton, whose lust to fight the Russians was being stoked by Baron von Wangenheim, the ex-Nazi who SS veterans had installed as Patton's groom.[36]

Habe's pieces reinforced countless other *Aufbau* items concerning the errors, disputes, and uncertainties about German reconstruction. Among them was the text of a speech by former Treasury Secretary Henry Morgenthau, who had been the most vigorous advocate in FDR's cabinet of a liberalized immigration policy and for a tougher stance toward postwar Germany. The text, published in April 1946, nearly a year after Germany surrendered, restated parts of the so-called Morgenthau Plan of 1944 to rebuild Germany as a basically "agricultural and pastoral" nation without the industrial capacity to ever again build a war machine. (Roosevelt had called it "nonsense.") The *Aufbau* piece was headed "Germany Remains the Problem." In a prior issue, Morgenthau had written that opening Palestine to European Jews was "the only solution" to the DP problem.[37]

Another piece on the situation in Germany was an excerpt of a powerful speech delivered in November 1945, six months after the end of the war, by Rep. Emanuel Celler, the Brooklyn Democrat who had struggled for years to open American doors to Hitler refugees and to liberalize the nation's immigration policies. (He would succeed on the latter twenty years later, when Lyndon Johnson signed Hart-Celler, the bill that finally repealed the racist national origins quotas that Congress had enacted in 1924.) Now he was attacking the AMG's neglect of the plight of the many homeless Jews in Germany, many of them DPs and camp survivors from Eastern Europe. Why, Celler asked, wasn't the AMG seizing the vast land holdings of the seven thousand Junker families who held about a fourth of Germany's agricultural land and parceling them out in small plots for farming to Holocaust survivors? Why weren't Nazis being thrown out of their big houses to make space for destitute DPs? America, moreover, should immediately set up consulates and give DPs and other victims of the Nazis first priority when they submit their (visa) applications, which should be processed without heart-rending delays.

And then, in a sort of codicil headed "Listen Mr. Attlee," he raised an equally important issue. Before the election that made you prime minister, Celler said, you made promises to the Jews; now honor them: Open the door to Palestine (and if you don't, tell us why not).[38] On the same page, Manfred George, in an initialed editorial, lambasted the creation of yet another Anglo-American Committee to study the Palestine situation. That piece was headed simply "NEIN." Six months later, *Aufbau* quoted (in English) British Foreign Secretary Ernest Bevin's speech to a Labour Party Conference: "Regarding the agitation in the United States, and particularly in New York, for one hundred thousand Jews to be put into Palestine, I hope it will not be misunderstood in America if I say with the purest of motives, that that was because they did not want too many of them in New York." George called it "an especially stupid" remark."[39] In effect, *Aufbau* said, you can't trust Bevin to do anything but put his Laborite agenda ahead of any humanitarian concern for Europe's homeless Jews.

More broadly, *Aufbau* deplored the use of the British Navy in the attempt to blockade the coast of Palestine against the inflow of undocumented Jewish immigrants—those who were caught were again interned, mostly in Cyprus: That was dishonorable and not worthy of the great tradition of the navy.[40] For *Aufbau*'s readers, and for Jews in general, Palestine and the rebirth of a Jewish homeland was an issue that was both deeply emotional and, for many, intensely personal. The case was perhaps articulated most clearly in an ad for a "Gigantic Tribunal" at Madison Square Garden dramatizing "the bloodstained evidence of the British betrayal of the Jews of Europe and Palestine." It was headed "Six Million Dead Jews Call for Judgment!"[41]

A New Confidence

On June 24, 1948, the Russians began their blockade of road and rail access to West Berlin. Ten days later, the Berlin Air Lift of food, fuel, and other supplies was fully under way—and so now undeniably was the Cold War. On June 25, in an event that—given Europe's postwar chaos and misery—was less coincidental than it seemed at the time, Truman, lambasting Congress for its inaction, signed a bill that opened America's doors to a few thousand more DPs. But because of its restrictive provisions, which effectively discriminated sharply against the Jews who had fled the pogroms in Eastern Europe after 1945, he did it reluctantly. Then in 1950, after intense lobbying by Jewish organizations and other human rights groups, and despite strong opposition from the right, Congress passed a significantly expanded law, cheered by Truman, allowing for the admission of some four hundred thousand European refugees, eighty thousand of whom were Jews. At the time, an estimated three hundred thousand refugees—Catholics and Jews who had fled from Eastern Europe, survivors of the concentration camps, and others—were still in DP camps. Australia, Canada, and some Latin American countries were also to take some of them.[42]

By the time Truman signed the 1950 bill, the state of Israel was already two years old, easing the pressure on the United States. Its founding, despite the vehement opposition of Secretary of State George C. Marshall and Defense Secretary James Forrestal—worried about U.S. oil interests in the Middle East—had been supported by Truman and recognized by him on May 14, 1948, only hours after Ben Gurion had proclaimed independence.

Just as important, the preceding two years had been marked by a series of events in the Middle East that dramatically altered the Holocaust-era image of

Aufbau front page, May 21, 1948: "The Great Goal," when Israel became an independent state. (courtesy of JM Jüdische Medien AG, Zurich)

the European Jews as helpless, passive victims and almost certainly boosted the shaky self-confidence of the refugees abroad. The Warsaw Ghetto uprising had already begun to change that image. Then, in July 1946, following an endless series of fruitless negotiations in London and countless special committee reports about Palestine, the Irgun—the Zionist paramilitary (read terrorist) organization headed by Menachem Begin (later Israel's prime minister)—blew up a wing of the King David Hotel in Jerusalem that housed British Army headquarters and the Palestine government offices, killing or severely wounding some ninety-four people (British civilians, Jews, and Arabs among them). Haganah, the prime Jewish defense organization in Palestine, called it "pure murder."[43] Manfred George, in one of many long *Aufbau* articles on the battles about the creation of a Jewish state in Palestine, saw it as a mad act of desperation that would probably hurt the cause, as many of his readers probably did also.[44] But it may not have hurt the confidence of Hitler's refugees.

In any case, the bombing of the King David Hotel was overshadowed a year later when the British, in maybe the most foolish act of their eroding hold on their Palestine mandate, seized and boarded the converted troopship *Exodus* thirty miles off the Palestine coast. The *Exodus* was carrying some 4,550 illegal Jewish immigrants (1,600 men, 1,200 women, and nearly 1,800 juveniles and children), two of whom were killed and thirty wounded in their desperate attempts to resist the British.

The refugees, part of the larger *Aliyah Bet* movement to take thousands of refugees, many of them from the European DP camps, to Palestine, were then loaded into other ships, and after weeks of miserable conditions, including twenty-four days in stifling heat in a French port during which they refused to leave the ships, they were taken to, of all places, Hamburg, Germany, where they were again interned, this time by the British in the British zone of occupation. *Aufbau*, in a story illustrated with a photo of Jewish prisoners seized off other ships in a British internment camp in Cyprus, called it "A Gruesome Act."[45] In an interview in a subsequent issue, Gerald Frank, an American clergyman who was on board, said it seemed to him that a quarter of the women were pregnant.[46]

And then, less than a year later, came the proclamation of Israel's statehood and the successful defense, extensively covered and cheered on the pages of *Aufbau*, by Israel's outnumbered defense forces against the combined armies of Egypt, Jordan, and Syria, which attacked the new nation. American Jews, Hitler refugees paramount among them, gave blood, contributed money through groups such as the United Jewish Appeal and Hadassah, and donated food through commercial outfits like Service for Palestine Inc., which proclaimed themselves the "official" shippers of kosher food to embattled Israel. When the war finally ended ten months later, after several failed attempts at an armistice, Israel controlled far more territory—Jaffa, the Galilee, parts of the Negev, West Jerusalem, and parts of the West Bank—than the 1947 United Nations partition plan called for. Not surprisingly, that struggle, the war for Israeli independence, also got extensive coverage in *Aufbau*.[47] In less than five years, the image of world Jewry had grown from helpless victims to that of some of the toughest and most resourceful fighters on earth. And the pride of Jews—Hitler refugees perhaps most of all—had risen with it.

But maybe the most powerful single confidence builder for the refugees, as for all American Jews—and maybe the best piece of propaganda ever for the nation of Israel, then ten years old—was Leon Uris's 1958 novel *Exodus* and the Otto Preminger film based on it, which opened in 1960. Preminger was also an Austrian Jewish immigrant; the writer of the screenplay, Dalton Trumbo, was one of the Hollywood Ten who had been blacklisted for his refusal to testify before the House Un-American Activities Committee not many years before. Neither the book nor the film was a great critical success—viewed today, the film is long, heavy handed, and often clumsy—but as someone later said, *Exodus* found its way into virtually every Jewish home everywhere. "Tailoring, altering and radically sanitizing the history of the founding of the State of Israel to flatter the fantasies and prejudices of American Jews," wrote columnist Bradley Burston in the Israeli daily *Haaretz* looking back on it a half century later, "Uris succeeded well beyond his own wildest dreams, essentially remaking his eager readers and himself as well. That is, he helped foment a significant change in his fellow Jews' perceptions of Israel and, indeed, of themselves."[48]

There would be other great confidence builders in the succeeding years— the swift and decisive Israeli victory in the Six-Day War in 1967 and with it the capture of more Arab territory—East Jerusalem, the West Bank, the Gaza Strip, the Golan Heights, and the Sinai Peninsula—that greatly enhanced Israel's security (and would later spawn all sorts of problems); as well as the dramatic rescue in 1976 by the Israeli Defense Force of 102 hostages at Entebbe from an Air France flight that had been seized by terrorists and flown to Uganda. The military victories were also important in promoting the ongoing fund-raising campaigns, with the strong backing of *Aufbau*'s Board of Directors, of the United Jewish Appeal and other Jewish organizations that were earmarked for the support of Israel. ("Let us not become guilty.") The danger was not over, said an ad published just ten days after the Six-Day War: "Israel is hanging in the gravest danger. [It] has been bled financially and economically. It cannot demobilize a single soldier; prisoners of war must be guarded; the many Arab residents of the conquered territories must be watched; wounded veterans must be cared for." There was the greatest need.[49] For many Jews, Hitler refugees especially, those campaigns—then and ever since—were one way of striking back. But coming at a time when the memory of Hitler and the death camps was still intensely personal for tens of thousands of immigrants, *Exodus* (the book and the film) may have had more impact than the actual, unhyped events on the ground did in the decades that followed. Significantly, it was a Nazi agent in *Exodus* who was portrayed as the chief instigator of the Arab revolt against the Jewish state.

★

Individually many of the "surviving remnant" from the death camps served as prosecution witnesses at the war crimes trials that began soon after Germany's surrender; collectively they reinforced the difficulty of determining who could be, as the term went, "de-Nazified" in Germany and Austria, and who could not. They and the millions who did not survive were accusing specters in the long hunt for concentration camp commanders and guards, the doctors who used the prisoners as human subjects for their experiments, and the Nazi officials and executives at Krupp, I.G. Farben, Siemens, and other corporations who organized and oversaw the industrialized mass murder that became the Holocaust and exploited the slave labor that the camps provided. And as witnesses to the collective monstrosity of the Nazis' crimes, they also reinforced the case for reparations for both the camp survivors and the refugees who had escaped.

For the refugees in the United States, many of whom were now immigrants—and in many cases citizens—there were dozens of other new questions, not just in their trips to the refugee relief agencies and their searches through the published "Looking For" items and the related items, placed by refugee relief organizations listing camp survivors searching for children, parents, or friends abroad who (presumably) had emigrated in time. Who was entitled to reparations and from whom? Given the new global situation, let alone a long list of humane considerations, should the United States, mindful of the errors the allies made at Versailles in 1919, help in the reconstruction of Germany, even as the Russians were hauling steel mills and manufacturing plants off from the East Zone?

Aufbau, which at the end of the European war had reflected the anger and doubts of many German refugees with heads such as its "Never Again Krupp," now became a strong supporter of a major American commitment to rebuild Europe's shattered economies. In an important piece headed "Protect the Marshall Plan" published in December 1947, as Truman's grand scheme was being debated, Manfred George, who at first had been uncertain about it, sought to counter both left-wing charges that the proposal was an exercise in

U.S. imperialism and the combination of isolationism and general American ho-hum indifference to the stakes involved. That defense rested most importantly on a recital of the desperate economic straits in which people in the major European nations, among them the French and British, as well as the Germans, found themselves. That year France had been nearly crippled by communist-led strikes in heavy industry, in the mines, on the railroads, and in other sectors of the economy. There had been sabotage of rail lines. Butter, sugar, and other basics could only be obtained at prices far beyond the reach of the average family. "One can't spend a week in France," George wrote, "without seeing how sick this country is." The high-stakes issue of whether the future of France lay with Charles DeGaulle or with the communist leader Maurice Thorez was of vital interest to the United States.[50] More immediately for the American refugees who still had—or might have—people in the rubble of Germany's cities, how in good conscience could they oppose anything that might make their lives a little easier?

*

From the late 1930s through the end of the war, as the preceding chapters should have made clear, America and its leaders, among whom FDR was regarded as a demigod, could do little wrong in the pages of *Aufbau*, even as the country kept its doors shut to the hundreds of thousands of Jews and other Europeans trying desperately to flee from Hitler. It devoted no end of space to encouraging its émigré readers to Americanize as rapidly as possible and provided endless columns of information and advice on getting there. In its cheerleading for America, although it attacked American nativists and Nazi sympathizers such as the white supremacists Gerald L. K. Smith and William Dudley Pelley, it regarded nativism, however deplorable, as prejudices confined to particular groups and individuals, not as a wider danger running through large parts of the population. But it did not fail to take note of anti-Semitism when it found it in its own backyard. In the fall of 1945, six months after Germany's surrender, it reported on a shop in Yorkville on Manhattan's East Side that was still peddling tracts titled "The Refugee Invasion of America through Immigration," others attacking the Jewish Justice Felix Frankfurter, and still others by a writer who, at a meeting of Nazi sympathizer Gerald L. K. Smith's America First Party, had called for the deportation of all Jews. The shop on East 86th Street was also selling pencils marked "Jew Money + Jew Deal + New Deal = War."[51] Two years later, the émigré Viennese playwright and literary agent Kurt Hellmer, in a series of *Aufbau* columns headed "Anti-Anti," took swipes at Smith, who had campaigned for the release of the Nazis convicted at

Nuremberg, and at the isolationist congressman (and prewar friend of leading Nazis) Hamilton Fish, whose militantly anti-communist monthly *Today's World* had published an anti-Semitic piece referring to the United States as being "in the yoke of the Jews," attacking the Anti-Defamation League, and (again) linking Jews and communists.[52] "Nazism and fascism, defeated in the theaters of the war," Hellmer would write, "have made room everywhere for a neo-Nazism and a neo-fascism, which are no less dangerous than their models."[53] For George, another target was Clare Booth Luce, a recent convert to Catholicism who attributed many of the evils of the contemporary world to the "unholy triumvirate" of communism, psychoanalysis, and relativity — meaning Marx, Freud, and Einstein, all of whom happened to be Jews.[54]

Hellmer's pieces almost certainly reflected the fears of Hitler refugees, whose experience, he said, "made room" for a heightened sensitivity to any sign of residual anti-Semitism, both in United States and in Europe. But *Aufbau* was also right in its warnings that, while the early neglect of the dangers of fascism and anti-Semitism might have been human error, a second such error was a crime. "Contemporary racism and anti-Semitism are not isolated phenomena," wrote Hulse, always the physician, in 1946, "they are not sui-generic diseases — they are symptoms of a cancer that seeks to corrupt our culture and just one of the many manifestations of fascism. . . . He who wants to counter anti-Semitism without the courage to expose and annihilate the people behind it will share responsibility for the next pogrom."[55] In the same vein, *Aufbau*, in a piece headed "Protection for the Land of Minorities," lauded Harry Truman for his creation in December 1946 of the President's Committee on Civil Rights.[56] Truman would later implement the committee's recommendation by ordering the desegregation of the federal work force and the armed forces. Neither turned out to be easy. Neither would be near completion during his lifetime.

In later years there was another concern — in some respects more unnerving because Jews, most of them Democrats and liberals and many of them victims of Nazi racism, had always believed they had been making common cause with blacks on civil rights — and that was the rise, or perhaps just the growing awareness, of black anti-Semitism and nationalism in the urban ghettos (at that time, maybe the irony of the name had not yet been widely noticed). In 1962, James Baldwin had started to shock upper-crust Americans about the nation's pervasive race problem with his powerful *New Yorker* essay — what one reviewer called a portrait of "white America as seen through the eyes of a Negro" — that would be the core of his *The Fire Next Time*, arguably the most important book on race of the twentieth century.[57] The following year, in a lengthy front-page review of Baldwin's play *Blues for Mr. Charlie*, then on Broadway, *Aufbau* editor Manfred

George took special note of African Americans' distrust of white liberals and the great gaps between the races, both of them with their flaws. The play, he said, was "frightening." Some day, he anxiously concluded, not only must the political bridges be crossed but those of human understanding as well. Two weeks later, returning to the topic in a piece headed "Before the Long, Hot Summer, the Radicalization of the Negro Revolt," he endorsed the moderate Bayard Rustin's efforts to "win back the blacks'" erstwhile white liberal allies who in many ways have withdrawn.[58]

But it was probably through the 1965 Rod Steiger film *The Pawnbroker*, one of the first movies about a Holocaust survivor in America, that many American Jews initially became aware of blacks' resentment against them. In the film, the hostility toward German-Jewish shopkeepers in black neighborhoods obviously conveyed a much broader social message. That fear was not put to rest by the findings of a researcher named Naomi Levine, duly reported in *Aufbau*, that in a representative sample of blocks in Harlem in 1968, blacks in fact owned 58 percent of the businesses.[59] It would only grow in succeeding years with the remarks of Rev. Jesse Jackson about "Hymies" and "Hymietown" in 1984 (for which he later apologized) and "Zionists who have controlled American policy for decades," and the blatant anti-Semitism of Louis Farrakhan and the Nation of Islam. And like others, *Aufbau* detected anti-Semitism in the opposition to the confirmation of Abe Fortas as Chief Justice in 1968 and, in a piece headed "How Could He Do This to Us?," recorded the embarrassment and hurt following disclosure of the ethical lapses that forced Fortas's resignation from the court.[60]

Maybe most galling for *Aufbau*'s editors, and probably for many Jews in New York in those years, was an introductory essay in the catalog for a show "Harlem On My Mind" at the Metropolitan Museum of Art—that most august of New York institutions—which again talked about the exploitation of Harlem blacks by Jewish storekeepers. Because Jews owned all the better grocery stores, the writer said, "The lack of competition . . . allows the already badly exploited Black to be further exploited by Jews." But the clincher may have been the conclusion that "Psychologically, Blacks may find that anti-Jewish sentiments place them, for once, within a majority. Thus our contempt for the Jew makes us feel more completely American in sharing a national prejudice." The uproar after *Aufbau* reported it in a story headed "Questions for the Metropolitan Museum" produced abject apologies from Thomas Hoving, the Met's director, and Robert Bernstein, the president of Random House, which published the catalog, a blast from Mayor John Lindsay, and a month later a formal retraction slip in the catalog.[61] Along the way, it also turned out that the offending essay was a slightly edited term paper written by a seventeen-year-old high school student.

At almost the same moment, *Aufbau* reported that another high school student had read a poem on the left-wing public radio station WBAI that began:

> Hey Jew boy, with that
> Yarmulke on your head.
> You pale-faced Jew boy. I wish
> You were dead.

And ended

> You came to America,
> Land of the free
> Took over the school system
> To perpetuate white supremacy.[62]

That it all happened just as the demagogic dirty trickster Richard Nixon, never beloved among Hitler refugees, was being inaugurated, and just two months after the end of a crippling New York City teachers strike laced with an "appalling amount of racial prejudice"[63] (in this case black parents versus teachers, many of them Jewish, led by a Jewish union president), made it apparent to many liberals — and not just immigrants and not just Jews — that one of the nation's most progressive political alliances was in jeopardy and, beyond that, that America, too, was still an imperfect paradise. At the same time, the paper's attention to domestic anti-Semitism and, more generally to a liberal agenda, also seemed to reflect a quarter century's evolution of the sensibility of its readers from that of German-Jewish immigrants to that of American Jews.

It's not clear how early *Aufbau*'s editors, much less its refugee readers, were aware of the investigations into alleged communist influence both in Hollywood and the labor unions (the CIO particularly) that had begun well before the war, or that the FBI had compiled extensive files on those it regarded as left-wing writers and artists in the émigré community, among them Mann, Brecht, and his close friend, the composer Hanns Eisler. Now, as the Chamber of Commerce and right-wing groups were warning about communist infiltration in the media and Rep. J. Parnell Thomas's House Un-American Activities Committee (HUAC) began to haul Hollywood writers and directors to its hearings into alleged communist influence in the movies, the worries grew apace. Eventually Eisler was deported and would join Brecht in East Germany.

Brecht testified at HUAC's hearings in 1947—he was not a citizen, he wrote Eisler, just a guest of the country, and thus had no choice. In any case, Brecht had never liked America. Although he obviously enjoyed a good life in California, he didn't want to delay his return to Germany—East Germany—which he had already planned. He left the day after he appeared before the committee.

In 1952, Thomas Mann, who was, next to Einstein, the best known of the German refugees, also went back to Europe, as did the poet Walter Mehring. But he would not go to Germany—there was no way to wipe the record of twelve years of Nazi crimes off the slate, he had written in a long open letter six years before declining several invitations to do so[64]—but to Switzerland, where he would live the rest of his life. He would make literary visits to Germany, as he had to the Goethe bicentennial in 1949. German was his language and his culture. But he would not live there.

Mann had a great devotion to many things American. He had become a U.S. citizen; had close American friends, among them Agnes Meyer, wife of *Washington Post* publisher Eugene Meyer (and mother of Katherine Graham, who would one day be the *Post*'s publisher); had visited FDR at the White House; had made consistent efforts through letters and personal appeals to government officials to help others get out of Nazi-occupied Europe; had castigated "humanists" such as the mythologist Joseph Campbell for their apparent indifference to the dangers of fascism; had recorded anti-Nazi talks for the BBC to be broadcast to Germany; and had, in many respects, become a leading voice for the émigré community.[65] (And, along the way, had been a great benefactor of *Aufbau*, in his view, probably the most significant repository of German culture in exile, contributing not only pieces and serving on its advisory board but also giving a major lecture in New York for *Aufbau*'s benefit.)

He may have always intended to return to Europe, where he was more culturally comfortable. "The old word Weltbürger [citizen of the world], or cosmopolitan, which appeared for a time old fashioned," he had said in a revealing speech during the war, "will again become honorable, and it is a German word." He was simultaneously part of the best in German culture and a citizen of the world.[66] But the rise of McCarthyism, now also Germanized to *McCarthyismus*, in the early 1950s and its threat to cultural freedom had dampened his enthusiasm for America. He had come under repeated attack as a communist from a self-styled Red hunter named Eugene Tillinger in a right-wing periodical called the *Freeman* and labeled in J. Edgar Hoover's FBI documents as "one of the world's most noted Communists." (Hoover's accusation was a flat lie, though Mann and *Aufbau* were almost certainly unaware of it when the paper ran a fawning article on Hoover in February 1950, a time, to be sure, when virtually all of the American press was still eating out of Hoover's hands. But it was a paean that *Aufbau*'s editors, some of whom had been hounded by secret policemen all over Europe, should have been a little more suspicious of.)[67]

Mann vigorously defended himself in, among other places, the pages of *Aufbau*, where he castigated "hysterical, blind, irrational anti-communism" as more "terrifying than indigenous communism. The Red hunter's insane pursuit and rage can only lead to the worst if we don't quickly awaken to it."[68] He defended Hollywood against McCarthyite attacks and castigated the HUAC when he was called as a witness. "As an American citizen of German birth," he told the committee, "I testify that I am painfully familiar with certain political trends. Spiritual intolerance, political inquisitions, and declining legal security, and all this in the name of an alleged 'state of emergency.' . . . That is how it started in Germany."[69]

Mann was hardly alone in his fears. Nor were former German leftists such as Brecht and Hanns Eisler who were ensnared by the Red-hunting congressional investigators, which were all covered in some detail in the pages of *Aufbau* under heads like "Politics in the Dark" and in Manfred George's "McCarthy Without Mask," published just before the start of the Senate's Army-McCarthy hearings that would effectively end McCarthy's career.[70] At about the same time, *Aufbau* cartoonist Wronkow would portray McCarthy giving the Hitler salute.

Many refugees heard frightening old echoes in the Red-hunting investigations, the revived Jew-communist links, the blacklisting and the sifting through old friendships and who-did-you-know associations, often going back to Weimar days, and the search through old movies, old poems, and art works for any hint of a leftist taint. Some, like the Hungarian-born photographer-painter László Moholy-Nagy, confronted unexplained delays in obtaining citizenship or getting other documents. Many were indeed frightened. If the witch hunters could come for State Department officials, highly regarded academics, and other influential people, they might come after anyone. But for most there was no better choice, no place to flee to again. If anything, it made many even more committed civil libertarians than their experience with the Nazis already predisposed them to. Hitler had attacked German leftists as "undeutsch." The echoes of "undeutsch" in "un-American," the critic Anthony Heilbut would write, "took the breath away."[71]

There's no way to know how many of the German Jews who had arrived before (and in a few cases during) the war vowed never to have anything to do with Germany or Germans again. Even before America entered the war, *Aufbau*'s editors had been unequivocal about the impossibility, as Hulse wrote, of returning to "a homeland that does not exist any more, that has been killed, defiled, destroyed."[72]

The full realization, at the end of the war of what the Nazis had done, seemed to make the issue altogether unequivocal. "Is there a future for Jews in Germany?" the Israeli journalist Robert Weltsch asked. Weltsch had been a leading Zionist writer in prewar Berlin, then became an *Aufbau* correspondent in Jerusalem, and later from his base as the correspondent of the Israeli paper *Haaretz* in London. "We cannot assume that there are Jews who are drawn to Germany. It smells of corpses here, of gas chambers and torture cells. . . . Germany is no soil for Jews."[73] Many refused to visit or buy German products—the Volkswagen was Hitler's people's car—or, if they had to visit, heard Nazi in every word of German spoken in their presence. But in the decades after the war, thousands returned to visit or vacation, and some did go back to stay, a few—such as Horkheimer and Adorno—to teach and revive their old academic institutes, many more to begin the process of reclaiming property or a business, or to connect with surviving relatives.

Some, who couldn't make a living in the United States, probably had no better choice than to return and try to reclaim whatever was left. A few, to make settlements quicker and easier, ended up in partnership with the sons of the people who had paid the bargain prices for their former shops or factories that the Nazis' laws had forced them to accept. *Aufbau*, among many others, had contended that the real debt had not been incurred by the individuals who had benefited from the systemic plundering of Jewish property, but by the whole nation and its people.[74] But since all such transactions, whether coerced or purportedly voluntary, were now under a legal cloud (and later subject to Allied-imposed restitution laws) some of the Nazi-era owners had an incentive to settle.[75] And so some businesses that had been Aryanized a decade or two before would be partially re-Judaicized. Latter-day company histories rarely mention the Aryanization or the Nazi years, except in some sanitized form of Newspeak (e.g., "In 1933, during a dramatic period of radical political changes and economical problems in Germany, the founders of the ROMIKA [shoe] brand had to abandon their business which they started in 1922").[76] But for many, as for Fritz Blum, born in Frankfurt in 1926 into a prosperous merchant family, "The material losses, the confiscation of property, the expropriation of all so laboriously achieved, the humiliation and deprivations and, ultimately, the withdrawal of citizenship of the country that had been our ancestral home for centuries—all fade into insignificance in light of the tragic sacrifice of human life. Twenty-nine of our family members and relatives—seventeen on my father's side and twelve and my mother's side—ranging in age from fourteen to fifty-nine, fell victims to Nazi atrocities. It took over fifty years to ascertain only some meager information about their gruesome fate."[77]

Some refugees returned as employees of American companies or as government or private-restitution lawyers, or as translators or technicians with the American Military Government, or as workers with UNRRA, the Joint, or other refugee relief organizations. Most of them, by the nature of their positions, were temporary. But, according to the best estimates, at least four thousand German Jews from the United States returned to stay, a small percentage of the 167,000 (another uncertain number) who had come between 1933 and 1946. Another twenty-five hundred, truly exiles, returned from Shanghai. Some, like Hermann Lewy, who had escaped from the French concentration camp at Saint Cyprien and had found no other place where he could settle, returned from Portugal in 1946 and was for a time interned by the American military in the miserable conditions of one of the DP camps.[78] And, ironically, thousands of Jews, fleeing the anti-Semitism in Eastern Europe, as well as a half-million Ukrainians, Estonians, Latvians, and Croats, also became DPs in Germany and Austria, though often only until they could find a way to move on to Palestine, the United States, or one of the nations of the British Commonwealth.

By 2003, according to the best estimates, 174,000 Holocaust survivors—again the definition is arbitrary—were living in the United States (511,00 were in Israel), of whom 140,000 arrived between 1945 and 1953.[79] Another 36,000 went to Canada in the same years, many of whom were probably also hoping that they would eventually get their U.S. visas. Most of the postwar arrivals came on converted American troop ships, which weren't designed for comfort to begin with and certainly hadn't become plusher since. One of them, Willie Herskovits, later told the sociologist William Helmreich, "There were about one thousand people on the boat and they were, I think, all Jewish. There were about two hundred people to a room and three beds, one on top of the others."[80]

That sounded a lot more like the 1890s than the luxury liners then plying the Atlantic (and also, maybe, a little hyperbolic). Many were met by representatives of HIAS, one of the organizations (another was USNA—United Service for New Americans) that often advanced the DPs' fares. Most of those who arrived before 1950, when Truman got the immigration law liberalized, were the beneficiaries of the mincy Displaced Persons Act that Congress passed in 1948 and which Truman, angry at its blatant anti-Jewish bias, nearly vetoed. But the Holocaust survivors were a different group from the prewar generation—there were many more Eastern Europeans, more people who had always worked with their hands, more Jews who had never assimilated into the larger culture and had never forgotten they were Jews. Many more spoke Yiddish (and thus connected somewhat more easily with those who had come in the first decades of the century), more were Orthodox, and fewer had benefited from (or maybe been handicapped by) *Bildung*.

And because they had been poorer, were less cosmopolitan, had lived in Poland, Hungary, Romania, the Baltics, and Russia, they also had been less likely to be able to escape. Which, of course, is also why some blamed the assimilated German Jews for their own misfortunes and, thus, in the words of Jack Wertheimer, a professor of American Jewish history, why some Jews regarded "the experience of German Jewry as a cautionary tale about the consequences of assimilation."[81] Their differences from the prewar German Jews were perhaps best symbolized, as the historian Manfred Jonas said, "by our amazement that they spoke Yiddish, and theirs that we did not."[82] They really didn't know each other.

And for similar reasons, there were fewer celebrities among them than there had been in the prewar generation. But more than a few distinguished themselves after. One was Tom Lantos, born in Budapest, who joined the resistance in Hungary at age sixteen, escaped twice from a Nazi labor camp, and later became the only Holocaust survivor to serve in the U.S. Congress. Another was Maj. Gen. Sidney Shachnow, a Jew born in Lithuania, who was brutalized in the Nazi concentration camp at Kovno and got to the United States in 1950. After he finished high school in Salem, Massachusetts, he enlisted in the army, served as a Green Beret in Vietnam, and became commander of a Special Forces unit in Cold War Berlin. Yet others included Jack Tramiel, born Jacek Trzmiel in Poland, a survivor of two Nazi camps who, as an immigrant, turned his little typewriter repair store in the Bronx into the hugely successful Commodore International computer company; the self-made billionaire philanthropists George Soros, a Jew born in Budapest who as a teenager had experienced both the Nazi and the Russian occupations; and the brothers Nathan and David Shapell, more about whom to follow.

What many had in common, notwithstanding their diversity, was that they were more unequivocally Jewish, something that the previous years never allowed them to forget. One of them, Esther Jungreis, the daughter of a Hungarian rabbi, who for six months had been a prisoner at Bergen-Belsen as a child, later became known as the "Jewish Billy Graham." Calling herself Rebbetzin Jungreis—she was married to a rabbi—she organized a major Jewish outreach organization, was a powerful lecturer at revival-style meetings, and wrote self-help columns and books, evangelizing her fellow Jews to study Torah and warning that assimilation was "a spiritual Holocaust." "We have a generation that has surpassed expectations in every field," she told an interviewer in 1997, "but when it comes to the Torah, we—the people of the book—have Jewish illiterates."[83] In the immigrant Jews' ongoing ambivalence/debates/uncertainty about where they belonged, she left no doubt which side she wanted them on.

Again, efforts were made to disperse the newcomers beyond New York, this time with somewhat more success. By mid-1949, the DPs had been settled in some three hundred communities—Cleveland, Ohio; McAllen and El Paso, Texas; Portsmouth, New Hampshire; Morristown, Tennessee; Richmond, Virginia; Hartford, Connecticut; and Kansas City—in forty-three states, some of which, like South Dakota, had lost people in the prior decades and were willing, if not eager, to get newcomers. Apparently some of that dispersal, along with loans for travel funds, had been arranged by HIAS with the immigrants in the DP camps before they left Europe. (Was the loan part of an implicit quid pro quo?) But it was probably also their very diversity and small-town backgrounds that made them less determined to live in the huge metropolitan areas of New York and Los Angeles.

And again, with the help of the Jewish Agricultural Society, some—almost certainly more than in the prewar generation—became farmers, often chicken farmers, in Petaluma, California; Vineland, New Jersey; and other places where Jews were already farming. (According to one estimate, the Jewish Agricultural Society settled twenty-five hundred Holocaust survivors on farms in New Jersey.)[84] "It was almost too good to be true," recalled Sol Finkelstein. "At the time, eggs were under government price support so you were guaranteed a good income no matter what. You didn't need much money to get started and the Jewish Agricultural Society was giving out low interest loans for becoming farmers. You could get a big, big mortgage at low, low interest and buy a house and five acres of farmland for just two thousand dollars. . . . So, we bought two chicken farms on Lake Road in Vineland, New Jersey."[85] During the 1960s, according to the Jewish Virtual Library, "the Jewish community [in and around Vineland] peaked at just over ten thousand people, with five synagogues in the city and another six in surrounding communities. The largest influx to the community was from several hundred survivors of the Nazi Holocaust, drawn to the area from large cities such as New York and Philadelphia with offers of assistance in the establishment of poultry farms and a quiet country life. These immigrants formed the Jewish Poultry Farmers' Association and a free loan society, as well as several diverse congregations." According to the Jewish Agricultural Society, ten percent of Holocaust survivors became farmers, which seems high but would explain the continuing series of ads in *Aufbau* from real estate brokers offering farms for sale.[86]

Some, like those in the prewar generation, started their own businesses, often in the little apartments in which they first lived, in part because when they first arrived they had trouble finding jobs and in part probably because they wanted to be independent. Some went into construction, among them (and maybe the name best known) Nathan Shapell, born Nathan Czapelski in a shtetl in Poland, who escaped from Auschwitz and after the war built housing for homeless Jews in Germany. He came to the United States with his wife in 1952, and with his older brother David and his brother-in-law, Max Webb, both also Holocaust survivors (Max and David first met in Auschwitz), started Shapell Industries, which became a major real estate developer in Southern California during the great boom that began in the 1950s. Subsequently, Nathan became a prominent figure on various state and presidential commissions on everything from low-income housing, prison conditions, and drug abuse to government efficiency and economic competitiveness. He was a large contributor to medical and educational institutions and, like his brother, deeply committed to causes commemorating the Holocaust, among them Yad Vashem (Israel's memorial to the victims), and, along with Jack Tramiel, a founder of the U.S. Holocaust Memorial Museum in Washington.[87]

By the end of the war, *Aufbau*'s back pages were full of help wanted ads for bookkeepers and other office workers, foremen in leather goods manufacturing, a "ruby polisher," salesmen, experienced machine operators in the garment industry, welders, watchmakers, nurses, cooks and bakers, and for all manner of household help, few of them upscale, but an indication of improving peacetime opportunities for German-Jewish immigrants. *Aufbau* ran a two-part piece by a physician named Hans Salzmann, "From Soldiers into Civilians," about the adjustment problems some returning GIs, especially those who had suffered a serious injury, might face in returning to civilian life.[88] But even those problems, similar to those confronting all returning veterans, indicated that they returned as Americans.

And as the story of the Shapells indicates, the arrival of the postwar wave of immigrants both fueled and benefited from the boom of the three decades after 1945, which, in turn, brought new energy and resources to Jewish philanthropic institutions. Six months after Israel proclaimed its independence, American Jews founded Brandeis University, signs, on the one hand, of the new Jewish self-confidence—and, with it, of economic and social success—and, on the other, as *Aufbau* reported, of the continuing arbitrary quotas that excluded Jews from the Ivy League and other selective colleges and universities (an ill-guarded secret) that remained part of admissions policy of some institutions into the 1960s.[89] The army, which at the start of the war had been closed to enlistment by enemy aliens, ran ads in *Aufbau*, in German, urging soldiers to reenlist and listed the benefits for doing so, including the pay ($50 a month for a private; $138 for a master sergeant) and the retirement benefits.[90]

But by then most veterans had other options, not least the GI Bill that Congress had passed and Roosevelt had signed in June 1944, more than a year before the war with Japan would end. It provided a range of benefits from unemployment compensation and home mortgages to loans for starting a business to tuition and other expenses for higher education, which is what it became best known for. According to the Veterans Administration (VA), "Thanks to the GI Bill, millions who would have flooded the job market instead opted for education. In the peak year of 1947, veterans accounted for 49 percent of college admissions. By the time the original GI Bill ended on July 25, 1956, 7.8 million of 16 million World War II Veterans had participated in an education or training program."[91]

There's no way to know how many of the men and women who, as *Aufbau* had put it, were once refugees and were now soldiers, were among the 7.8 million who eventually took advantage of the education benefits of the original GI Bill, but, given the immigrants' orientation toward learning—the legacy of the old *Bildung*—there must have been more than fifteen thousand, proportionately more than in the general population of ex-GIs. The Jewish quotas at the upper-crust colleges didn't begin to loosen until the 1950s, and, at places like Yale, weren't eliminated until the 1960s. But for those thousands, and often for their families, the GI Bill and the colleges it made accessible—among them many state universities and big urban institutions like NYU, City College, and Brooklyn College particularly—was yet another gate to assimilation and Americanization.

What the VA summary left out—and what was hardly recognized at the time, and still isn't—is that the GI Bill's benefits went overwhelmingly to whites, in part because blacks couldn't get mortgages from many banks in many neighborhoods, in part of because of racial and social prejudice in university admissions, and in part because the American school system didn't prepare them or told them to not even try. That, too, was an old American story. Most immigrants, once they qualified as "white"—once not easy for Italians, Slavs, Armenians, or people from the Middle East (or Jews)—could probably make it into the economic and social mainstream faster than most blacks.[92]

McCarthy, McCarran, and the Rosenbergs

The backlash began in earnest in 1950—backlash against Roosevelt and the New Deal, against immigration, especially Jewish immigration, and against anything that was faintly left wing. It was the year that Alger Hiss, a long-time State Department official, was convicted of perjury for denying his role in an alleged Soviet spy ring. It was the year that the movie industry writers and directors known as the Hollywood Ten began to serve one-year prison sentences for their refusal to testify before HUAC—most would be backlisted by the Hollywood studios for many years after. It was the year that Sen. Joseph McCarthy of Wisconsin gave his speech in Wheeling, West Virginia, attacking Secretary of State Dean Acheson for harboring communists in the State Department, thereby sparking the era of Red baiting—accusations, hearings, investigations—that gave the world a new synonym for demagoguery.

The shadows looming behind it all were Stalin, the Cold War, and the bomb. The Red Scare of the 1950s, fueled in considerable measure not only by J. Parnell Thomas and HUAC, McCarthy, Richard Nixon, and other American demagogues but by the high-profile trials of the Soviet spies, real and alleged: of Klaus Fuchs, the son of a Lutheran pastor, and of Julius and Ethel Rosenberg and Ethel's brother, David Greenglass, all American-born Jews. America had felt momentarily secure after the war in its sole possession of the bomb, but that ended in August 1949 when the Soviets, apparently aided in part by secrets the spies had delivered, detonated their first A-bomb. For the refugees in America—and no doubt for a great many American Jews—it was hard to miss the echoes of the old Jew-communist libel. But for many, McCarthyism and the Cold War also turned what had been nearly unbridled enthusiasm for their new country into anxiety and disillusionment. They had seen too much of this before and had ignored it until it was too late. From the start, *Aufbau* went after McCarthy, pointing out that at least some of the claims on his initial "list" of 205 alleged communists in the State Department, later changed to fifty-seven, and then again to eighty-one, came verbatim from a pamphlet by a hate-monger named Joseph Kamp, described by the American Legion (hardly a left-wing organization) as engaged in "pamphleteering to create religious hostility." In its accusations of "communist infiltration," *Aufbau* quotes the Legion, "[Kamp's Constitutional Educational League] makes malicious and irresponsible charges against . . . respected groups and individuals who are working to strengthen and improve our democracy."[93] *Aufbau* followed with two pieces on the former Soviet spy Louis Budenz and the other ex-communists who were now working with McCarthy.

Also in 1950, Congress passed the Internal Security Act, which for all practical purposes outlawed the Communist Party. Its principal author, Sen. Pat McCarran of Nevada, was obsessed with the threat of communist subversion and had been a major force in blocking all efforts to admit more Hitler refugees and Holocaust survivors in the years before. Two years later, pairing up with

Rep. Francis Walter of Pennsylvania, like McCarran a right-wing Democrat, he coauthored the Immigration and Nationality Act of 1952—forever after the McCarran-Walter Act—that slightly modified the national origins quota system but did not end its racist criteria. It ended the categorical exclusion of Asians but set the quota so low as to be almost meaningless, and it gave preference to certain occupations, most notably Spanish Basque sheepherders who were much in demand by McCarran's Nevada rancher constituents. But McCarran, certain that communists were more likely to come from southern and eastern Europe (and were often Jews), left little doubt who it was that he most wanted to exclude. "We have in the United States today hard-core, indigestible blocs which have not become integrated into the American way of life," he famously said, "but which, on the contrary are its deadly enemies. Today, as never before, untold millions are storming our gates for admission and those gates are cracking under the strain. The solution of the problems of Europe and Asia will not come through a transplanting of those problems en masse to the United States."[94]

Truman vetoed the bill. "Seldom," he said, "has a bill exhibited the distrust evidenced here for citizens and aliens alike." It was racist and a barrier to the alleviation of the European DP problem.[95] But Congress, with the help of votes from Democrats, overrode the veto, and it passed. Combined with the Internal Security Act, the law also provided for the deportation of aliens, including naturalized aliens, who were communists, suspected subversives, or had "become a member of any organization membership in which at the time of naturalization would have raised the presumption that such person was not attached to the principles of the Constitution . . . and not well disposed to the good order and happiness of the United States," and it banned any such persons from entering the country, even as visiting artists and scholars.[96] Those who would be excluded under its provisions in succeeding years included Graham Greene, Jan Myrdal, Gabriel García Márquez, Pablo Neruda, Doris Lessing, and countless other internationally recognized writers, artists, and intellectuals. It became a major embarrassment abroad for the United States.

Aufbau campaigned relentlessly against the Act. In a front-page "open letter" to the president published June 20, 1952, shortly after Congress passed the act, headed "Your Veto Is Needed," Manfred George wrote as the "mouthpiece of hundreds of thousands of immigrants from German-language countries" who were "deeply shocked by the unjust and hostile attitude toward naturalized citizens as well as prospective immigrants which is inherent in this legislation." Among other things, he said, the bill "gives consular and immigration officials unlimited power to exclude, and unlimited authority to deport whomever they please with virtually no recourse to any impartial authority for the victims concerned." On the same page, it also ran pieces by Rep. Jacob Javits, a liberal

Republican in the days when there still were such politicians; by Sen. Herbert Lehman, a Democrat, whom Javits would later succeed in the Senate; and by Msgr. Joseph O'Grady, secretary of the National Conference of Catholic Charities. This law, Lehman said, "is not to be believed."[97]

The following week, shortly after Truman, calling the law "disgraceful," issued his veto, the paper ran a long list of organizations that opposed it, from the National Catholic Welfare Conference and the NAACP to the CIO (but not the American Federation of Labor) and the United Auto Workers. There were also three more pieces from outsiders, two in English, by Robert F. Wagner Jr., then the Borough president of Manhattan, and Edward Corsi, the New York State Industrial Commissioner, who called the act "Pure Racialism." A third, in German, by Monroe Sheinberg, the head of the ADL in New York, was headed "Three Lies," each of which would have been familiar a half-century before or a half-century later: Immigration brought with it a large number of criminals; the immigrants competed for jobs and available housing with Americans; immigrants depress the American standard of living. For some two hundred years, Sheinberg said, America had grown and prospered from its streams of new settlers. Now there was a new iron curtain, not the familiar one of Soviet communism but the iron curtain of Pat McCarran, trying to strangle immigration.[98]

At the same time, like many of the immigrant Jews it served, *Aufbau* became increasingly concerned with the case of the alleged atom spies Julius and Ethel Rosenberg, who had been sentenced to die in 1951 and whose case, then being appealed, had become an international cause célèbre. Jean Paul Sartre called it "a legal *lynching* which smears with blood a whole nation." And inevitably the debate about the McCarran-Walter Act and the anti-Semitism that had long driven its author became entangled with the anti-Semitism that the Committee to Secure Justice in the Rosenberg case claimed had motivated the Rosenbergs' conviction and the death penalty that followed. In the same issue that *Aufbau* ran the Wagner, Corsi, and Sheinberg pieces, its editors, well aware of the long dismal history of charges about Jewish cabals, carefully negotiated this thorny ground, pointing out that the judge, Irving Kaufman, the chief prosecutor, and another key member of the Rosenberg prosecution team, Roy Cohn (soon to become famous as chief counsel to McCarthy's Investigations Subcommittee — and later mentor to a young Donald Trump), were all Jewish, which could hardly have been coincidental. Cohn later claimed that it was through his influence that Judge Kaufman got the case, a claim that was never verified. But there was no doubt that Kaufman favored the prosecution.

Aufbau's editorial warned against any facile likening of the Rosenberg prosecution to the murder of Jewish innocents in the Holocaust, which it suggested the Communist Party, hoping to ensnare Jews in its "political nest," was trying to do. In the same piece the editorial also took a swipe at Rabbi Benjamin Schultz of the American Jewish League Against Communism, which was firmly on the other side in the case and who, the editorial said, had crept out of the gunk of fascist elements and was likewise compromising the cause of the Jewish people.[99] The debate about the convoluted Rosenberg case went on for decades. One of the things that *Aufbau*'s editors couldn't have known was that David Greenglass, Ethel Rosenberg's brother, whose testimony was a key element in her conviction, later admitted that he had lied to protect his own wife.

What was beyond debate was that McCarthyism and the long list of related investigations, trials, loyalty oaths, and blacklisting (federal and state) that came with it cast a shadow of doubt on the more-or-less unqualified faith in America's freedoms and opportunities that many refugees had once wanted so passionately to believe in. Similar to the investigations into alleged communist influence in Hollywood, the Rosenberg trial and the McCarran-Walter Act, so much of it involving Jews and Jewish issues, made the echoes of the years before Hitler became chancellor all the louder. And beyond that there was the cross between sheer insensitivity and the polite but unmistakable residual American anti-Semitism that Hitler's Holocaust should have laid to rest. In 1947, when Darryl F. Zanuck, a Nebraska boy who wasn't remotely Jewish, started to film *Gentlemen's Agreement*, based on Laura Z. Hobson's best-selling novel about upper-crust American anti-Semitism, many of his fellow Hollywood powers, already intimidated by the oncoming shadow of McCarthyism, urged him to abandon the project: Why stir up trouble? Zanuck disregarded the warnings and produced what turned out to be Fox's biggest hit of the year. It opened just two weeks before the Hollywood Ten were indicted for their refusal to testify before J. Parnell Thomas's House Committee.[100]

But as the association of any immigrant group with the hysteria of the moment—criminals, anarchists, communists, terrorists—continued, so did the debate about whether the United States is, or was founded as, a Christian nation. Two years after it passed the McCarran-Walter Act, Congress, prompted by Eisenhower, wrote the words "under God" into the Pledge of Allegiance. We were not like the godless communists. But to many Jews, it was also clear just whose God it referred to. All that notwithstanding, in a piece in July 1953, Manfred George rejected arguments from a European critic that, with such things as the death sentence imposed on the Rosenbergs, there was a "new America" as opposed to the "old America" of the Roosevelt years, which the world had respected. In a democracy, George responded, "so long as the freedom to struggle is guaranteed, democracy will inevitably lead to the victory of progressive forces."[101] Yet, ironically, on the same page, *Aufbau* ran an article about the McCarran-Walter Act, headed (in German) "An Attack on the Bill of Rights."

Thirty years later, in May 1985, in what still seems a gratuitous insult, Ronald Reagan paid his ceremonial visit to the Bitburg military cemetery in West Germany, where some Waffen SS Nazis are buried. That it coincided with the fortieth anniversary of VE Day hardly mitigated the insult to the millions of people, not only Holocaust survivors, who knew only too well from their own bitter experience and that of their families what the SS represented. Reagan had intended to use it—as German Chancellor Helmut Kohl had urged—as a token of German-American reconciliation. After the uproar that followed the announcement of the visit, when Elie Wiesel told him to his face that Bitburg "is not your place," and especially after Reagan issued a statement, doubling down on the insult, that because they were drafted, the SS soldiers were "victims, just as surely as the victims in the *concentration camps*," he also went to Bergen-Belsen.

Aufbau's editors were incensed, covering the story as intensely as its resources, then already dwindling, allowed. Reagan's decision to follow the Bitburg visit with the visit to the Bergen-Belsen death camp, which happened to coincide with the fortieth anniversary of the liberation of the camp, only made things worse. Could Hitler's soldiers, asked *Aufbau* coeditor Henry Marx in a signed editorial, be equated with the victims of the death camps? "The president is proud of his steadfastness [in going to Bitburg, despite the uproar] in a hateful thing. There are times when obstinacy isn't strength, but only perversity."[102] Visiting Bitburg may have been one of the dumbest things Reagan ever did.

Wiedergutmachung (Restitution)

In the sometimes tangled knot of great issues for the Hitler-era refugees in America and elsewhere abroad—nativism, immigration, and residual anti-Semitism in America; Zionism and the progress of the infant state of Israel; the fate of the friends and relatives left behind; the fate of Europe, and Germany particularly; and the prosecution of a list of war criminals that seemed to grow longer by the day—probably none proved more difficult at the start, and few would eventually be more satisfactorily (and more surprisingly) resolved, than *Wiedergutmachung*,[103] the reparations and restitution of expropriated property and rights—sometimes *Aufbau* called it "atonement"—for the victims of German persecution and their descendants.[104] What may be most surprising is that despite an enormous level of political and bureaucratic stonewalling, in some cases years of it, it was the West Germans—uniquely the West Germans, not the East Germans, not the Austrians, not the French, not the Swiss, and, of course, never Stalin's Russia—that so acknowledged their culpability.

Aufbau's bold headline in 1951, "Chancellor Adenauer Admits: We Are Complicit" fairly summarized it: "Unspeakable crimes have been committed in the name of the German people, calling for moral and material indemnity," Adenauer told the German Parliament, when he began to break the ice in September 1951. "The Federal Government are prepared, jointly with representatives of Jewry and the State of Israel . . . to bring about a solution of the material indemnity problem, thus easing the way to the spiritual settlement of infinite suffering."[105] The speech came at a time when the full scope of the Nazis' crimes was just becoming clear, when many of the criminals had not yet been found, and when many in the West, including many victims of the Nazis, weren't at all sure that the toxin had been purged from the German bloodstream—and when some were certain it never could be—and when much of Germany still lay in ruins. But all those things gave Adenauer's speech even greater significance. Given in response to demands from Jewish organizations abroad and from the Israeli government, it reflected an uncertain blend of genuine shame, maybe even good will, and shrewd political calculation—even statesmanship—from a nation eager to reestablish its economic viability and its international standing as a democratic society.

Manfred George called it "a good start." The words have been spoken, George said, and they bind Adenauer's successors as well. And they're a sharp "reminder in the hide of an East Germany that still remains silent." Now if the words lead to real reparations, both to the victims and in aid to Israel, "then maybe we could speak further about the future configuration of the relations between Jews and Germany."[106]

Many Jews continued to be distrustful of the motivation and, in the refusal of some ever to have anything to do with Germany again, even spurned the chance to collect the reparations that they were eligible for. "Reconciliation?" wrote Louis Freimann in a letter to *Aufbau*, one of many such letters, shortly after Adenauer's speech. "No. Never!" There might have been a few exceptions, he wrote. "All the rest, including the Chancellor were Nazis." "I still hear the voices of those who are gone," wrote another in the same issue, "telling us that if you survive this hell, tell the world that in a people of sixty million, there were maybe five hundred thousand good ones. There will be no reconciliation with the German people in my time."[107] Reports like the front-page story in the following issue about the reconstitution of Nazi groups, then said to number two hundred thousand former party members, headed "It's Already Gone This Far," didn't do much to allay the concerns.

Aufbau front page October 5, 1951, with a quote from German Chancellor Adenauer's declaration: "We are complicit." (courtesy of JM Jüdische Medien AG, Zurich)

Nor did the sensational case of Philip Auerbach, the restitution commissioner in Bavaria with a somewhat compromised background as a former concentration camp inmate, who was charged and later convicted on many counts of paying false claims to Jewish victims of the Nazis. That three of his judges were former members of the Nazi Party and that the trial itself inevitably fanned another wave of German anti-Semitism didn't help the cause. George, who interviewed Auerbach in Munich, where the trial took place, concluded that "here there was no longer any talk of right and wrong but only about political intrigue and hate."[108] A few days after he was sentenced in August 1952 to thirty months in prison, Auerbach committed suicide.

There were all sorts of difficulties in getting the restitution process—actually several processes—running and delivering the promised funds,[109] reinforcing the suspicions of Holocaust victims about German intentions and Germany's festering anti-Semitism, and *Aufbau* was full of stories about the problems and the ways to negotiate the bureaucratic hurdles. In the early years after the war, West German politicians had dragged their feet in passing the clear restitution laws that the American occupation authorities demanded, and once restitution statutes were enacted, German officials invented all manner of ways to impede the process and wherever possible deny claims. (The East Germans in the Russian zone, in full denial and suffused in the fog of Marxist doctrine, did nothing.) "Restitution," Felix Guggenheim would say in 1972, "was something you fought for, and you mostly did not get what you should get. . . . It was a hard fight, and you didn't have to say thank you for it."[110]

The archives are full of affidavits, letters between American and German lawyers, copies of old records, deeds, and bills of sale certifying a claimant's right to the stolen property. There were lists, year by year, of what an applicant had been paid in the Weimar years, pay and pensions that he or sometimes she or a murdered spouse had lost in the Hitler years. And as today's headlines make clear, some of the questions are still not settled, particularly the contested provenance of great art, much of it now in major museums both in Europe and abroad, some looted or sold under duress, some not. One issue of *Aufbau* in the fall of 1947 carried a dozen ads from lawyers and accountants, most of them former practitioners in Germany, offering to represent émigrés seeking restitution. And, of course, there was a book, advertised in *Aufbau*, called *Restitution Laws (Wiedergutmachungsgesetzen)* by Hans Strauss, J.D., available for $1.80, plus twenty cents for shipping and four cents New York sales tax. It could be ordered from, of all sources, *Aufbau*'s old nemesis, the parent company of the *Staats-Herold*.[111]

One of those restitution lawyers, though not an advertiser, was *Aufbau*'s occasional columnist Robert Kempner, who, as a former prosecutor in the

Weimar years (and later a member of the prosecution team at the Nuremberg war crime trials), probably knew more about German law than anyone else. But there were many others, some of whom had practiced in Germany and were now associated with American firms.

For a time between the late 1940s and the 1960s, *Aufbau* ran a fortnightly page "Problems of the *Wiedergutmachung*" under a standing head, which in the 1960s became "*Wiedergutmachung*: A Roadmap for all Concerned."[112] The intricacies of the restitution laws, the decisions in the courts, and countless other details were a major issue. Perhaps the most obvious of those problems—beyond the fact that at first even the Germans didn't recognize their responsibility, and that often there was a question of legal ownership—was that so much had not simply been stolen or sold, often under duress, to Aryans (Aryanized) but destroyed. Moreover, anyone who had lived in what became East Germany after the war got nothing until Germany was reunified in 1990, forty-five years after the end of the war, or from the Swiss banks, or in France, until 2000, and never at all in most places in Eastern Europe.

Nonetheless, little on the international stage in the half-century after the war turned out to be as successful either for the German government or the recipients as was the wholly unprecedented program of restitution. In 1962, the prolific Kurt Grossmann, who was then deeply engaged on behalf of Hitler refugees in the fight for restitution, reported that 825,000 claims were still unsettled. But nearly 2.3 million had been.[113] Through the sixty postwar years, the Claims Conference, formally the Conference on Jewish Material Claims Against Germany, that grew out of the negotiations that followed the Adenauer speech, distributed more than sixty billion dollars from Germany: for lifetime pensions to some 278,000 Holocaust survivors; for rebuilding Jewish communities in Europe; for Israel; for one-time payments to thousands of others; for welfare services and social care programs to elderly and needy survivors; for efforts to find and recover art and other cultural objects looted by the Nazis, among them, most recently, the collection of Cornelius Gurlitt in Munich which, when it was discovered in 2012, was said to be the largest collection of looted art in private hands.[114] In addition, partly through Kempner's efforts, additional millions were paid by German companies such as Flick, whose subsidiary made gunpowder, in compensation for the slave labor they exploited during the war.[115]

Tens of thousands depended on those *Wiedergutmachung* payments, and some still do. "My mother's family received restitution for the furniture design, manufacturing and interior design businesses they owned," wrote a woman now living in California who was brought to this country from Brussels by her German-Jewish parents as a young girl. "My grandparents lived off the restitution payments for the remainder of their lives."[116] For the old people, Guggenheim said, "the *Wiedergutmachung* was a sensational and important thing that all of a sudden every month comes one hundred or two hundred dollars, and it helped them face old age easier."[117]

In addition, thousands of Jewish refugees and camp survivors who had been former German citizens dealt directly with the restitution offices set up by Germany or sometimes through the United Restitution Organization (URO—a legal aid society to help claimants of limited means living outside Germany) to recover both in restitution and compensation some part of what was due to them from Nazi Germany. By 1967, the URO had helped Hitler victims secure an additional five hundred million dollars in indemnification payments or property. Later, in settlement of a set of lawsuits, an additional five billion dollars was paid to 140,000 former slave laborers, Jews and non-Jews, in German industry.[118] But beyond financial restitution, *Wiedergutmachung*—and making amends in a broader sense—became an essential part of Germany's foreign policy orientation. Nearly three quarters of a century after the Holocaust, Germany would be far and away the world's greatest refuge for the Syrians and the other victims of the murderous wars in the Middle East.

There's no way to know how many of those who vowed never again to buy anything made in Germany—no Volkswagen, no Leica, no Rosenthal china, no Solingen cutlery—maintained that vow, even after German reunification. A few regarded any *Wiedergutmachung* money from the German government as "blood money," a question that was fiercely debated among the refugees in America and even more fiercely in the Israeli Knesset, where the vote to negotiate with Germany finally passed in January 1952 by the relatively close vote of 61 to 50. But for those who benefited from the *Wiedergutmachung*, boycotting all things German would have been difficult. As Anne Clara Schenderlein, now a research fellow at the German Historical Institute in Washington, summarized, "The practicalities of restitution demanded an involvement of German-Jewish refugees, and the organized refugee community in particular recognized the importance that a good relationship with Germany would hold for them."[119] Some also recognized, in Schenderlein's words, "the German government's need for their public good will and acted upon it to influence German conduct and further its own interests, asserting that their experiences as victims of Germany entitled them to be expert observers and judges of matters of Nazism and anti-Semitism and the overall democratization process in West Germany."[120] And then there were those who again did business with Germans, "importers," as Guggenheim would say, "who all of a sudden saw a chance to represent, say, Rolleiflex here, and could not be as anti-German as they were before."[121]

For Adenauer's government, restitution and good relations with the American-Jewish community and with German refugees and Holocaust survivors particularly was a strategic foreign policy test and, given the considerable number of officials in the German foreign office who remained from the Nazi era (many of them probably full-blown Nazis), that was not always easy. In the summer of 1950, there had been an intense debate at the American Federation of Jews from Central Europe during which "Rabbi Max Grüenewald harshly criticized attempts to interact with Germans that would minimize what had happened, stating that the 'graves were still too fresh.'"[122]

For many of Hitler's victims, both those who came before the war and for the camp survivors who came later, the issue of reconciliation would likely never to be put to rest. Others, maybe particularly those who had gotten away relatively unscathed, managed to forget. In July 1951, *Aufbau* launched the series "Jews and Germans," which raised the question whether the divide could be bridged in a single generation. As part of it, Manfred George, in a reflection of the misgivings of German émigrés about their former homeland, conducted a long interview with West German President Theodor Heuss, in which George noted the progress of German reconstruction and the related benefits of the Marshall Plan, and Heuss, whose office was largely ceremonial, expressed guarded optimism about the country's future, hopes for its relations with France, and the prospects for European recovery.[123] All of which, of course, was what his job required. But, in fact, it was already happening. In 1950, French Foreign Minister Robert Schuman had proposed the formation of a joint European Coal and Steel Community, which was created in 1951 and would become the base of the European Economic Community, the Common Market. Initially composed of Belgium, France, Italy, Luxembourg, the Netherlands, and West Germany, the European Community (EC) was launched in 1958, just a little more than a decade after Germany's defeat.

More immediately, by the early 1950s, some refugees were making trips back to Germany, most at first to find surviving relatives or to represent American organizations, or to try to negotiate with German officials for restitution, among them people who later confessed that being there almost made them sick.[124] At about the same time as the 1951 Heuss interview—also roughly the time of Adenauer's speech—the major international airlines were flying daily to German cities, and as Germany rebuilt, more emigrants returned to revisit old neighborhoods or just on vacation. In a survey of Jews in Washington Heights in the mid-1960s, 53 percent said they had traveled to Germany since the war, some, at least, on business or to petition for restitution payments—but still a surprising number. Two-thirds said they'd been to Israel.[125]

Both sets of numbers indicate that compared to the images of struggling, depressed refugees of the 1930s and 1940s, things had improved considerably. They also indicated that while many were still determined never again to have anything to do with Germany, and some were frightened or nauseated even to hear German spoken, a growing number did go. Conversely, the West German government, eager to establish good relations with its exiled Jews, did a lot abroad through its consulates to foster them and to reassure the American-Jewish community that it did not tolerate the anti-Semitic incidents that still occurred all too frequently in West German cities.[126] Before the end of the 1960s, the mayor of Mainz ran an ad inviting *Aufbau* readers to visit the city where Gutenberg invented the art of printing, the city of Hamburg promoted itself as a center of world commerce, and quite a few others, Berlin among them, sponsored return visits by refugees who might want to see again the places they'd come from. Among the ads for upscale Swiss winter resorts in Interlaken, Lugano, and Grindelwald, there were ads for hotels in Stuttgart, Kiel, Karlsruhe, Frankfurt, and Berlin. The Berlin Philharmonic—under the imperious off-and-on Nazi Party member Herbert von Karajan, who had been officially de-Nazified in Austria in 1946—listed an outline of its complete 1969 European concert schedule, most of it in Germany.[127] There were ads from Avis telling readers that "even in Europe you don't have to go without your car"; and from Swissair, Lufthansa, KLM, and Pan Am (all in German) inviting readers, in Pan Am's 1969 ad (complete with a photo of a VW Beetle), to have

> a nice long drive through the countryside. We deliver the country. And the car. And a good amount of free kilometers. With Pan Am's three week "Freewheeler Holiday Tour" to Germany—for only $338. And that's not all you get for this low price. You'll get the round-trip jet flight from New York to Frankfurt, twenty overnight stays in a lovely guesthouse in Paderborn, and a car with one thousand kilometers free of charge.
>
> Think about how wonderful it will be to once again experience the beauty of Germany.[128]

In later years, there would also be ads for the German newspaper *Die Welt*, from the Austrian tourist industry touting *Sommer in Österreich*, and for the Leipzig University Chorus.

Beginning in the late 1980s, the American Jewish Committee expected to be cosponsoring conferences in New York and Bonn, then West Germany's capital, with Atlantic Bridge (Atlantik Brücke), the private German group created in 1952 to foster improved German-American relations—in this case, specifically between Germans and American Jews. The sponsors, not surprisingly, identified the Holocaust as the central issue, whose dark shadow just wouldn't go away. "[That] the Germans after some early delays have found their 'way to Israel,'" wrote *Aufbau* coeditor Henry Marx, "doesn't mean they've found their 'way to the Jews.'" The first meeting, in November 1987, came just two years after Ronald Reagan's visit to the Bitburg cemetery and amid what *Aufbau* called the "Waldheim Affair." But the conferees also agreed that the emphasis had to be on the future, not the past, and, on that score at least, time seemed to be in their favor.[129]

Just as the Bonn conference was getting under way, Marx reviewed the German-Austrian docudrama *The Wannsee Conference*, then showing in New York (and advertised in the pages of *Aufbau*), which was based on the minutes of the meeting of Nazi leaders in January 1942, where the industrialized genocide called the Final Solution was planned. The film ran just eighty-five minutes, precisely the length of the Wannsee meeting that decided on the murder of millions. The film, said Marx, would be therapeutic for some, painful for others. But he was encouraged that it was Germans who had made it and were "showing this greatest crime against mankind in all its inhumanity." So the film must be welcomed. "It's not often enough, and not thoroughly enough that this frightful past can be discussed so that it does not fall into forgetfulness."[130] And it was another sign that the Germans were confronting that frightful past.

✶

In the years immediately after the war, tens of thousands of German Jews, and often their children, had struggled their way through West German restitution bureaucracies, some with success, many more in the early postwar days—despite the determination of the Allied occupying powers to require restitution—without. Sometimes the German officials were unresponsive; often the process took years. The documents in support of their claims—what they had lost, how much, and sometimes even where (with realigned borders)—were laced, in Atina Grossmann's words, with stories cataloguing "the proud defensiveness of those forced to prove what had once been self-evident—schooling, degrees, social position, truncated bright futures—as well as the hurdles to emigration, the difficulties of starting anew in old professions, and the fees and costs associated with new licenses and degrees."[131] Until Adenauer's speech, and often for decades after, denial and resistance were more common than acknowledgment. German courts were often unsympathetic, ordering restitution payments set at small fractions of the value of the Aryanized property.

But by the end of the 1950s, Israel had received a lump-sum payment of some $745 million for the purchase of oil and raw materials (the latter mostly from Germany), and many individuals had gotten lump-sum payments for property or bank accounts stolen by the Nazis; others had gotten life-time commitments for the pensions they would have received had they retained their positions as officials, teachers, or judges in the German bureaucracy. Atina Grossmann, born in 1950 and then living in New York with her refugee family, recalled that:

> My father (a restitution lawyer) took a great measure of bitter pleasure in pulling as much money as he possibly could out of the young Bundesrepublik, and even at a very young age I was acutely aware of the sudden turn in my family's own fortunes in 1957, when the restitution money (*Wiedergutmachungsgeld*) for our own family and for my father's clients, and his commissions, started rolling in. My father embarked on his first journey back to Europe, and I still remember the smooth suede of the elegant leather handbags he brought back from Spain for my mother, and the aura of the Continent and some long-lost luxury entering our cramped New York apartment. Something significant had definitely shifted for German-Jewish refugees in New York. The fabled *Sommerfrische* (summer holiday) suddenly moved from small inns with a German-speaking clientele and hearty Central European cooking (some kosher, some not) in the rolling hill towns of the Catskills such as Tannersville and Fleischmanns to the authentic nostalgically remembered Alps and the grand hotels of Zermatt, Sils Maria, or Arosa. The final approval of restitution legislation by the Bundestag in 1956 marked the slow end of the German-Jewish Catskills. And I could palpably, physically, sense the relief that washed through the Café Éclair, the Tip Toe Inn, the afternoon *Kaffeeklatsches* of the Yekke community in New York, as the money and the pensions began to arrive, bank accounts expanded, and a certain sense of security, mixed always with the pain of irretrievable loss (of which I was less clearly aware), settled into refugee life.[132]

Some had reclaimed the businesses—often the modest remains of the businesses and sometimes in strange partnership with the sons of the prior owners—that had been Aryanized by the Nazis and had rebuilt them. Many still struggled, but others, half Aryanized themselves, were collecting German Expressionist paintings and riding in their chauffeur-driven BMWs to the summer music festival in Salzburg (though rarely to the Wagner festival at Bayreuth) and to their winter cottages on the Costa del Sol. By that time, Germany had become a major element not only in the Western Alliance—it had joined NATO in 1955, just a decade after Hitler's defeat—but was astonishing the world with the speed of its economic recovery, already known as "the German miracle." Paradoxically, the near-complete destruction of many German

cities, and much of the country's industry and infrastructure, combined with
the help of the Marshall Plan, probably facilitated the modernization, both of
plant and industrial practices, on which postwar Germany thrived.

★

As might be expected, the end of the war, the destitution of many of its survivors, and the establishment of the new State of Israel reenergized the lively
prewar care package industry. But it now offered not just little—and not so
little—packets of food, but vacuum cleaners, General Electric and Westing-
house refrigerators, washers, Philco radios, sewing machines, and other durable
household goods. During the immediate postwar years, there was a joke in New
York about the wife in Palestine who asked her husband why he kept cursing
as he was trying to assemble a baby carriage from a kit they'd ordered from
England. "No matter how I put this damn thing together," he replied, "it always
comes out a machine gun."

Service for Israel Inc. offered packages of everything—fresh frozen meats,
vegetables, coffee, sugar, marmalade, chocolate—air shipped, ranging from
$10.50 for a "Standard" twelve-pound package to $38.50 for a fifty-five pound
"Family" package. Hudson Shipping Co. promised to deliver hundred-pound
shipments of flour to Vienna in forty-eight hours for $14.50, or packages of
food—ham, bacon, butter, cheese, and condensed milk, nothing kosher here—
for $11.40. American Fuel Relief for Austria offered to ship five-hundred-kilo
loads of coal to Vienna for $18.50 (one thousand kilos for $36), delivery guaranteed in four to six weeks or your money back. Swiss banks were advertising
their services in transferring funds, in buying and selling foreign currency, and
in "commercial and financial transactions with Israel." At the same time (July
1951), the United Jewish Appeal (UJA) was running full-page ads pointing out
that one thousand Jews were arriving every day from the danger zones in Romania, the Arab countries, and North Africa, who now had a chance to realize
their dreams at last. But they desperately needed help.[133]

The UJA campaign and the other philanthropic organizations providing
aid, and the individual food packets and the appliances for Israel in the early
1950s, were just small precursors of the billions in financial and military support
that the United States would provide Israel in the years following. In part, that
aid was certainly strategic—Israel was both a key ally and the only beachhead
of democracy in the region. But for America's Jews, and its immigrant European Jews especially, it was a sign of their own newfound strength, political
clout, confidence, and, yes, Americanization. Not so coincidentally, it was also
in the early 1950s that the lobbying arm of the American Zionist Council

morphed into what became the very powerful American Israel Public Affairs Committee (AIPAC). And for a country that in the 1930s and 1940s—meaning some thirty years before—had turned its back on hundreds of thousands of desperate refugees trying to flee almost certain death, those billions in American aid for Israel were also a form of *Wiedergutmachung*, now much too late, but all that could be done.

*

Manfred George died on December 30, 1965. By that time his paper had just passed its prime and much of what he had committed *Aufbau* to had been achieved or was in the process of realization. Tens of thousands of his fellow refugees, like George himself, had become American citizens. They, and often their children, had had the satisfaction of contributing to the Allied war effort in the defeat of both Germany and Japan, had been part of the American Military Government in Germany, and had since established themselves in every major American city and in hundreds of smaller places as well and were well on their way to success in their businesses and professions, more than a few in major positions of leadership. Many had also become beneficiaries of German restitution payments, living in part on the pensions they would have been entitled to had they not been fired from their jobs as professors, teachers, and civil servants and driven out of their country by the Nazis. Palestine had been partitioned and part had become the state of Israel. West Germany, despite all the well-justified doubts of thousands of George's fellow immigrants of the prior years, was on its way to becoming the most successful democracy on the European continent. The European Economic Community had been created a few years before and seemed to be thriving. And, despite the ongoing bureaucratic difficulties, Germany and its citizens were paying billions in restitution and other forms of *Wiedergutmachung* to hundreds of thousands of Hitler's victims and to countless communities and institutions that had been the victims of the Nazis. More fundamentally, as Andreas Mink, one of *Aufbau*'s last editors, would later write, "As a forum for Jewish refugees from Hitler's expanding German Reich, [*Aufbau*] helped to shape a common identity for Jews from all parts of the former Weimar Republic, Austria, and Czechoslovakia, who had previously been rooted in various regional cultures and milieus. This identity was based on more than Jewish tradition and the experience of persecution; it also included a 'liberal and democratic attitude' in the American sense."[134]

The magnitude of the paper's success might paradoxically, even ironically, be measured by the decline in its circulation in the 1970s, 1980s, and 1990s, as fewer German-speaking Jews arrived, as there were no more camp survivors, and as increasing numbers of its readers learned English, became American-ized, or simply passed away—another fact reflected in the growing number of death announcements on *Aufbau*'s pages that replaced the vanishing classifieds. Most of the children of those readers, who quickly became fluent in English if they hadn't been born in the United States, never went near *Aufbau*. You can still find people who knew readers of the *Aufbau*, their parents or uncles or aunts or maybe a grandparent, but rarely any who read the paper themselves.

The paper continued to publish, from 1966 to 1984 under the editorship of Hans Steinitz, who had succeeded George, and then for twenty years under several others. It reduced its publication schedule roughly in symmetry with its rise in the 1930s, from weekly to fortnightly, then to monthly, with increas-ing emphasis in its last years on news summaries, commentaries, essays, re-views, and, in reflection of its straitened resources, less hard news. As early as 1964, it published a German-language guide to the New York World's Fair—seventy-five thousand copies—offering advertisers "a unique opportunity to reach a large and prosperous segment of the World's Fair market."[135] Later, it created the Aufbau Heritage Foundation to solicit contributions from readers and other friends in the declining German-Jewish émigré community which, judging from the list of contributors, many of them now children of refugees, had itself dispersed all over the country—and indeed the world. Frankfurt on the Hudson was the past. "What if," in the words of one of its ads, "this singular voice, which has spoken for us in all this time were suddenly silenced and dis-appeared forever from our midst?" It even ran occasional ads from retailers in Yorkville, once regarded as hostile territory, among them one for Schaller and Weber's Gold Medal Meat Products on Second Avenue—certainly not kosher butchers.[136] For a time in the 1970s it also got support from the West German government, which took out "large numbers of subscriptions."[137] But the demo-graphics were unavoidable. In 2004, it was taken over by a Swiss company that now publishes it as a glossy illustrated monthly called *Aufbau: The Jewish Monthly Magazine*, which is very different from its predecessor but still lists the year of publication according to the old count, which began in 1934. But *Aufbau* had outlived its readership. What was remarkable was that through nearly forty-five years—its peak years—it had only two editors, George and Steinitz, itself a tribute to the strength and commitment of its board and its parent New World Club.

In 1994, *Aufbau*'s New York publisher Jerry Brunell, an insurance broker who worked as a volunteer in its waning days—he had arrived in New York as a thirteen-year-old refugee in 1938 (he was then Gerhart)—told a *Times* re-porter that "not only did I read it. I became an American because of it." In the same story, Will Schaber, one of its last editors, a democratic socialist, though not a Jew, who had fled when Hitler came to power, remarked on the irony that while Germany was dominated by the Nazis, the best of German culture was "to a great extent being sustained by a newspaper founded by Jews who were persecuted and forced into exile."[138] When the *Times* interviewed the editors in 1994, there were no computers in the office, just typewriters, and on the walls, the photos of the three old heroes that had hung there almost from the beginning: Roosevelt, Einstein, and Thomas Mann.

In February 2004, two months before its last issue as the old *Aufbau*, it published a seventieth anniversary issue, a sort of summing up, about half of it in English, with contributions from and interviews with established figures, some of them like the historian Fritz Stern, who belonged to what the physicists Gerhard Sonnert and Gerald Holton called (in the same issue) the "second wave," men and women brought to this country as children. Tellingly, some of the issue was also devoted to pieces, like "Young Germans Still Struggle with the Past," on the emigration of Soviet Jews to Germany, yet another irony of history, and on how the Germans were dealing with their own flares of anti-Semitism. But more was on Jewish life in contemporary Germany (where *Aufbau*, in its effort to survive, had been trying to build circulation and support). It may even have been true, as *Aufbau*'s publisher said in 1999, "Sixty-five years later, we carry the culture back to Germany."[139]

But sadly, some pieces in that seventieth anniversary issue were not much more than thinly veneered nostalgia about the paper's past. In its March issue the following month, it warned that because of technical problems, the next issue would be delayed and then, a month later, it was gone. Henceforth, *Aufbau* would be the rich historical archive of a generation whose impact on American culture and democracy would be far greater than its numbers.

The end testified to the successful completion of the mission it had set for itself at the beginning. Although the Holocaust would not be forgotten, certainly not by Jews, and while the outcroppings of neo-Nazism didn't go unnoticed, the condemnation of contemporary Germany and contemporary Germans as the eternally attainted culprits was a thing of the past. But maybe just as telling, if less obvious, was the fact that at the end, none of *Aufbau*'s few remaining editors—Andreas Mink (born in 1958 in Baden-Baden) or Monika Ziegler (also a German-born gentile)—was a Hitler refugee, even in the "second wave," or could have been, and few were even Jewish. There were countless Jewish journalists in America, some of them, as noted earlier, part of the second wave, but they were fully assimilated and few were literate in German. That, too, testified, to *Aufbau*'s success, and to America's.

5

Legacy

---

*   *   *

It's impossible to imagine contemporary America, or indeed much of the world, without the changes brought by the prewar Hitler refugees, their American children, and the postwar Holocaust survivors who followed them—changes now so intrinsic they are no longer remarkable in the nation's everyday life or indeed in the history of Israel. What, asked the French historian Jean-Michel Palmier in his magisterial study *Weimar in Exile,* "would America have been without them? There is no domain of culture or of science—biological research, the visual arts, cinema, theater, art history or economics—to which these émigrés did not give a sharp boost."[1] That may be slightly hyperbolic. And while Palmier refers most obviously to the influence of intellectuals and artists, his conclusion can just as well apply to the larger sweep of the whole generation. There is no way to calculate the extent to which ordinary immigrants, the younger ones especially—people who arrived in their teens or twenties (or were brought as young children) and had not been demoralized by the loss of career and status in the Hitler years—became professionals: architects, industrial designers, doctors, nurses, psychiatrists, teachers, social workers, professors, journalists, publishers, rabbis, lawyers, civil servants of every description, craftsmen, engineers, insurance brokers, real estate developers, garment manufacturers, and other business people, many of whom had started their own firms, and slipped seamlessly into American communities in every corner of the country and into American life, and did it in spite of the ethnic bias they often faced. From the start, many refugees-*cum*-immigrants felt duty bound to contribute to the United Jewish Appeal and other established Jewish philan-thropic organizations, in part to show gratitude for the help they'd gotten, in part to show they were making it, and in part, maybe, just because they were Jewish. They became major donors to, and pillars on the boards of, countless social service agencies, synagogues, theaters, museums, colleges, orchestras, and philanthropies. That, too, was part of Americanization. And inevitably they brought a cosmopolitan sensibility that prewar America, its provincialism protected by two oceans, so often lacked.[2]

The places they had first clustered in—most of them—are now the homes of people, many of them also immigrants, from other cultures, speaking other languages, eating different food, and listening to different music. The Éclair is gone; the hotels in the Catskills and the Adirondacks—those that remain—cater to a very different clientele. In 1987, *Aufbau* ran a hopeful piece contending that "after a considerable decline" the outlook for Yiddish in America had im-proved.[3] But even after the infusion brought by the Eastern Jews who survived the Holocaust, and excepting only a few ultra-Orthodox communities such as the Yiddish village Kiryas Joel in Orange County, New York, Yiddish is barely managing to survive. In 2011, an estimated 160,000 people in America (1.5 mil-lion worldwide), most of them elderly, spoke Yiddish at home. But would con-temporary American architecture be what it is without non-Jewish Hitler refu-gees like Gropius and Breuer, or the Bauhaus? The list of Hitler refugees who became major figures in America is endless: Henry Kissinger, Felix Rohatyn, Madeleine Albright, Max Frankel, Henry Grünwald, Peter Gay, Erich Fromm, Claude Levi-Strauss, Billy Wilder, Peter Lorre, and Art Spiegelman. How much strength did the American civil rights movement in the 1950s, 1960s, and 1970s gain from Jews, and from the Hitler refugees especially, who of all the white people in America probably best understood the stakes? Would social theory be the same without Theodor Adorno, Ludwig Marcuse, Erich Fromm, and the other refugees of the Frankfurt School? To what extent did Albert Einstein, Hans Bethe, Leo Szilard, Edward Teller, and all the rest energize American science? The prestige of Einstein himself, whose science was rarely understood by nonscientists and who was often the subject of cartoons and wisecracks about absent-minded geniuses, did much to reduce the nation's historic anti-intellectualism and make the country a little safer for science.

How deeply did émigré intellectuals such as the libertarian economist Ludwig von Mises (also a Jew, the "von" to the contrary notwithstanding) and the political philosopher Eric Voegelin, born in Cologne but educated in Vienna and lifelong friend of Friedrich Hayek (a disciple of Mises and a hero of libertarian economists), influence American neoconservatism in the latter half of the twentieth century and maybe beyond? What of Leo Strauss, born an Orthodox Jew in Prussia, who became a central figure at the University of Chicago, America's temple of intellectual conservatism? Harry Jaffa, who wrote much of Barry Goldwater's 1964 convention speech with the lines "extremism in the defense of liberty is no vice" and "moderation in the pursuit of justice is no virtue," was a Strauss disciple from his days at the New School when Strauss taught there.

During the administration of George W. Bush, the "Straussians," former students of Leo Strauss at Chicago, among them Paul Wolfowitz, Bush's so-called idea man, and William Kristol, editor of the *Weekly Standard*, were thought to be the dominant influences in the aggressive U.S. foreign policy that led to the Iraq war. (Here, too, criticism of the so-called Leo-Conservatives was tinged with an edge of anti-Semitism.) Was Donald Trump, with his call to "make America great again" the sort of reactionary whose politics grew out of their misreading of the libertarian classics of Vienna school economics, maybe even an effort by American right-wingers to make themselves a little more respectable with a layer of highfalutin European ideology? "The path that led from the seminar rooms in Chicago to the right-wing political-media-foundation complex in Washington," wrote Mark Lilla, a professor of humanities at Columbia, "has transformed American politics over the past five decades."[4]

And then there were the somewhat more questionable contributions of the architect and urban planner Victor Gruen, born Viktor David Grünbaum in Vienna, generally recognized as the father of the shopping mall (which he later disowned). How do we gauge the much-debated influence of a whole generation of refugee (but not all Jewish) psychoanalysts and psychotherapists—such as Alfred Adler (to whom we apparently owe the inferiority complex), Heinz Hartmann, Erik Erikson, and Helene Deutsch, who had been Freud's assistant in Vienna, and other Vienna-trained American analysts—on American psychiatry? The Nazis had declared psychoanalysis "a degenerate Jewish science."

As early as 1934, Ernest Jones was telling the International Congress of Psychoanalysis that half of Germany's analysts had already fled.[5] It was, the psychiatrist Jeffrey Lieberman wrote, as if the "Vatican and its cardinals had shifted the site of the Holy See from Rome to Manhattan," bringing with them "the dogmatic and faith-based approach to psychiatry that Freud had espoused, discouraging inquiry and experimentation." (And, Lieberman might have added, resisting the use of psychotropic drugs.) All the émigré analysts were Jews trained by Jews, he wrote, working with mostly Jewish clients. "It would be hard to imagine a therapy less suited to the treatment of people with severe mental illness."[6] What it did do was give birth to a whole new strain of American humor: Where would Woody Allen have been without it? Every shrink joke for a half century had a Germanic name or German accent. "So," said the doctor. "Now vee may perhaps to begin. Yes." That was Philip Roth in *Portnoy's Complaint.*[7]

More broadly, to what extent did the refugee German professors, many of them as Prussian as they were Jewish, who were often shocked by the intellectual shallowness of their first American students, reshape American academic life? To what extent did the American high school, for all its academic flabbiness, become a little less just the place, as Robert Hutchins would famously say, "where the band practices"? The émigré historian George L. Mosse, who was born in Berlin, recalled an experience he shared

> with many much-older refugee professors, who had been educated in Germany, and who often commented upon the ignorance of their students, their lack of aesthetic judgment and sophistication, and at the same time their freshness, their eagerness to learn. At that point I had little interest and almost no knowledge of a German-Jewish legacy, and instead pointed to the lamentable state of the American high school and of departments of education devoted to the notion that school was not an instrument of learning or of personal development but an engine for socialization. Many U.S.-born colleagues joined the fight in order to save so-called subject matter from being drowned by the emphasis upon method, upon "how to do things," then the staple of teachers' training.[8]

The list runs on. Would Mahler have become a staple of America concert halls without Bruno Walter? Would the music in those concert halls have reached anything close to the quality it did without the standards set by the émigrés Toscanini, Klemperer, Szell, Horowitz, Serkin, Rubinstein, the influential musicologist Alfred Einstein (no relation to Albert), and so many others? Would as many Americans even have been exposed to classical music had it not been for the broadcasts of the NBC Symphony under Toscanini? (In 1950, NBC even chartered a special train to take the whole orchestra on a national concert tour. It would be hard to imagine such a thing today.) Schoenberg's influence was already enormous when he arrived in California, but it was certainly extended in America, particularly through his work with John Cage and Lou Harrison. (In California, he also played with George Gershwin, but that was tennis, not music.) What would have become of classical ballet in America without George Balanchine, the Georgian-Russian émigré from Saint

Petersburg? Would there have been a Neue Galerie in New York devoted to German Expressionists and Vienna Secessionists had it not been for Otto Kallir, who brought the work of those artists to America and whose original establishment in Vienna was called the Neue Galerie? Would the hope for a Common Market and a European community, a United States of Europe, been dreamed as it was, or maybe even at all, had it not been for the bitter experiences and the enhanced global perspective of the Hitler refugees, many of whom now thought of themselves as Europeans? Do we have any more imaginative riffs on the comic strip than Art Spiegelman's *Maus*, an immigrant's telling of his family's Holocaust story—funny, moving, deeply Jewish—or any more telling and ironic narrative about it?

Hannah Arendt, who had worked for Zionist organizations in France just before the war, had long worried that partition of Palestine into Jewish and Arab states, rather than creating an amalgamated multiethnic state, would lead to eternal friction in the Middle East; on that, the warning now seems prophetic. But would there have been an Israel without American Jews, German Jews paramount among them? And if so, would it have survived in the midst of four hundred million Arabs and a Western world not yet free of its historic anti-Semitism if it did not enjoy the political influence, the money, and, most of all, the moral authority of those European refugee Jews? How much was American Judaism itself reshaped by those refugees, the Orthodox Jews from the camps especially? Conversely, said the literary scholar Guy Stern, "the German Jewish in America have been consistently in the van as a detoxifier of the corrosive poison made in Germany."[9]

The monuments are well known—Brandeis University, the Leo Baeck Institute, the Holocaust Memorial Museum, the Wiesenthal Center, the USC Shoah Foundation (founded by the Hollywood producer Steven Spielberg, which has filmed interviews with fifty-two thousand survivors of the Holocaust and of the more recent genocides in Nanjing and Rwanda). "This is something that I was put on this earth to do—not just to make movies, but to tell this truth to people, especially young people," Spielberg told interviewer Maria Shriver in 2014. He said he used the proceeds from his Oscar-winning film *Schindler's List* to fund it.[10] Selfhelp, started by a handful of émigré volunteers to help fellow refugees—its mission, it says, has always been "to serve as the last surviving relative of victims of Nazi persecution"—is now a major social service enterprise engaged in providing housing for low-income seniors and ancillary services in support of independent living for a diverse population. Some are Holocaust survivors—in 2016 there were still 110,000 in the United States; 50,000 in New York City. But in recent years its low-rent apartments have housed a growing percentage of Chinese, Koreans, and other Asians in the Queens neighborhoods where, aided both by the German restitution money provided by the Claims Conference and by state funding, Selfhelp first built those apartments for Holocaust survivors.[11] In 2016, the president of Selfhelp's board of directors, Raymond V. J. Schrag, was the son of one of Selfhelp's émigré volunteers who worked for what was then a shoestring organization in the 1940s. Among his predecessors as president in that earlier era was the Protestant theologian Paul Tillich.

One other monument probably belongs on this list. In November 2016, the German government bought the house in Pacific Palisades that Thomas Mann had built for himself and that he lived in for ten years before he moved back to Europe — not to Germany, but to Switzerland. The price was nearly fourteen million dollars. It had been advertised as a "tear down," which caused the uproar in Germany that led to the purchase. After a two-year renovation, it was reported, the German culture ministry "planned to turn the five-bedroom house into a center for trans-Atlantic dialogue that offered residencies for academics and artists."[12] German Foreign Minister Frank-Walter Steinmeier was quoted as saying it was a symbol "for many Germans who worked toward a better future for their country, paved the way for an open society and laid the foundations for common transatlantic values."[13] This, too, was reconciliation.

There's no way to estimate the wider influence that the three to four hundred thousand immigrants from the Nazi era had on American culture, much less the impact of their children. Lucy Steinitz, the U.S.-born daughter of Hans Steinitz, who succeeded George as *Aufbau*'s editor and was then running a Jewish social service agency in Baltimore, probably spoke for many of her peers when she wrote that whatever efforts the second generation makes "to preserve the legacy of German Jewry will probably focus on the years of Nazi terror and destruction rather than on the philosophical or cultural mores which preceded the war. The Holocaust still overpowers us and numbs us; it overshadows prewar history and binds all Jews together in a single destiny. . . . I identify much more closely as a child of the Holocaust than as a descendant of Goethe, Schiller or the German-Jewish *Bildung*."[14] That's probably true for many, if not most.

But how many in that second generation have nearly forgotten even the Holocaust? How many have again nearly forgotten that they're Jews or the racism that still infects the country to which their parents or grandparents fled three quarters of a century before? Have they forgotten, or did they even know about the collective insanity — the denial of reality, the exploitation of political lies, racism, bigotry, and Orwellian language — that drove their forebears here?

The election campaign of 2016 and the anger and divisions that led to it have again led some to ask, as it was eighty years ago: Could it happen here? There are many differences, but it makes the questions raised by Hitler's refugees resonate as they have at no time since they arrived in America.

∗

How much *Aufbau* did to facilitate the Americanization of the refugees, the DPs, the camp survivors, and others who came after the war—or even the Americanization of the old Weimar left before the war—can never be accurately measured, although there's hardly anyone who didn't acknowledge it. How much it did to waken them from what Frederick Lachman, *Aufbau*'s columnist on Jewish history, called "the teary, sentimental" dream of returning to the cultural, intellectual pre-Hitler years for which some so passionately longed is even harder to estimate.[15]

Yet in the larger culture there are elements of both legacies. Given the exposure that American GIs had to the world, the GI Bill and the vastly broadened access that young postwar Americans had to higher education, the impact of television and other new media, the ease of travel, and the chill that the Cold War and the bomb cast over the nation, any such calculation is virtually impossible. But there's not much doubt that post-1945 America was a radically different, vastly more cosmopolitan place than it had been before the war. It was technology that narrowed the Atlantic Ocean, but it was in considerable measure the refugees, some not Jewish, like Thomas Mann, who, in encompassing the two cultures, brought them a bit closer together. Mann, like some others, was simultaneously repulsed by McCarthyism and drawn by the long tradition of European culture of which he was a major example. Similarly, for many others, what had been, in the critic Anthony Heilbut's words, "an initial full-throated, albeit consciously willed, devotion (the word is not hyperbolic; President Roosevelt was virtually canonized by refugees who usually regarded themselves as instinctive skeptics)" soured to a "final disillusionment and the attendant revisions of the loving schemes and estimations of the previous decades."[16]

But notwithstanding the Red hunts and despite the nation's seemingly deep undercurrents of racism and its twenty-first-century pockets of anti-Semitism (too much of it, shockingly, on the left), it's hard to underestimate the gains in civil rights and civil liberties of the past three-fourths of a century, gains that were owed to many things, but not in small part to the doors that the Hitler refugees and the Holocaust survivors helped to open and the moral authority they brought to the cause. If there are any admission quotas in higher education now, they're designed to favor rather than exclude disadvantaged groups (although they may, in the process, handicap other disadvantaged groups). University presidents with names like Shapiro, Levin, and Marx are now as common as the Plimptons, the Butlers, and the Lowells once were, maybe more so. And could anyone who recalls the days after World War II—when college English Departments were the private preserves of WASPs and when great American-born Jewish critics like Alfred Kazin felt like aliens during their brief stints as visiting professors in places like Amherst—have imagined an immigrant Jew named Gundersheimer as president of the Folger Shakespeare Library, probably the most celebrated repository of material on the English Renaissance in the world? The same is generally true in corporate boardrooms and in the upper reaches of Wall Street law firms. If there are still glass ceilings, it isn't Jews, not Jewish men anyway, who are bumping against them. When Richard Rovere wrote his semi-facetious piece "The American Establishment" in 1962, which he described as "a more or less closed and self-sustaining institution that holds a preponderance of power in our more or less open society," it was populated almost entirely by WASPs. On the eve of the 2012 election, the blog the *Daily Beast* noted that for the first time in U.S. history there was no WASP on either of the major party presidential tickets: A black incumbent president, itself of course without precedent, and a Catholic vice president against a Mormon and a Catholic. It also noted that none of the major leaders in the federal government, not the Speaker of the time, John Boehner, or the president pro-tem of the Senate, Harry Reid, was a WASP. Nor was there a WASP among the nine justices of the Supreme Court. Until well after World War II, we used to talk about the Court's "Jewish Seat," occupied, most famously by Louis D. Brandeis and then his friend Felix Frankfurter, who also happened to be an immigrant from Vienna, albeit in an earlier era, both Zionists. In 2012, there were (and as of 2018 still were) three Jews on the court: Stephen Breyer, Ruth Bader Ginsburg, and Elena Kagan.[17]

It would be impossible to credit any of that to one single group or force; the Holocaust itself did much to discredit anti-Semitism, at least among the elites, though, as noted earlier, it took nearly two decades after the Nazis' defeat to end quotas at places like Yale and longer than that in many corporate boardrooms. But with the extraordinary talents and reputations so many German Jews brought with them and, in comparison to any prior generation of immigrants, their urbanity and cosmopolitanism—and because, as the historian Manfred Jonas said, "they did not on the whole, carry their Jewishness like a badge"—they "were able to penetrate American society more effectively and more rapidly than many other immigrant groups. . . . They quickly appeared in respectable numbers in the arts, the media, and the universities, and they joined social, cultural and even political associations in surprising numbers."

But as he also said, anything definable as "German-Jewishness" (whatever that might be) "seems to me a thing of the past."[18]

Yet, whoever suggested that there would ever be such a thing, anymore than there had been an American "Catholic Irishness" or a "Catholic Polishness" brought on by immigrant generations past? The German-Jewish impact was significant precisely because it blended so easily into—and so smoothly influenced—the American culture that evolved after the war, a culture and a society that have been partially purged of their provincialism and xenophobia, and have slowly become a little less insular. American cosmopolitanism suffered a severe blow in the years after the election of 2016, but the nation has suffered, and recovered from, similar setbacks before.

Neither Hitler's refugees, nor even the horrors of the Nazi genocide were the only elements in the evolution of that postwar world or of the globalism, the war crimes laws, and the moral standards that are now part of it, however much they're currently disregarded. Nonetheless, they were certainly an element in that development. A good part of the contemporary argument in the West for the admission of Syrians and other Middle Eastern refugees uses the West's callousness toward the European Jews in the Hitler years as a shameful example of policies that should never be repeated. The xenophobic and nativist arguments against admitting refugees from the Middle East echo the arguments made three-fourths of a century ago against admission of the Hitler refugees: for saboteurs and fifth columnists, read terrorists; for communists, read Muslims.

It's been nearly three centuries since Benjamin Franklin warned that Pennsylvania was becoming a "Colony of Aliens who will shortly be so numerous as to Germanize us instead of our Anglifying them and will never adopt our Language or Customs any more than they can acquire our Complexion."[19] A few years later, Jefferson worried about immigrants from foreign monarchies who "will infuse into American legislation their spirit, warp its direction and render it a heterogeneous, incoherent, distracted mass."[20] No need to say that while there was bilingual instruction in the schools of Pennsylvania during the colonial era (and again) in the American Midwest in the years before World War I, the country has never been Germanized or Italianized, never been overrun by unreconstructed monarchists (or communists or Muslims imposing Sharia law).

America had its years, even decades, when, in Arthur Schlesinger's words, it had too much pluribus and not enough unum. Much of the country is now bilingual. But so is Canada, and Switzerland is tri-lingual, which are two of the most stable and successful nations on earth. But generally it's been the uncommon genius of America, this sometimes self-proclaimed nation of immigrants, to assimilate and acculturate its newcomers even as they have acculturated it. Because of their high level of education and worldliness, that's probably been even more emphatically true of the Hitler refugees and survivors than for any generation of immigrants since the mid-nineteenth century. In part, the Nazis made it a bit more easy: Despite their first misgivings about the crudeness of American culture, there could never have been a contrast as stark between the regime they escaped and the one that greeted them when they arrived. More important, as a great many writers pointed out, in contrast to many other places, the immigrants could be wholeheartedly Jewish and American at the same time. Unlike even the best years in the Weimar era, or any other time in Germany, in America there was little tension between them.

Countering that assessment, the historian Jack Wertheimer offered an unequivocal dissent. In the face of the strong possibility among all American Jews of over-assimilation and forgetting that one was Jewish altogether, the history of Jews in Germany was a dark cautionary tale. "For a while German Jews assimilated in an unprecedented manner," he wrote. "And then they were punished brutally. . . . German Jews were taught a lesson by the Nazis that all Jews must remember: assimilation cannot work; the only protection Jews have is to concern themselves with the fate of their coreligionists . . . escape from Jewishness is impossible."[21] For a great many Jews, that sense was probably among the most important reasons for their unwavering support of Israel, even as its governments veered ever farther to the right and away from the democratic-socialist idealism of its founders. But it also seemed to reinforce Arendt's argument that as long as the Jews had no state of their own, their rights were always at risk.

*

There was hope for another form of unity in the dream of a united postwar Europe, a United States of Europe, that had been advanced by the Hungarian politician Richard Nikolaus Eijiro, Count of Coudenhove-Kalergi, as early as 1923 with his book *Pan Europa* and his "Pan European Union" organization to which it led and which were widely credited as the ideological base of European integration.

Aufbau first took up the idea in 1940. In 1942, in the middle of the war, Wilfred Hulse wrote about the need for the world's nations to yield some of their sovereignty to an international organization, first in Europe and then globally. "It was the only way," he wrote, "to end the burden of nationalism. . . . It would be something entirely new and unprecedented, and the only guarantee of peace in the world."[22] *Aufbau* covered Eijiro's campaign and the growing international support for a European union more intensely in the years immediately following the war, both with staff-written pieces and with guest articles by people like FDR's former Interior Secretary Harold Ickes, always an *Aufbau* favorite.[23] It was tragic, Einstein wrote in his message to *Aufbau*'s memorial service for FDR after the president's death in 1945, that "he wasn't able engage his unique abilities in the solution of the problems of international security, and tragic especially for us Jews that this man with his acute sense of justice did not live long enough for the decisive negotiations that would determine [the future] for our sorely tested people."[24] When the first meetings of the UN took place in 1946, Manfred George endorsed the hope that eventually it would evolve from a league of sovereign states into a world government.[25] A European Union was the first big step.

Given their experience in the 1930s and 1940s, a great many Hitler refugees were taken with the idea. This was the best way to prevent any recurrence of German aggression, the best way to prevent yet another 1914 and another 1939 and, very likely, the likeliest resolution of the refugees' ambivalence about identity. The way not to be a German—either present or former, West or East— and to celebrate your historic *Kultur* was to be, or have been, a European. Pan-Europe promised to do away with many of the horrors associated with the prewar period: the terror of national borders and the layers of officialdom and documentation associated with them—the passports and visas, the douaniers, the stops at every frontier post, the inspection of baggage, eventually, maybe, even to end the need to change francs, French, Belgian, Luxembourg, into deutschmarks, or lire into guilder in entering every new country. That the last, as it was finally established—a single currency without the fiscal institutions to manage it—might become a dubiously and possibly dangerous excessive economic indulgence didn't dampen the enthusiasm of the European leaders that led to it. "Europe with its military customs officials and passport scrutinizers," Thomas Mann had written during a brief vacation in Holland in 1939, "seems to us narrow, overcrowded and ill-tempered."[26]

What was certain is that even as they were Americanized and assimilated into American life (with, in the words of one contemporary, "a speed and thoroughness unparalleled in the history of immigration"),[27] the refugees and their children became voices both for a new cosmopolitan outlook in America and Europe and evidence of the terrible damage that xenophobia and provincialism could inflict. Because they were seamlessly part of so many other things— as Americans, as Holocaust survivors, as former Europeans, as mainstays of the Western culture that they helped bring to the New World—there is no way to isolate their impact from all the other things they are part of. But there can

hardly be much doubt that, as much as any prior generation of American immigrants, and perhaps more, they enlarged that New World, and often the old
as well. For America, as for many other parts of the twenty-first century neo-
nationalist world—the world of ISIS, of Brexit, of Trump, Assad, Putin, Mugabe,
Duterte, and the world's other despots—perhaps the most urgent hope is that
the sensibilities and outlook that Hitler's refugees brought to the world and the
lessons of their time will never be forgotten.

Sources and Acknowledgments

Given the centrality of *Aufbau* to the concerns, life, and culture of German-speaking immigrants in the Hitler years and in the decades after the war, it's surprising that the paper hasn't gotten more attention. It's particularly surprising because the rich social and educational background of that generation made it almost unique in the history of American immigration over the past one-and-a-half centuries.

There have been a number of insightful academic studies, among them Dagobert Broh, "The History of the Newspaper *Aufbau*, 1934–1948" (unpublished doctoral dissertation in the Department of History at Concordia University, Montreal), and Anne Clara Schenderlein, "'Germany on Their Minds'? German Jewish Refugees in the United States and Relationships to Germany, 1938–1988" (unpublished doctoral dissertation in the Department of History, University of California, San Diego). Both have been extremely helpful in my research for this book.

But no one, to my knowledge, has used the paper itself as a window into or as a guide to the generation of German-speaking immigrants to which it was addressed during the seventy years of its publication. I'm grateful to Jüdische Medien AG in Zurich for granting me the rights to reproduce some of its pages as illustrations in this book. I'm especially indebted to the Leo Baeck Institute in New York, which has digitized every issue of the paper and has thousands of telling letters and memoirs of German exiles. And I'm particularly appreciative to LBI archivists Frank Mecklenburg and Michael Simonson for their unending encouragement and assistance.

I also drew on many other published sources, many of which are cited in the notes. Those I found particularly helpful are Steven M. Lowenstein, *Frankfurt on the Hudson*; Abraham J. Peck, ed., *The German-Jewish Legacy in America, 1938–1988: From Bildung to the Bill of Rights*; Will Schaber, ed., *Aufbau Reconstruction: Dokumente einer Kultur im Exil*; Mark W. Anderson, *Hitler's Exiles: Personal Stories of the Flight from Nazi Germany to America*; Valerie Popp, *"Aber hier war alles anders . . .": Amerikabilder der deutschsprachigen Exilliteratur nach 1939 in den USA*; Ruth E. Wolman, *Crossing Over: An Oral History of Refugees from Hitler's Reich*; David S. Wyman, *The Abandonment of the Jews: America and the Holocaust, 1941–1945*; Jean Michel Palmier, *Weimar in Exile: The Antifascist Emigration in Europe and America*; Anthony Heilbut, *Exiled in Paradise: German Refugee Artists and Intellectuals in America from the 1930s to the Present*; Paul Mendes-Flohr, *German Jews: A Dual Identity*; Walter Laqueur, *Generation Exodus: The Fate of Young Jewish Refugees from Nazi Germany*; Timothy Snyder, *Black Earth: The Holocaust as History and Warning*.

Additional sources include Maurice R. Davie, *Refugees in America: Report of the Committee for the Study of Recent Immigration from Europe*, published in 1947; Jeffrey S. Gurock, ed., *American Jewish Life* (volume 4 in *American Jewish History*); William B. Helmreich, *Against All Odds: Holocaust Survivors and the Successful Lives They Made in America*; Hannah Arendt, *Eichmann in Jerusalem: A Report on the Banality of Evil* and *The Origins of Totalitarianism*; Erich Maria Remarque, *The Night in Lisbon*; Anna Seghers, *Transit*; Peter Schrag, *Not Fit for Our Society: Immigration and Nativism in America*; Otto Schrag and Peter Schrag, *When Europe Was a Prison Camp: Father and Son Memoirs, 1940–1941*; Marcel Bervoets, *La Liste de Saint-Cyprien*; Hildegard Bachert, *A Memoir*; Lion Feuchtwanger, *The Devil in France: My Encounter with Him in the Summer of 1940*; Varian Fry, *Surrender on Demand*; Sheila Isenberg, *A Hero of Our Own: The Story of Varian Fry*; Lisa Fittko, *Escape through the Pyrenees*; Ronald Weber, *The Lisbon Route: Entry and Escape in Nazi Europe*; Neill Lochery, *Lisbon: War in the Shadows of the City of Light, 1939–1945*; Elisabeth Marum-Lunau, *Auf der Flucht in Frankreich: "Boches ici, Juifs là-bas"*; Ludwig Marum, *Briefe aus dem Konzentrationslager Kislau*; Susan Zuccotti, *The Holocaust, the French and the Jews*.

In addition I relied on interviews and conversations with surviving Hitler-era refugees who came to this country as children or teenagers, among them Hildegard Bachert, the art scholar and gallery owner; Marion Lust-Cohen, who had worked for Selfhelp; Veronica Kaufman; and, of course, my own recollections. Deidre Cooney Bonifaz's essay about the émigrés who were guests at Morning Star Farm ("A Haven in Whately") and my conversations with her also provided important background. I'm also grateful to my long-long-ago student associate Werner Gundersheimer for permission to quote from his unpublished memoir. And I'm indebted to Caroline Waddell Koehler and her colleagues at the United States Holocaust Memorial Museum for the use of photos in their archives; to Marina Mahler for permission to use the photo of Franz Werfel and her grandmother, Alma Mahler; and to the Library of Congress for the use of a number of photos in its vast collection.

I also want to thank my longtime agent and friend, Ellen Levine, for her belief in this project at a shaky time for book publishing and for putting up with my impatience and sticking with me. Also I'm indebted to Professor Marion Kaplan of New York University and, again, to Frank Mecklenburg of the Leo Baeck Institute, both for their encouragement and for their very helpful comments on an early draft of this book. Finally a special thanks to Patricia Ternahan, who edited and massaged the illustrations, read various drafts, and never ceased to believe in this project when I was almost ready to give up. As so often in the past, she was right.

Notes

The first epigraph on page v comes from an email from Max Frankel to me. Frankel, born in Germany, arrived in New York with his parents as a refugee in 1940. He was a career journalist and executive editor of *The New York Times* from 1986 to 1994. The second epigraph is from Hans Steinitz, "Aufbau, Neubau, Brückenbau," in Will Schaber, ed., *Aufbau Reconstruction: Dokumente einer Kultur im Exil* (New York: Overlook Press, 1972), 14.

Introduction

1. Maurice R. Davie, *Refugees in America: Report of the Committee for the Study of Recent Immigration from Europe* (New York: Harper, 1947), 23. The numbers, based on an analysis of federal data from the U.S. Immigration and Naturalization Service, are the most credible I've been able to find.

2. Tekla Szymanski, "Aufbau: Unser Aller Tagebuch" (Our Everybody's Diary), at http://www.tekla-szymanski.com/deutsch/germ14aufbau.html (accessed October 2016).

3. Ludwig Wronkow, "The Circulation of the *Aufbau*," *Aufbau*, December 22, 1944, pp. 27–28. His estimate, as suited any circulation manager, was almost certainly too optimistic.

4. Dagobert Broh, "The History of the Newspaper *Aufbau*, 1934–1948" (PhD thesis, Montreal, Concordia University, 1996), 99. The numbers are from the Audit Bureau of Circulations.

5. Quoted in Szymanski, "Aufbau."

6. Hannah Arendt, *Eichmann in Jerusalem: A Report on the Banality of Evil* (New York: Penguin, 1977), 58–59. Robert Weltsch was then the editor of the semi-weekly *Jüdische Rundschau* in Berlin.

7. See, e.g., Oscar Handlin, "Jewish Resistance to the Nazis," *Commentary*, November 1, 1962.

8. Manfred George, "Why We Publish *Aufbau*," *Aufbau*, December 22, 1944, p. 17.

9. "10 Commandments for New Immigrants," *Aufbau*, November 1, 1936, p. 6.

10. Wilfred C. Hulse, "Emigrant Jews and German Culture," *Aufbau*, January 26, 1940, p. 3.

11. Manfred George, "A Serious Question," *Aufbau*, January 1, 1939, p. 2.

12. Hans Steinitz, "Aufbau, Neubau, Brückenbau," in Schaber, *Aufbau Reconstruction*, 16.

13. Even the name change wasn't easy. In the November 1, 1940, issue of *Aufbau*, his name appeared both as Manfred George and Manfred Georg.

14. *Aufbau*, August 16, 1940, p. 11.

15. "Interview with Carey McWilliams," *Aufbau*, May 14, 1943, p. 15. Culbert Olson, a one-term governor, was the only Democrat elected to that office in California in the twentieth century before 1958.

16. This is a fearfully complex issue, factually and morally: Was it ever justified if, in order to save some, an organization betrayed others? Could any deal with the SS ever be trusted? What, under the dreadful conditions that confronted the Jewish leaders in Budapest, could be done? For an extended discussion, see, e.g., Randolph L. Braham, *The Politics of Genocide: The Holocaust in Hungary* (Detroit: Wayne State University Press, 2000), 74 ff.

17. "You're Not a German Anymore," *Aufbau*, January 9, 1942, p. 1. My parents and I were officially denaturalized in 1940.

18. Herbert R. Strauss, "Interview with Felix Guggenheim," January 6, 1972, DigiBaeck, Leo Baeck Institute Oral Histories, https://www.lbi.org/digibaeck/results /?term=Felix Guggenheim&qtype=basic&dtype=any&filter=All&paging=2 (accessed December 2017). Hillel Aron, "The Forgotten History of LA's Forgotten Exiles, Which Included Bertolt Brecht and Thomas Mann," *LA Weekly*, August 20, 2016.

19. It was "'All quiet' on the front of our foreign-born movie colony," wrote Hans Kafka, in "Hollywood Calling," *Aufbau*, September 14, 1945, p. 16.

20. Sigrid Schneider, "The German Press in Parisian Exile" (book review), *Aufbau*, April 8, 1988, p. 26.

21. "Our Boys Club," *Aufbau*, December 4, 1942, p. 4.

22. "Berlin-Vladivostok-Yokohama-New York," *Aufbau*, August 9, 1940, p. 3.

23. "Negro Jews in Harlem," *Aufbau*, June 14, 1940, p. 10.

24. "We're driving (traveling) to the Bear Mountains." There were no "Bear Mountains," only Bear Mountain, a popular weekend destination for New Yorkers.

25. Skat, the three-player game, is apparently still among the most popular card games in Germany.

26. Vera Craener, "U.S.A. Profile: Julius Rosenwald," *Aufbau*, July 26, 1940, p. 7.

27. E.g., Rudolph Stahl, "Immigration into the USA," *Aufbau*, November 1, 1938, p. 6; *Aufbau*, March 1, 1939, p. 1.

28. "The Truth about Refugee Immigration," *Aufbau*, July 15, 1939, p. 1; David S. Wyman, *The Abandonment of Jews: America and the Holocaust, 1941–1945* (New York: The New Press, 2007).

29. "The Truth about Refugee Immigration," p. 1.

30. "Charles Osner, Typewriters," ad, *Aufbau*, September 5, 1941, p. 17; James Barron, "Mary Adelman, 89, Fixer of Broken Typewriters, Is Dead," *New York Times*, November 24, 2017.

31. *Aufbau*, March 1, 1940, p. 7. Lippmann was offering new suits for $37.50 and alterations to suits and overcoats to conform to American styles.

32. Frank Rice, "Swim American," *Aufbau*, February 23, 1940, p. 6.

33. *Aufbau*, November 20, 1987, p. 20.

34. "Appeal . . . Give Quickly, Give a Lot," ad, *Aufbau*, September 5, 1941, p. 21.

35. "In the Camps of the Refugees—Reports of American Journalists," *Aufbau*, April 4, 1941, p. 1.

36. "Release from Gurs—$25," *Aufbau*, February 7, 1941, p. 1. Many of the inmates at Gurs, though hardly all, were German Jews who had been driven out of the Rhineland by the Nazis—in essence deported to France, which of course didn't want them.

37. Robert Kempner, "The Situation in Gurs," *Aufbau*, December 6, 1940, p. 2. Three hundred dollars in 1940 was roughly the equivalent of $3,600 in 2014.

38. Lion Feuchtwanger, *The Devil in France: My Encounter with Him in the Summer of 1940* (New York: Viking, 1941), 220–21.

39. "An Exchange of Letters," *Aufbau*, March 15, 1940, p. 3. Hulse was then identified as the chairman of the "*Aufbau* Committee."

40. *Aufbau*, May 24, 1940, p. 2.

41. E.g., "Freedom's Battle against Hitler," *Aufbau*, January 31, 1941; "An Important Jewish War Goal," *Aufbau*, February 7, 1941, p. 4.

42. "Kaddish for the Dead President," *Aufbau*, April 27, 1945, p. 7.

43. Grace Tully, "FDR Was My Boss," *Aufbau*, February 24, 1950, p. 1. Other installments followed.

44. Bernard Postal, "Thomas Jefferson, to Whom All Men Were Equal," *Aufbau*, April 9, 1943, p. 8.

45. Wilfred C. Hulse, "Homesickness," *Aufbau*, September 6, 1940, p. 7.

46. Tekla Szymanski, "*Aufbau*: Our Common Diary," in *Jüdischer Almanach* (Frankfurt: Suhrkamp, 2005), 108.

47. Quoted in Niall Ferguson, *Kissinger, 1923–1968: The Idealist* (New York: Penguin, 2015), 164.

48. George, "Toward the Southeast—The March to Palestine," *Aufbau*, November 9, 1945, p. 3.

49. *Aufbau*, May 21, 1948.

50. *Aufbau*, June 9, 1967, p. 1; *Aufbau*, June 16, 1967, p. 1.

51. "The Furtwängler Case," *Aufbau*, April 18, 1947, p. 1.

52. In one of the odder pieces on Furtwängler, headed "Enough of the Furtwängler Swindle," the Swiss writer Otto Maag charged that the conductor's orchestras were full of Gestapo spies. *Aufbau*, March 22, 1946, p. 32.

53. E.g., Robert Weltsch, "The Last 'Big' Nazi," *Aufbau*, April 19, 1946, p. 9.

54. Ernest Landau, "The Fiasco of De-Nazification," *Aufbau*, June 10, 1949, p. 25.

55. Kurt Grossmann, "The International Red Cross and the Jews," *Aufbau*, June 11, 1948, p. 5.

56. Josef Burstin, "Yiddish Theatre News," *Aufbau*, January 15, 1943, p. 11.

57. "Letters to the Editor," *Aufbau*, January 5, 1940, p. 11.

58. Jan Logemann, Andreas Joch, Corinna Ludwig, Ashley Narayan, and Barbara Reiterer, "Transatlantic Perspectives: Europe in the Eyes of European Immigrants to the United States, 1930–1980," *Bulletin of the German Historical Institute* 48 (Spring 2011): 85.

Chapter 1. A Community of Fate

1. Among them, Otto Schrag, my father, in 1940–41.

2. Werner Gundersheimer, *Coming Across: A Child's Odyssey* (copy of unpublished memoir provided to author, © 2012 by Werner Gundersheimer).

3. *Aufbau*, June 30, 1944, p. 15.

4. See, e.g., "Places on Ships and Rescue Work," *Aufbau*, August 22, 1941, p. 5.

5. A reporter who visited the ship before its departure from Lisbon described "the acute suffering for the majority of the passengers due to the overcrowding, the insufficient crew and the complete inadequacy of the ship's sanitary, cooking, sleeping and health facilities. Many passengers were already suffering from the poor quality of the food and water, and all were affected by the lack of sufficient sanitary facilities." "Refugee Ship Navemar Sails from Lisbon for Cuba and New York," Jewish Telegraph Agency, August 18, 1941.

6. Henry James, *The American Scene* (Boston: Harper Brothers, 1907), 84.

7. Liane Gutman, "Memoir," in Robert B. Kahn, ed., *Reflections of Jewish Survivors from Mannheim* (New York: Mannheim Reunion Committee, June 1990).

8. Hans Nanotek, "Last Day in Europe," *Aufbau*, April 4, 1941, p. 9.

9. Varian Fry, *Surrender on Demand* (New York: Random House, 1945), 170–78, 189–91; Sheila Isenberg, *A Hero of Our Own: The Story of Varian Fry* (New York: Random House, 2001), 165–69.

10. Gundersheimer, *Coming Across*; Peter Gay, *Die Republik der Aussenseiter; Geist und Kultur in der Weimarer Zeit, 1918–1933* (Frankfurt: S. Fischer Verlag, 1960); Peter Gay, "The German-Jewish Legacy—and I: Some Personal Reflections," in Abraham J. Peck, ed., *The German-Jewish Legacy in America, 1938–1988* (Detroit: Wayne State University, 1989), 17.

11. Günter Gaus, "In Person," German television interview with Hannah Arendt (1964) at https://www.youtube.com/watch?v=J9SyTEUi6Kw (accessed November 2016).

12. Judy Hodgkiss, "Einstein's Friend, Walter Rathenau: The Agapic Personality in Politics and Personality," *The Schiller Institute*, June 2012, http://www.schillerinstitute .org/educ/hist/2012/rathenau.html (accessed November 2016).

13. Paul Mendes-Flohr, *German Jews: A Dual Identity* (New Haven: Yale University Press, 1999), 63, 91.

14. Born letter to Einstein, June 2, 1933, https://archive.org/stream/TheBornEin steinLetters/Born-TheBornEinsteinLetters_djvu.txt (accessed December 2017).

15. And, in testimony to the reflexes of bureaucracies, on the list of internees at the French concentration camp at Saint-Cyprien, the only middle names were Israel. The French had simply used the racist appellation that their erstwhile German foes had given Jews.

16. "Involuntary German Nationals," *Aufbau*, December 5, 1941, p. 4.

17. Ludwig Haas died in 1930, before he could see how prophetic his advice was.

18. Joseph Tanfani, "Donald Trump Warns That Syrian Refugees Present 'A Great Trojan Horse' to the U.S.," *Los Angeles Times*, October 19, 2016.

19. Wyman, *The Abandonment of the Jews*, 5.

20. Henry Pachter, "On Being an Exile," *Salmagundi* 10–11 (Fall 1969–Winter 1970): 12–51.

21. "In the Last Minute of the Election Campaign," *Aufbau*, November 1, 1936, p. 4.

22. Gundersheimer, *Coming Across*.

23. Y.W.C.A. National Board, *Public Affairs News Service*, series 3, bulletin 7, March 23, 1939.

24. Hilde Walter, "Everything Is Always Different," letter, March 3, 1941, in Mark M. Anderson, *Hitler's Exiles: Personal Stories of the Flight from Nazi Germany to America* (New York: The New Press, 1998), 224.

25. Fred K. Hoehler, *Europe's Homeless Millions*, Foreign Policy Association Headlines Series no. 54 (November–December 1945).

26. The Fry and Fittko stories are dramas in their own right. For more: Fry, *Surrender on Demand*; Isenberg, *A Hero of Our Own*; Lisa Fittko, *Escape through the Pyrenees* (Evanston: Northwestern University Press, 1991).

27. "They Took Hold and Did It," interview with Prof. Julius Hirsch, *Aufbau*, December 22, 1944, pp. 43–44.

28. Quoted in Edward Bahr, *Weimar on the Pacific: German Exile Culture in Los Angeles and the Crisis of Modernism* (Berkeley: University of California Press, 2007), 31.

29. For a brief introduction to Polanyi's work and influence, see Robert Kuttner, "The Man from Red Vienna," *New York Review of Books*, December 21, 2017, pp. 55–57.

30. Davie, *Refugees in America*, 437 ff. Among them, Fermi, Einstein, Pauli, Mann, and Otto Meyerhof. Not all on Davie's list were Jewish or refugees.

31. Hannah Arendt, "We Refugees," *Menorah Journal* 31 (1943): 69–77.

32. In the wartime summer of 1944 or 1945, I lived in a cabin provided by the American Friends Service Committee while doing farm work near Moorestown, New Jersey, and attended Quaker meetings. I was thirteen or fourteen at the time.

33. "Solidarity in Emigration?," *Aufbau*, January 1, 1937, p. 1.

34. Valerie Popp, *"Aber hier war alles Anders . . .": Amerikabilder der deutschsprachigen Exilliteratur nach 1939 in den USA* (Würzburg: Königshausen & Neumann, 2008), 60.

35. Henry Bierig, letter to Robert B. Kahn, October 22, 1989, *Mannheim Reunion Collection*, http://archive.org/stream/mannheimreunionf002#page/n9/mode/1up (accessed September 2016).

36. Davie, *Refugees in America*, 120.

37. W. Robert Rhee, "Work in the Fields," *Aufbau*, October 2, 1942, p. 16.

38. Selfhelp board meeting minutes, March 30, 1939, and November 30, 1939, among others in Selfhelp's archives, New York.

39. Michael E. Dobkowski, "A History of Selfhelp Community Services, Inc." (unpublished paper in the archives of SelfHelp, New York), p. 4.

40. Vera Craener, "Women Adapt," *Aufbau*, December 22, 1944, p. 26. My mother had gotten my father out of the French camp at Saint-Cyprien.

41. Hilde Scott, "Everyday Problems: Working in a Foreign Household," *Aufbau*, December 22, 1939, p. 11.

42. Wilfred C. Hulse, "Disappointment in New York," *Aufbau*, August 2, 1940, p. 9.

43. "Successful Immigrants," *Aufbau*, May 24, 1940, p. 13; "Refugees as Pioneers: New Methods, New Jobs," *Aufbau*, May 10, 1940, p. 2.

44. "Living Standards and Immigration," *Aufbau*, May 3, 1940, p. 5.

45. E.g., "Immigration and Unemployment," *Aufbau*, May 17, 1940, p. 7.

46. "Who Has Provided Work?," *Aufbau*, August 15, 1939, p. 12.

47. Alfred Gottschalk, "The German-Jewish Legacy: A Question of Fate," in Peck, *The German-Jewish Legacy in America*, 84.

48. Davie, *Refugees in America*, 86.

49. Quoted in Szymanski, *"Aufbau*: Our Common Diary."

50. Richard Dyck, "New Immigrants Learn English: Snapshots from a Language School," *Aufbau*, August 9, 1946, p. 24.

51. Helmut Pfanner, *Exile in New York: German and Austrian Writers after 1933* (Detroit: Wayne State University Press, 1983), 139 ff.

52. Carl Zuckmayer, "Amerika ist Anders," in Zuckmayer, *Die Langen Wege. Betrachtungen* (Frankfurt: Knut Beck and Maria Guttenbrunner-Zuckmayer, 1996), 172. Cited in Popp, *"Aber hier war alles Anders . . . ,"* 51.

53. Ibid.

54. Hildegard Bachert, *A Memoir* (New York: Galerie St. Etienne, 2010), 13.

55. Ludwig Marcuse, "Resisting America," from *Mein Zwanzigstes Jahrhundert* (Munich: Paul List Verlag, 1960), excerpted and translated in Anderson, *Hitler's Exiles*, 174.

56. Carol Ascher et al., "Fragments of a German-Jewish Heritage in Four 'Americans,'" in Peck, *The German-Jewish Legacy in America*, 182.

57. "Now or Never: The Historic Battle for Civil Rights," *Aufbau*, March 13, 1964; "All Men Are Created Equal," *Aufbau*, May 14, 1954, p. 1.

58. Werner Cahnman, "A German Jew in a Negro University," *Aufbau*, April 19, 1946, p. 19.

59. Guy Stern, "German Culture, Jewish Ethics," in Peck, *The German-Jewish Legacy in America*, 30.

60. Bruno Frank, "Jews Must Retain the German Language," *Aufbau*, December 27, 1940, p. 9.

61. See, e.g. Benjamin Lapp, "The Newspaper *Aufbau*, Its Evolving Politics and the Problem of German-Jewish Identity, 1939–55," in *Leo Baeck Institute Yearbook* 58 (2013): 161–74.

62. Albert Einstein, "Statement," *Aufbau*, December 27, 1940, p. 9.

63. Manfred Jonas, "A German-Jewish Legacy," in Peck, *The German-Jewish Legacy in America*, 55.

64. H. O. Gerngross, "Lincoln and the Jews," *Aufbau*, February 16, 1940, p. 3.

65. E. G. O., "Immigrants among One Another," *Aufbau*, June 1, 1939, p. 5.

66. Gottschalk, "The German-Jewish Legacy."

67. Carl Zuckmayer, "Call-up to Life," *Aufbau*, March 20, 1942, p. 3.

68. Popp, *"Aber hier war alles Anders . . . ,"* 62.

69. Quoted in Steven M. Lowenstein, *Frankfurt on the Hudson: The German-Jewish Community of Washington Heights, 1933–1983, Its Structure and Culture* (Detroit: Wayne State University Press, 1989), 50.

70. Interview with Heinz Pinner, conducted by Herbert A. Strauss, Los Angeles, January 1, 1972, LBI New York, AR 25385, Digibaeck, http://www.lbi.org/digibaeck /results/?qtype=pid&term=1331811. Cited in Anna Clara Schenderlein, "Germany on Their Minds? German Jewish Refugees in the United States and Their Relationships to Germany, 1938–1938" (unpublished dissertation, University of San Diego, 2014), p. 75.

71. "Immigrants—a Reorientation in Spirit," *Aufbau*, December 1, 1936, p. 1.

72. Ernest Stock, "From the American Scene: Washington Heights," *Commentary*, June 1, 1951.

73. Letter to Ludwig Strauss, September 11, 1912, in the Ludwig Strauss Archive in the Jewish National and University Library, Jerusalem. Quoted in Mendes-Flohr, *German Jews*, 52.

74. See, e.g., Hans Lamm, "Our Polish Brothers," *Aufbau*, April 5, 1940, p. 12.

75. Michael Wurmbrand, "Tilting against Windmills in the U.S.: An Attack on German-Speaking Jews," *Aufbau*, August 9, 1946, p. 21.

76. "To a Jew, this role of the Jewish leaders in the destruction of their own people is undoubtedly the darkest chapter of the whole dark story. [. . .] In the matter of co-operation, there was no distinction between the highly assimilated Jewish communities of Central and Western Europe and the Yiddish-speaking masses of the East. In Amsterdam as in Warsaw, in Berlin as in Budapest, Jewish officials could be trusted to compile the lists of persons and of their property." Arendt, *Eichmann in Jerusalem*, 117–18.

77. Oscar Maria Graf, "Germans against Nazis," *Aufbau*, September 15, 1940, p. 9.

78. Robert B. Goldmann, "The Wagner Question: Can Music Be Anti-Semitic?," *Aufbau*, July 19, 2001, p. 8.

79. *Aufbau*, July 6, 1945, p. 32.

80. Martin Gumpert, "Immigrants by Conviction," *Survey Graphic* 10 (September 1941): 487; cf. Martin Gumpert, *First Papers*, 1941, chap. 3. Cited in Davie, *Refugees in America*, 85.

81. Davie, *Refugees in America*, 373.

82. Milton Mayer, "The Case against the Jew," *Saturday Evening Post*, March 28, 1942. Manfred George, "The Case against *The Saturday Evening Post*" (in English) and "The Shot into the Mirror" (in German), *Aufbau*, April 3, 1942, p. 1.

83. Irving Howe, "The *Saturday Evening Post* Slanders the Jewish People," *Labor Action* 6, no. 14 (April 5, 1942): 4.

84. Charles Coughlin, untitled radio address, January 8, 1939, at Internet Archive, www.archive.org/details/Father_Couglin (accessed August 2009).

85. Charles A. Lindbergh, "Geography, Aviation and Race," *Reader's Digest* (November 1939), 64–67.

86. Author interviews with Marion Lust-Cohen, long-time Selfhelp worker, June 17, 2016, and October 1, 2016.

87. Alfred Gottschalk, "The German-Jewish Legacy: A Question of Fate," in Peck, *The German-Jewish Legacy in America*, 85.

88. Kurt Hellmer, "War Film in Yorkville," *Aufbau*, July 26, 1940.

89. Lowenstein, *Frankfurt on the Hudson*, 25.

90. "Café Éclair Guestbook, 1940–1992," in *Guide to the Papers of Alexander and Marianne Selinger, 1899–2000*, AR 25016, Leo Baeck Institute, http://digifindingaids.cjh.org/?pID =476073 (accessed November 2017).

91. Ascher et al., "Fragments of a German-Jewish Heritage in Four 'Americans,'" 180.

92. Among them, some of my relatives and friends of my parents.

93. Carl Zuckmayer, "A Part of Myself," in Anderson, *Hitler's Exiles*, 274.

94. Ibid.

95. Vera Craener, "Seeing Vicki Baum Again," *Aufbau*, April 24, 1942, p. 21.

96. "Victory Lingerie," *Life*, October 22, 1945, p. 89 ff.

97. Vera Craener, "'Rhapsody in Blue': Sky Blue Cotton Signifies 'Summertime,'" *Aufbau*, June 29, 1945, p. 20.

98. "Go West Young Immigrant," *Aufbau*, September 1, 1939, p. 17.

99. *Aufbau*, October 15, 1939, p. 12.

100. "Should I Go West?," *Aufbau*, May 14, 1943, p. 15.

101. "Information Here!," *Aufbau*, September 6, 1940, p. 8.

102. "Alaska Suggested as Haven by Ickes," *New York Times*, November 24, 1938. *New Horizons for Alaska: A Survey of Economic Conditions and Resources for Future Development of the Territory* (Washington: U.S. Department of the Interior, 1938), 73, https://archive .org/details/alaskaprojectcol1330unse (accessed September 2016).

103. Frank Bishop, "Alaska—Land of the Future," *Aufbau*, July 1, 1939, p. 11; "The Alaska Project Again Ripe for Discussion," *Aufbau*, September 1, 1939, p. 13.

104. "The Alaska Project Again Ripe for Discussion," 13.

105. James M. Mead, "Land of Hope," *Aufbau*, November 29, 1939, pp. 1, 15.

106. *Aufbau*, December 7, 1945, p. 3.

107. Richard Dyck, "On the Threshold of Freedom," *Aufbau*, January 18, 1946, p. 3; "The Fort Ontario Experiment: Did It Succeed?," *Aufbau*, February 1, 1946, p. 19.

108. *Aufbau*, January 26, 1940, p. 14. The Jewish Agricultural Society ad ran in many issues. Photo, *Aufbau*, February 2, 1940, p. 1; "The Good Earth," *Aufbau*, February 9, 1940.

109. Jewish Telegraph Agency, "Agriculture Society Stresses Need of Increasing Jewish Farm Population," March 5, 1941, http://www.jta.org/1941/03/06/archive /agriculture-society-stresses-need-of-increasing-jewish-farm-population (accessed June 2016).

110. "Jewish Farmers in America," *Aufbau*, May 2, 1947, p. 13.

111. Manfred George, "Wild West Today," *Aufbau*, September 17, 1950, p. 5; *Aufbau*, February 24, 1950, p. 15; *Aufbau*, April 7, 1950, p. 17.

112. Ted Malone, "The Story of Sgt. Eric G. Newhouse," *Aufbau*, September 15, 1944, p. 15. Newhouse, tail gunner in a Flying Fortress, apparently regarded every shot at an enemy plane as retribution for what the Nazis had done to his family before he fled, by a long circuitous route, to America.

113. Anna Seghers, *Transit* (New York: New York Review of Books, 2013), 38–39. *Transit* was first published in 1944. Seghers was also the author of *The Seventh Cross*, published in the United States in 1942 and the basis of a 1944 movie starring Spencer Tracy, both among the few depictions of concentration camps in either medium up to that time.

114. Part of my father's story, documented in his dossier from Saint-Cyprien. Otto Schrag and Peter Schrag, *When Europe Was a Prison Camp: Father and Son Memoirs, 1940–41* (Bloomington: Indiana University Press, 2015), 127.

115. From an affidavit relayed to the Emergency Rescue Committee, September 3,

1941, quoted in Elisabeth Marum-Lunau, *Auf Der Flucht in Frankreich: Boches ici, Juifs là-bas* (Teetz: Hentrich & Hentrich, 1997), 273.

116. S. Frohman ad, *Aufbau*, December 20, 1940, p. 7.

117. "Departures from Germany," *Aufbau*, September 15, 1939, p. 25.

118. "Mailbox," *Aufbau*, August 14, 1940, p. 7.

119. Gerald Holton and Gerhard Sonnert, "Younger, but Still Successful," *Aufbau*, February 16, 2004, p. 30. Holton, one of the great innovators in the teaching of college physics, was born in Berlin in 1922, got to England in one of the Kindertransports in 1938, and came to the United States in 1941. Holton and Sonnert are the authors of *What Happened to the Children Who Fled Nazi Persecution* (New York: Palgrave Macmillan, 2006) and other studies of the "second wave" of young immigrants.

120. Sam Roberts, "Vera Katz, Mayor Who Oversaw Portland's Flowering, Dies at 84," *New York Times*, December 13, 2017.

121. Harry Ettlinger, "Ein Amerikaner" (unpublished memoir, 2002, in the archives of the Leo Baeck Institute), p. 23, http://collections.ushmm.org/search/catalog /irn517818 (accessed August 2016).

122. Ernest Stock, "From the American Scene." This was Kissinger's high school.

123. Davie, *Refugees in America*, 164.

124. Lowenstein, *Frankfurt on the Hudson*, 126.

125. Peter Gay, "On Becoming an American," *Salmagundi* (Winter 1976/77).

Chapter 2. A Generation with Double Vision, 1933–41

1. Wilfred Hulse, "Jewish Emigrants and German Culture," *Aufbau*, January 26, 1940, p. 3.

2. Peter Mayer, "Reflections on Aufbau's Handbook for Immigrants," *Aufbau*, February 26, 2004, p. 40. This seventieth anniversary edition was, in fact, a kind of swan song for the paper, which died almost immediately after.

3. *Aufbau*, August 18, 1950, p. 7.

4. *Aufbau*, July 26, 1946, p. 6.

5. Gaus, "In Person."

6. Hans Steinitz, "Aufbau, Neubau, Brückenbau," 13.

7. "Five Years Aufbau," *Aufbau*, November 29, 1939, p. 2. The piece bore the initials of Wilfred Hulse, both a regular columnist and a leader in its parent German-Jewish Club.

8. "An Explanation," *Aufbau*, January 1, 1935, p. 1.

9. "In Celebration of the Heine Memorial," *Aufbau*, February 1, 1935, p. 1.

10. "Herod the Great," *Aufbau*, May 1, 1935, p. 6.

11. Joseph Maier, "Jewish Youth in America," *Aufbau*, August 22, 1941, p. 12. Maier, who was born in Leipzig in 1911 and came to the United States in 1933, would become a translator and interrogator of a number of high ranking Nazis at the Nuremberg war crimes trials and later a distinguished sociologist at Rutgers.

12. "Observations on the Party Meeting in Nuremberg," *Aufbau*, October 1, 1935, p. 5.

13. "Illegal Report from Germany," *Aufbau*, November 1, 1935, p. 1.

14. "Forced Labor for Germany's Jews," *Aufbau*, October 15, 1939, p. 1.

15. "Following Stettin-Königsberg—Nazis Must Pay," *Aufbau*, February 23, 1940, p. 1; "Nine Hundred East Prussian Jews Frozen to Death," *Aufbau*, March 1, 1940, p. 1.

16. Grossmann, "From Countries of Persecution to Safety: 25 Years' Refugee Problem" (unpublished manuscript in Leo Baeck Institute, Kurt Grossmann Collection), http://archive.org/stream/kurtgrossmanncol20gros#page/n0/mode/1up (accessed December 2017), p. 17.

17. Wyman, *The Abandonment of Jews*, 321. A fuller (though somewhat myopic) account is in Laurel Leff, *Buried by the Times: The Holocaust and America's Most Important Newspaper* (New York: Cambridge University Press, 2005). But oddly enough, Wyman, while often citing "the Jewish press" in his 458-page book, never mentions *Aufbau*, which covered virtually every facet of this story.

18. "Mass Extermination of Jews Confirmed," *Aufbau*, July 7, 1944, p. 1.

19. "Crisis in France" and "Panic in Warsaw," *Aufbau*, August 21, 1942, p. 1; "Internment of All Jews in France," *Aufbau*, September 11, 1942, p. 1; "Laval as Hitler's Lackey," *Aufbau*, September 11, 1942, p. 3. Laval, a career politician and one-time socialist, was head of Vichy's collaborationist government at the time.

20. "Reversal in Twelve Hours," *Aufbau*, October 1, 1936, p. 1.

21. "The 'Neutral' *New Yorker Staats-Zeitung*?," *Aufbau*, December 1, 1935, p. 5; "Is the *Staats-Zeitung* Nazi? A Necessary Discussion," *Aufbau*, February 9, 1940, p. 1.

22. "The 'Neutral' *New Yorker Staats-Zeitung*"; "Again, Our Dear *Staats-Zeitung*," *Aufbau*, April 1, 1936, p. 5.

23. "The *Staats-Zeitung* on a New Path," *Aufbau*, December 1, 1938, p. 6.

24. *Aufbau*, February 1, 1939, p. 1.

25. Alan Cranston, "Where Does the Foreign Language Press Stand," *Aufbau*, August 28, 1942, p. 5. Cranston, then head of the Foreign Division of the OWI, later became a U.S. Senator from California.

26. "What's the *Staats-Zeitung* Trying to Prove: A Strange Article on the Model-Ghetto Theresienstadt," *Aufbau*, October 5, 1945, p. 32.

27. Manfred George, "Charlie Chaplin in 'The Great Dictator,'" *Aufbau*, October 18, 1940, p. 9.

28. "Concerning the Label 'Emigrant,'" in John Willett and Ralph Manheim, eds., *Bertolt Brecht Poems, 1913–1956* (London: Methuen, 1987), 301.

29. "Immigrants—a Reorientation in Spirit," *Aufbau*, December 1, 1936, p. 1.

30. Manfred George, "Why We Established *Aufbau*," *Aufbau*, December 22, 1944, p. 17.

31. Thomas Mann, "Time and Patience," *Aufbau*, November 29, 1939, p. 1.

32. Thomas Mann, "The Prize of Peace," *Aufbau*, December 18, 1942, p. 5.

33. "The Big Test," *Aufbau*, November 1, 1938, p. 1.

34. *Aufbau*, December 1, 1938, pp. 5, 7; *Aufbau*, March 1, 1939, p. 6.

35. Harold L. Ickes, "Make Democracy Work to Halt Intolerance" and "I Will Never Forget You, St. Louis," *Aufbau*, June 15, 1939, p. 1.

36. Stahl, "Immigration into the USA."

37. "Letter from Cuba," *Aufbau*, September 1, 1939, p. 15.

38. "'The Alien Horde,'" *Aufbau*, January 26, 1940, p. 3.

39. Peter Schrag, *Not Fit for Our Society: Immigration and Nativism in America* (Berkeley: University of California Press, 2010), 14, 212–13.

40. *Aufbau*, September 4, 1942, pp. 14–15.

41. Deirdre Bonifaz, "A Haven in Whately: The Refugees Who Came to Our Farm," in Peter L. Rose, *The Dispossessed: An Anatomy of Exile* (Amherst: University of

Massachusetts Press, 2005), 203–33. Jimmy Cooney, a passionate pacifist, was the publisher, editor, and printer (on a hand press) of a literary magazine, *The Phoenix*, that published some of the early works of the novelists Henry Miller and Jean Giono and the diarist Anaïs Nin. My father was one of their guests. Later the Cooneys became life-long friends.

42. *"Aufbau* Summer Resort Guide" and "How Much Do I Tip?," *Aufbau,* June 18, 1943, pp. 13, 18.

43. "A Report from Hell," *Aufbau,* July 1, 1939, p. 5.

44. Ludwig Marcuse, "Love or Hate?," *Aufbau,* August 15, 1939, p. 7.

45. "With the First Settlers," *Aufbau,* May 17, 1940, p. 10. The Evian Conference, prompted by FDR, had been organized to try to find places for the hundreds of thousands of Jews trying to escape Hitler. The Dominican Republic and Costa Rica were the only countries that agreed to take any. In fact, the number of Jews emigrating to the Dominican Republic never got much greater than the five hundred families.

46. "15,000 Alsatian Jews on the Road," *Aufbau,* August 16, 1940, p. 1; "Shipped to Southern France," *Aufbau,* November 1, 1940, p. 1.

47. Goldmann, "World Crises and Judaism," *Aufbau,* August 23, 1940, p. 1.

48. EDI, "Nazism," *Aufbau,* April 1, 1936, p. 6.

49. "Bonn Readies a Law against Lying about the Holocaust," *Aufbau,* April 12, 1985, p. 3.

50. Robert A. Khan, "Why Do Europeans Ban Hate Speech? A Debate between Karl Loewenstein and Robert Post," *Hofstra Law Review* 41, no. 3 (2013): 545–84.

51. Aryeh Neier, "Engagement and the German-Jewish Legacy," in Peck, *The German-Jewish Legacy in America,* 117–20.

52. Henry Cabot Lodge, "Lynch Law and Unrestricted Immigration," *North American Review* 152, no. 414 (May 1891): 609.

53. *Aufbau,* February 16, 1940, p. 1; *Aufbau,* February 23, 1940, p. 3.

54. S. Aufhäuser, "What Is a Closed Shop?," *Aufbau,* September 6, 1940, p. 17.

55. "The Presidential Election," *Aufbau,* October 18, 1940, p. 4.

56. Wilfred Hulse, "Democracy versus Dictatorship," *Aufbau,* July 26, 1940, p. 9.

57. E.g., "Enough Groping Around in the Past," Willkie ad, *Aufbau,* November 1, 1940, p. 3.

58. "Who Still Doesn't Have 'First Papers'?," *Aufbau,* May 24, 1940, p. 3.

59. In 1964, however, *Aufbau* published an interview with Sen. Margaret Chase Smith of Maine about her intention to run for president. "A Woman Will Become President," *Aufbau,* February 7, 1964, p. 7.

60. W. M. Citron, ed., *Aufbau Almanac: The Immigrant's Handbook* (New York: German-Jewish Club, 1941).

61. Manfred George, "Selected Out—This War, Too," *Aufbau,* September 15, 1939, p. 1.

62. George, "Selected Out" and "Our Stand in the War against Hitler," *Aufbau,* September 15, 1939, pp. 1, 2.

63. "FIVE MILLION Jews Are Under Fire in the German-Russian War," *Aufbau,* June 27, 1941, p. 1.

64. Curt Riess, "Thomas Mann—Interview," *Aufbau,* June 7, 1940, p. 7.

65. "The Falling Veil," *Aufbau,* September 15, 1939, p. 4.

66. *Aufbau,* October 1, 1939, p. 1.

67. "The 'Stürmer' about the Nazi Crimes in Poland," *Aufbau*, November 1, 1939, p. 3. The *Stürmer*, the Nazi paper, *Aufbau* said, was celebrating the murder of Jews in Poland.

68. W. M. Citron, "Help for Polish Jews," *Aufbau*, October 1, 1939, p. 6.

69. Kay R. Gilbert, "At the Last Minute: The Refugee Conference in Washington," *Aufbau*, October 15, 1939, p. 10.

70. "Congress Hears JTA Reports on Atrocities, Read by Dickstein," Jewish Telegraph Agency, January 25, 1940.

71. "Instructions to German Agents: Now Only Anti-Semitic Propaganda!," *Aufbau*, January 12, 1940, p. 1.

72. "Ghetto State by the Grace of Hitler," *Aufbau*, October 15, 1939, p. 1.

73. "At the Outposts," *Aufbau*, January 12, 1940, p. 1.

74. "Palestine Barrier," *Aufbau*, January 12, 1940, p. 1.

75. W. C. H. (Wilfred C. Hulse), "Test of Nerves," *Aufbau*, October 1, 1939, p. 3.

76. W. C. H. (Wilfred C. Hulse), "Ann Morrow and Charles Lindbergh Pray for Peace," *Aufbau*, December 29, 1939, p. 7.

77. "How Is the War Going?," *Aufbau*, September 6, 1940, p. 1; W. A. Citron, "The Week in the U.S.A.," *Aufbau*, September 6, 1940, p. 3.

78. "We Are Again Sending Money to Your Relatives in Europe," Modern Tours, Inc., ad, *Aufbau*, August 22, 1941, p. 3.

79. "Food Packages to Germany: I Accuse," in Letters, *Aufbau*, November 1, 1939, p. 19.

80. "Why No Food to Germany?," *Aufbau*, March 15, 1940, p. 3.

81. Schenderlein, *Germany on Their Minds?*, 130.

82. The number is entirely plausible. At the end of the war, twenty thousand Jews lived in the Shanghai Ghetto, more elsewhere in Shanghai, nearly all of whom went to Palestine after the defeat of Japan. Among those who did not were the German-born economist Michael Blumenthal, who served for two years as President Carter's treasury secretary, and the Harvard constitutional law professor Lawrence Tribe, who was born in Shanghai.

83. "Hollywood Calling," *Aufbau*, August 2, 1946, p. 21. Kafka had the title as "The Duchess of Amalfi."

84. Vera Craener, "What's with Rationing?," *Aufbau*, December 25, 1942, p. 20.

85. Craener, "Women Adapt."

86. *Aufbau*, October 25, 1940, p. 7. Bibo had been a passenger on the ill-fated *St. Louis* and was forced back to France. The poem was written at the French concentration camp Saint-Cyprien, where my father was also interned. But Bibo did not survive. He died at Auschwitz.

87. My translation of the first two stanzas of "Das Eisenbahngleichnis," a poem first published in the satirical magazine *Simplicissimus* in 1931. Kästner was a prolific writer and journalist, best known for *Emil and the Detectives* and other children's stories. The Nazis burned his books, but he remained in Germany.

88. Franzi Ascher, "The Refugee's Summer Night," *Aufbau*, May 17, 1940, p. 11. My translation.

89. Shalom Ben Chorin, "Faust Twice in Hebrew," *Aufbau*, June 30, 1944, p. 17.

90. "'The Mortal Storm'—A Gripping Anti-Nazi Film," *Aufbau*, June 28, 1940, p. 9.

91. "Film-Panorama," *Aufbau*, December 4, 1942, p. 12.

92. *Aufbau*, March 14, 1941, pp. 14–15.

93. "The Great Moment," *Aufbau*, February 17, 1950, p. 32.

94. Ernst Mandowsky, "Tragedy in the Family of Bruno Walter," *Aufbau*, September 15, 1939, p. 10.

95. "A Blow against the Guiltless" (reprint, in English, of an editorial in *The Nation*), *Aufbau*, July 11, 1941. The headline was in German.

96. See, e.g., "The Battle Over Visas," *Aufbau*, August 22, 1941, p. 1.

97. E.g., "The Regulations for Reporting (Foreign) Assets,—Who Must Report, What and How . . . ," *Aufbau*, August 29, 1941, p. 1.

98. Morris Rothenberg, "The Imperative Problem of Jewish Statesmanship," *Aufbau*, September 5, 1941, p. 4.

99. "Law against Fifth Column—For, Not against, Non-Citizens," *Aufbau*, July 5, 1940, p. 1.

100. "Anti-Alienism and Anti-Semitism" and "A Needed Measure against a Fifth Column," *Aufbau*, May 31, 1940, pp. 1, 3.

101. Francis Biddle, "NO HYSTERIA!," *Aufbau*, June 21, 1940, p. 1.

102. "Spies among Refugees?," *Aufbau*, September 6, 1940, p. 3.

103. "Sabotage Training in the Villa Rathenau—Hoover Warns of New Attempts," *Aufbau*, May 14, 1943, p. 1. The Rathenau villa, in Berlin, which once belonged to the murdered Weimar foreign minister Walter Rathenau, became a Nazi spy training center.

104. "We're Waiting" (editorial), *Aufbau*, August 8, 1941, p. 4.

105. W. C. H. (Wilfred C. Hulse), "US Unity—Get American Names?," *Aufbau*, July 1, 1940, p. 9.

106. "G-JC (German Jewish Club): On Searching for a New Name," *Aufbau*, September 27, 1940, p. 7.

107. Bachert, *A Memoir*, 14.

108. W. C. H. (Wilfred C. Hulse), "Again the German Language," *Aufbau*, June 7, 1940, p. 7.

109. *Aufbau*, May 17, 1940, pp. 1, 2. There was, of course, no certainty about those numbers. They were certainly increasing rapidly when they appeared and were probably far too low.

110. Walter Lippmann, "Zero Hour," *Aufbau*, May 24, 1940.

111. Lippmann column of February 13, 1942, quoted in Richard Reeves, *Infamy: The Shocking Story of the Japanese American Internment in World War II* (New York: Picador, 2015), 50.

112. Henry R. Luce, "The American Century," *Aufbau*, April 18, 1941, pp. 13–16. The piece first ran in the February 17, 1941, issue of *Life*.

113. "Unwanted Alsatians," *Aufbau*, August 8, 1941, p. 5.

114. Marguerite Gilbert, "I Fled Belgium," *Aufbau*, June 7, 1940, p. 1.

115. Hertha Pauli, "Flight," *Aufbau*, October 11, 1940, p. 3.

116. *Aufbau*, July 12, 1940, p. 1.

117. Michael R. Marrus and Robert O. Paxton, *Vichy France and the Jews* (New York: Basic Books, 1981), 343.

118. "Letter from Shanghai," *Aufbau*, January 12, 1940, p. 3.

119. "A Jewish Army?," *Aufbau*, June 21, 1940, p. 1.

120. Paul Hurwitz, "A Jewish Army throughout the World," *Aufbau*, October 25, 1940, p. 1.

121. "On the Question of a Jewish Army," *Aufbau*, November 1, 1940, p. 1.

122. Hannah Arendt, "The Jewish Army—the Beginning of Jewish Politics?," *Aufbau*, November 14, 1941, p 1.

123. Hannah Arendt, "Ceterum Censeo," *Aufbau*, December 26, 1941, p. 2.

124. "New World—New Lives," *Aufbau*, May 17, 1940, p. 10.

125. Ibid.

126. Manfred George, "The Road to Freedom," *Aufbau*, September 5, 1941, p. 4.

127. Quoted in Peter Schrag, *California: America's High-Stakes Experiment* (Berkeley: University of California Press, 2006), 64.

Chapter 3. Friendly Enemy Aliens, 1941–45

1. "United We Stand," *Aufbau*, December 11, 1941, p. 1.

2. "Calling All Immigrants," *Aufbau*, April 10, 1942, p. 1. The subheads were in both English and German.

3. Dorothee Schneider, "Aufbau-Reconstruction and the Americanization of German-Jewish Immigrants, 1934–1944" (unpublished master's thesis, University of Massachusetts, 1975), pp. 19 ff., http://scholarworks.umass.edu/theses/2576 (accessed November 2017).

4. Wilfred C. Hulse, "I Like America," *Aufbau*, March 1, 1940, p. 7. Only the head was in English.

5. See, e.g., Otto Schrag and Peter Schrag, *When Europe Was a Prison Camp: Father and Son Memoirs, 1940–41* (Bloomington: Indiana University Press, 2015); Anne Grynberg, *Les camps de la honte: Les internés des camps françaises, 1939–1944* (Paris: La Découverte, 1991).

6. Hannah Arendt, "We Refugees," *Menorah Journal* 31 (1943): 69–77, reprinted in Marc Robinson, ed., *Altogether Elsewhere: Writers in Exile* (Boston: Faber and Faber, 1994), 110–17.

7. Hannah Arendt, "Those Deprived of Their Rights and the Degraded," *Aufbau*, December 15, 1944, p. 13; Hannah Arendt, *The Origins of Totalitarianism* (New York: World, 1951), 267–302.

8. Quoted in Anna Schenderlein, "German Jewish 'Enemy Aliens' in the United States during World II," *Bulletin of the German Historical Institute* 60 (Spring 2017): 101. From Undated Document, Felix Guggenheim Collection, Box 108, Felix Guggenheim Papers, Correspondence, 1942–1944, National Defense Migration Hearings and German Aliens.

9. "Refugees Seek Clarification," Letters, *New York Times*, December 22, 1941.

10. Albert Einstein et al., "Open Letter to President Roosevelt," February 1942, in Anderson, *Hitler's Exiles*, 251.

11. For which he received a personal thanks from Roosevelt. Correspondence between President Franklin D. Roosevelt and Arturo Toscanini, reproduced in a press release of April 20, 1943, entitled "President Roosevelt Lauds Toscanini for His Devotion to Cause of Liberty," NBC Arch., NBC Press Release.

12. Frank Testimony, Hearings before the House Select Committee Investigating National Defense Migration, 77th Congress, 2nd Sess., Part 31, p. 11725.

13. "Thomas Mann's Testimony before the Tolan Committee" (in English), *Aufbau*, March 13, 1942, p. 3.

14. Strauss, "Interview with Felix Guggenheim," 32.

15. "More Than 300,000 Aliens Have Been Screened," *Aufbau*, May 8, 1942, p. 1.

16. "To Naturalize Soldiers—Army Will Speed Grant of Citizenship to Aliens in Service," *New York Times*, May 20, 1942. *Aufbau* cheered it even before the president had signed it: "Congress Determines: Aliens in the Army Will Become Citizens," *Aufbau*, March 27, 1942, p. 1.

17. "The Right to Naturalization," *Aufbau*, December 15, 1944, p. 4.

18. "Attorney General Francis Biddle: Loyal Non-Citizens Safe," *Aufbau*, December 19, 1941, p. 1.

19. "No Concentration Camps for Non-Citizens," *Aufbau*, December 12, 1941, p. 16.

20. Presidential Proclamations 2525 and 2526 of December 7, 1941, and December 8, 1941. *Regulations Controlling Travel and Other Conduct of Aliens of Enemy Nationalities* (Washington: U.S. Department of Justice, 1942).

21. Biddle, "Employment of Aliens in Private Industry," *Aufbau*, January 2, 1942.

22. Schenderlein, *Germany on Their Minds?*, 137.

23. Elow, "We Aliens," *Aufbau*, January 9, 1942, section 2, p. 1. My translation.

24. "No Reason to Panic," *Aufbau*, February 13, 1942, p. 1.

25. Reeves, *Infamy*, 39–54.

26. "Sorrow Comes to the West Coast: The Curfew Regulations and Their Consequences," *Aufbau*, April 3, 1942, section 2, p. 7. But the story was at the front of the West Coast section, not on the front page.

27. Strauss, "Interview with Felix Guggenheim," 31.

28. E.g., Lawrence E. Davies, "Japanese Begin Evacuation Trek," with the subhead "Good Humor Prevails," *New York Times*, March 23, 1942.

29. Schenderlein, *Germany on Their Minds?*, 159.

30. "Curfew Law Ended on West Coast for German Aliens," *Aufbau*, January 8, 1943, section 3, p. 1. The area to which DeWitt applied the curfew happens to be the most heavily Democratic region in the nation today.

31. "Axis Agents and Loyal Immigrants," *Aufbau*, February 6, 1942, section 2, p. 3.

32. "No Measures against 'Loyal Aliens,'" *Aufbau*, May 1, 1942, p. 1.

33. "'Discrimination against Aliens a Breach of Contract,'" *Aufbau*, June 11, 1943, p. 2.

34. "To Whom It May Concern," *Aufbau*, May 17, 1940, p. 4. Wilfred C. Hulse, "Written in the Margin: Again the German Language," *Aufbau*, June 7, 1940, p. 9.

35. "Blast Rommel," *Aufbau*, April 9, 1943, p. 19.

36. "The Share of Jews in High Government Positions in the U.S.A.," *Aufbau*, April 17, 1942, p. 3.

37. Vera Craener, "Miss America 1945—Bess Myerson, Child of Jewish Immigrants," *Aufbau*, September 14, 1945, p. 32.

38. "What Will Happen to the Refugees in France?," *Aufbau*, April 24, 1942, p. 1.

39. "Will Emigration Come to a Complete Standstill?," *Aufbau*, December 26, 1941, p. 1.

40. "The Odyssey of the Serpa Pinto," *Aufbau*, January 2, 1942, p. 1.

41. Ibid.

42. "McNutt Demands—Employ Aliens," *Aufbau*, April 23, 1943, p. 1.

43. Gottschalk, "The German-Jewish Legacy," 84.

44. "What's Going On in Boston?," *Aufbau*, October 22, 1943, p. 1.

45. "'Enemy Aliens' after Germany's Defeat," *Aufbau*, May 18, 1945, p. 4.

46. "Campaign for Roadmaps, City Maps and Other Important Military Information," *Aufbau*, December 25, 1942, p. 6.

47. Pvt. Charles N. Ermann, "We Are in the Army Now," *Aufbau*, March 14, 1941, p. 28.

48. Watson B. Miller, "Foreign Born in the United States Army during World War II, with Special Reference to the Alien," *Monthly Review* (Washington, U.S. Immigration and Naturalization Service), October 1948, p. 51.

49. "From 'Krankenschwestern' into 'Nurses,'" *Aufbau*, January 15, 1943, p. 20.

50. "Our Boys Club," *Aufbau*, December 18, 1942, p. 26.

51. "Yesterday Refugees—Today Soldiers," *Aufbau*, December 22, 1944, p. 11.

52. "'E' for Excellence," *Aufbau*, June 25, 1943, p. 28.

53. Schiller Cohen, "My Toughest Air Battle," *Aufbau*, October 1, 1943, p. 1.

54. Wilfred C. Hulse, "With One Foot in Germany," *Aufbau*, January 12, 1945.

55. Schenderlein, *Germany on Their Minds?*, 199.

56. Mort Horvitz, "Foreign-Born GIs Were Liberators," *The Jewish Veteran*, n.d., at http://www.archive.org/stream/harveynewtonooreelo2#page/n621/mode/1up.

57. Ernest Michel, "Memoir," in Kahn, *Reflections of Jewish Survivors from Mannheim*, 7.

58. Steven Karras, "Bernard Fridman," in *The Enemy I Knew: German Jews in the Allied Military in World War II* (London: Zenith Press, 2009), 62.

59. Schenderlein, *Germany on Their Minds?*, 203.

60. Ettlinger, "Ein Amerikaner," 50.

61. Niall Ferguson, *Kissinger: 1923–1968: The Idealist* (New York: Penguin, 2015), 123.

62. "Our Boys Club," *Aufbau*, January 22, 1943, p. 21.

63. "Immigrants—Outstanding Soldiers," *Aufbau*, December 7, 1945, p. 17; "Julius Klein—Dead at 82," Jewish Telegraph Agency, April 11, 1984, http://www.jta.org /1984/04/11/archive/julius-klein-dead-at-82 (accessed August 2016).

64. Like much of the nation in those years, *Aufbau* was focused on the war and on the circumstances of its own readership. There was little on American racism until later.

65. E.g., "I Was a War Prisoner of the Nazis," *Aufbau*, October 15, 1943, p. 1.

66. "Invisible Emissaries: The Organization of a Jewish Underground in Europe," *Aufbau*, October 1, 1943, p. 1.

67. "My Stance on Zionism," *Aufbau*, May 8, 1942, section 2, p. 10. Heinrich Schnitzler, the son of Arthur, who died in 1931, provided the letter to *Aufbau*. Arthur would have been eighty when the letter was published.

68. Chaim Weizmann, "The Present and Future of the Jewish People," *Aufbau*, May 15, 1942, p. 3.

69. "A Historic Resolution," *Aufbau*, October 1, 1943, p. 5.

70. "The Nazis Must Pay," *Aufbau*, January 8, 1943, p. 1.

71. *Aufbau*, December 11, 1942, p. 1.

72. *Aufbau*, May 4, 1945, p. 1.

73. "Protests! Against Amnesty for War Criminals," *Aufbau*, June 23, 1950, p. 1.

74. Manfred George, "V-E Day: 5 Years, 8 Months, 5 Days of War," *Aufbau*, May 11, 1945, p. 2.

75. "Berchtesgaden Can't Become a Kyffhäeuser (Monument)," *Aufbau*, October 19, 1943, p. 28.

76. Manfred George, "The Russian Victory and German Questions," *Aufbau*, January 26, 1945, p. 1.

77. Manfred George "Inside Germany," *Aufbau*, July 26, 1945, p. 1.

78. Manfred George, "Teaspoons and Medicine Bottles," *Aufbau*, March 28, 1947, p. 1.

79. Manfred George, "To Get Europe's Trust," *Aufbau*, October 17, 1947, p. 1.

80. "The Charges against I.G. Farben," *Aufbau*, May 9, 1947, p. 1.

81. Margarete Buber-Neumann, "Prisoner of Stalin and Hitler," *Aufbau*, June 3, 1949, p. 3; June 10, 1949, p. 9; June 17, 1949, p. 9. Buber-Neumann was the divorced wife of the Zionist-humanist philosopher Martin Buber's son.

82. Manfred George, "Adenauer in the USA," *Aufbau*, April 10, 1953, p. 4.

83. "Which Is the Real German People?," *Aufbau*, November 5, 1943, p. 9.

84. Friedrich Wilhelm Foerster, "German Megalomania," *Aufbau*, January 15, 1943, p. 3.

85. "Emil Ludwig Warns about the German Junkers," *Aufbau*, June 18, 1943, p. 4.

86. Emil Ludwig, "What Should Happen to Germany," text of a speech delivered in Los Angeles, *Aufbau*, July 24, 1942.

87. "Hollywood Calling," *Aufbau*, June 30, 1944, p. 5.

88. Manfred George, quoted in Marjorie Lamberti, "German Antifascist Refugees in America and the Public Debate on 'What Should Be Done with Germany after Hitler,' 1941–1945," in *Central European History* 40, no. 2 (June 2007): 279–305.

89. *Aufbau*, May 18, 1945.

90. Manfred George, "The State of Things," *Aufbau*, December 7, 1945, p. 2.

91. "A.F. of L.: For Palestine—against Immigration," *Aufbau*, October 15, 1943, p. 1.

92. E.g., St. Etienne ad, *Aufbau*, December 22, 1944, p. 33.

93. Jane Kallir, *Saved from Europe: Otto Kallir and the History of the Galerie St. Etienne* (New York: Galerie St. Etienne, 1999), 23–39.

94. Author interview, September 30, 2016. See also Corey Kilgannon "75 Years with a Manhattan Gallery and No Sign of Stopping," *New York Times*, October 30, 2015.

95. E.g., "Use Less Gas in Your Home," ad, *Aufbau*, January 15, 1943, p. 7.

96. "Wise Gets Confirmations," *New York Times*, November 25, 1942; "Slain Polish Jews Put at a Million," *Times*, November 26, 1942.

97. "Battle in the Warsaw Ghetto," *Aufbau*, May 14, 1943, p. 1.

98. Thomas Mann, "The Death of Franklin Delano Roosevelt," *Aufbau*, April 20, 1945, p. 1.

99. *Aufbau*, May 11, 1945, p. 18.

100. "5,000 Save Themselves in Spain," *Aufbau*, January 1, 1943, p. 1.

101. "52,000 Belgian Jews Deported," *Aufbau*, June 18, 1943, p. 1; Leni Yahil, *The Holocaust: The Fate of European Jewry, 1932–1945* (Oxford: Oxford University Press, 1991), 436.

102. E.g., "Freed in Buchenwald," *Aufbau*, May 25, 1945, p. 1.

103. E.g., "First Signs of Life," *Aufbau*, June 15, 1945, p. 37.

104. *Aufbau*, June 15, 1945, p. 7.

105. *Aufbau*, August 17, 1945, p. 16.

106. "The Destruction of the World: Will Atomic Warfare Hasten or Hinder It?," *Aufbau*, October 5, 1945, p. 5.

107. Albert Schweitzer, "Reverence for Life," *Aufbau*, February 24, 1950, p. 1.

108. "The Career of Lise Meitner: Other Co-workers on the Atomic Bomb," *Aufbau*, August 10, 1945, p. 6.

109. James R. Oestreich, "For Rudolf Bing at 88, Operatic Drama Lingers," *New York Times*, March 11, 1990.

110. Manfred George, "The Case of Kirsten Flagstad," *Aufbau*, February 3, 1950, p. 3.

Chapter 4. In the Shadow of the Holocaust, 1945–65

1. Simon H. Rifkind, "The Truth about the Jewish DPs," *Aufbau*, April 1, 1946.

2. "A Great General," *Aufbau*, December 28, 1945, p. 4; Eric Lichtblau, "Surviving the Nazis, Only to Be Jailed by America," *New York Times*, February 7, 2015, p. SR3.

3. Robert W. Abel and Ernest W. Moser, "Open Letter to the Chairman of the Joint Jewish Distribution Committee," September 26, 1945, in the *Papers of the Gundersheimer-Siegel Family* at the Leo Baeck Institute-Center for Jewish History, http://digifindingaids.cjh.org/?pID=1926870#subserI-2 (accessed August 2016).

4. Manfred George, "Closed Doors," *Aufbau*, July 6, 1945, p. 1.

5. "Don't Let Them Go Under," *Aufbau*, December 7, 1945, p. 1.

6. "Nazis Deceiving G.I.s" and "Mrs. Roosevelt's Impressions of the Camps," *Aufbau*, February 22, 1946, pp. 1, 3.

7. Report of Earl G. Harrison, in Resources, U.S. Holocaust Memorial Museum, https://www.ushmm.org/exhibition/displaced-persons/resourcI.htm (accessed August 2016). Also "Report Is Sent to Eisenhower," *New York Times*, September 30, 1945.

8. Leonard Dinnerstein, "The United States and the Displaced Persons," in Yisrael Gutman and Avital Saf, eds., *SHE'ERIT HAPLETAH, 1944–1948: Rehabilitation and Political Struggle*, Proceedings of the Sixth Yad Vashem International Historical Conference, Jerusalem, October 1985 (Jerusalem: Yad Vashem, 1990).

9. Harry Truman, "Statement and Directive on Displaced Persons," December 22, 1945, Jewish Virtual Library, http://www.jewishvirtuallibrary.org/jsource/Holocaust/truman_on_dps.html (accessed August 2016).

10. Arendt, *Eichmann in Jerusalem*, 119.

11. Richard Dyck, "Conversation with Leo Baeck," *Aufbau*, December 21, 1945, p. 1.

12. "The Pogrom Mentality in Germany," *Aufbau*, August 1, 1947, p. 1.

13. *Aufbau*, June 15, 1945, p. 3.

14. "Specialists with the Occupation: The Employment of German-speaking U.S. Citizens," *Aufbau*, June 22, 1945, p. 1.

15. Manfred George, "Fear of the Sergeant-Major," *Aufbau*, September 28, 1951, p. 1.

16. See, e.g., Harald Freiling, "Three German Teachers Are Studying American Instruction about the Holocaust," *Aufbau*, December 4, 1987, p. 10.

17. Jennifer Bormann, "Aufbau, a German-Jewish Newspaper as 'Heimat' in Exile," *Transatlantic Perspectives*, July 6, 2011, http://www.transatlanticperspectives.org/entry.php?rec=90 (accessed November 2016).

18. *Aufbau*, January 17, 1969, p. 21.

19. AJ Committee News, press release, July 7, 1997.

20. Richard Pollak, *The Creation of Dr. B: A Biography of Bruno Bettelheim* (New York: Simon and Schuster, 1997), 227–30, 358–62. It might have been more plausible to associate the German Jews' fate to their training as good, obedient Germans and their deference to authority; not a "ghetto mentality" but something closer to its opposite.

21. "New Trial for Ilse Koch in the Fall," *Aufbau*, June 17, 1949, p. 1.

22. *Aufbau*, May 8, 1964, p. 30; "Four Questions for the Compensation Authorities," *Aufbau*, May 9, 1969, p. 23.

23. *Aufbau*, April 24, 1964, p. 1.

24. Robert Kempner, "Help for Nazi Murderers," *Aufbau*, May 23, 1969, p. 1; "Cold Waivers for Nazi Criminals," *Aufbau*, May 30, 1969, p. 1.

25. Robert Kempner, "Goering Was the Incendiary," *Aufbau*, March 25, 1988, p. 3.

26. Heiner Lichtenstein, "Two Austrians Head the List of War Criminals," *Aufbau*, November 6, 1987, p. 3.

27. Henry Marx, "Not a Single Member of the People's Courts Has Been Convicted," *Aufbau*, July 18, 1986, p. 1.

28. Paul Hesslein, "The Drill Field of the Nazi Underground," *Aufbau*, October 19, 1945, p. 1.

29. See, e.g. Hermann Pichler, "Waldheim—An Austrian Tragedy," *Aufbau*, June 20, 1986, p. 4; "The Austrian Jewish Community Assails the Anti-Semitism of the OVP (Austrian People's Party)," *Aufbau*, July 4, 1986, p. 2; "The Jewish Community in Vienna Takes a Stand on Waldheim's Installation," *Aufbau*, July 18, 1986, p. 1; Leslie Maitland Werner, "Waldheim Barred from Entering the U.S. Over Role in War," *New York Times*, April 28, 1987.

30. Heiner Lichtenstein, "Elie Wiesel as Witness in the Trial of Klaus Barbie," *Aufbau*, June 19, 1987. *Aufbau* had also followed the Mengele story. Mengele had escaped to South America and ended up practicing medicine in Paraguay. He was never brought to trial. "Days of Retribution: Concentration Camp Doctor in Paraguay," *Aufbau*, February 7, 1964.

31. "Petain and Louis XVI," *Aufbau*, August 17, 1945, p. 4.

32. Gershon Sholem, "Neither of Us Was There," and Hannah Arendt, "You Misunderstood Me," *Aufbau*, December 20, 1963, pp. 17–18. *Aufbau* said that it had imposed a hiatus on its coverage of the heated debate that Arendt's book produced. The pieces in this issue, drawn from the *Neue Zürcher Zeitung*, where they first appeared, ended that hiatus. The Hahn and Kempner articles were published on March 29, 1963, and April 12, 1963.

33. "Albert Schweitzer on the Hochhuth Debate," *Aufbau*, March 6, 1964, p. 4.

34. Schenderlein, *Germany on Their Minds?*, 300.

35. E.g., Hans Habe, "Our Defeat in Germany," *Aufbau*, March 28, 1947, p. 3.

36. Arthur Allen, "The Problem with Trump's Admiration of General Patton," *Politico*, December 26, 2016, https://www.politico.com/magazine/story/2016/12/trump-general-patton-admiration-214545 (accessed January 2018).

37. Henry Morgenthau Jr., "Germany Remains the Problem," *Aufbau*, April 26, 1946, p. 1; Morgenthau, "The Only Solution," *Aufbau*, November 16, 1945, p. 1.

38. Emanuel Celler, "What Can America Do? Toward the Rescue of the Jews of Europe," *Aufbau*, November 16, 1945.

39. Manfred George, "Mr. Bevin's True Hardships" and "Bevin's Slur," *Aufbau*, June 21, 1946, pp. 1, 3. Bevin's quote was surrounded by indignant responses from New York's two U.S. Senators, Robert Wagner and James Mead, from Mayor William O'Dwyer, and from City Council President Newbold Morris.

40. Richard Dyck, "'Operation Cyprus': The Closure of Palestine by Land and by Sea," *Aufbau*, August 16, 1946, p. 1.

41. *Aufbau*, February 22, 1946, p. 9.

42. Anthony Leviero, "Truman Signs Bill Easing DP Entries: 415,744 Get Refuge," *New York Times*, June 17, 1950; "U.S. Policy toward Jewish Refugees, 1941–1952," *Holocaust Encyclopedia* (Washington: U.S. Holocaust Museum), https://www.ushmm.org/wlc/en /article.php?ModuleId=10007094 (accessed August 2016).

43. "Assassination in Jerusalem," *Aufbau*, July 26, 1946, p. 1.

44. Manfred George, "An Injustice without Equal," *Aufbau*, August 2, 1946, pp. 1–2.

45. "A Gruesome Act," *Aufbau*, July 25, 1947, p. 1.

46. Gerald Frank, "I Was on Board the Exodus 1947," *Aufbau*, August 1, 1947, p. 1.

47. E.g., Richard Dyck, "Israel's Battle for Freedom," *Aufbau*, May 21, 1948, p. 9; map, p. 1; photos, p. 3; "An Ambulance for Tel Aviv," *Aufbau*, May 28, 1948, p. 3; "Behind the Scenes with the Egyptian Army: Parade Ground Troops or a Powerful Force?," *Aufbau*, May 28, 1948, p. 5; "Blood for Israel" (photo), p. 25.

48. Bradley Burston, "The 'Exodus' Effect: The Monumentally Fictional Israel That Remade American Jewry," *Haaretz*, November 9, 2012.

49. "*Aufbau* Calls: The Armistice Is Not the End of the Crisis," *Aufbau*, June 16, 1967, p. 11.

50. Manfred George, "Protect the Marshall Plan," *Aufbau*, December 26, 1947, p. 3.

51. "Nazi Propaganda in Yorkville," *Aufbau*, September 28, 1945, p. 3.

52. Kurt Hellmer, "Anti-Anti," *Aufbau*, June 7, 1946, p. 40, and December 19, 1947, pp. 13–14.

53. Kurt Hellmer, "Anti-Anti," *Aufbau*, August 2, 1946, p. 6.

54. Manfred George, "Clare Doesn't Like Albert," *Aufbau*, January 2, 1948, pp. 1–2.

55. W. C. H. (Wilfred C. Hulse), "Resisting Anti-Semitism?," *Aufbau*, April 19, 1946, p. 19.

56. "Protection for Minorities in the Land of Minorities," *Aufbau*, January 3, 1947, pp. 5–6.

57. James Baldwin, "Letter from a Region in My Mind," *New Yorker*, November 17, 1962, https://www.newyorker.com/magazine/1962/11/17/letter-from-a-region-in -my-mind (accessed December 2017). *The Fire Next Time* was published in January 1963.

58. Manfred George, "Black and White at the Brink," *Aufbau*, May 1, 1964, p. 1; *Aufbau*, May 15, 1964, p. 7.

59. Otto Leichter, "Negro Anti-Semitism" and "Negro Businesspeople Dominate Harlem," *Aufbau*, September 20, 1968, pp. 1, 3. Nor, of course, did it mitigate the resentment of Korean and other Asian shopkeepers in Los Angeles twenty years later.

60. "Intrigues against Abe Fortas," *Aufbau*, September 27, 1968, p. 1. Fortas, whose nomination faced intense opposition from southern conservatives in the Senate, was never confirmed. Later, hit with ethics charges, he resigned his seat as an associate justice. Hans Steinitz, "Justice without Earl Warren," *Aufbau*, May 16, 1969, p. 3; "How Could He Do This to Us?," *Aufbau*, May 23, 1969, p. 5.

61. "Questions for the Metropolitan Museum," *Aufbau*, January 17, 1969, p. 1. The piece ran just below a friendly farewell to Lyndon Johnson, who would leave office three days later. See also "Museum in the Crossfire," *Aufbau*, January 24, 1969, p. 1, and Schaber, *Aufbau Reconstruction*, 91–93.

62. "The Anti-Semitic Poem of a Schoolgirl," *Aufbau*, January 24, 1969, p. 1. At that time, Jack Greenberg, a Brooklyn-born Jew, who had, with Thurgood Marshall, argued the Brown case and many other major civil rights cases, was head of the Legal Defense

and Education Fund of the NAACP. But there were already protests because he was white (and Jewish) and in 1984 he left the LDF for a teaching job.

63. The quote is from an official report on the strike. Henry Raymont, "City Panel Finds 'Appalling' Signs of Racial Bigotry," *New York Times*, January 17, 1969, p. 1. *Aufbau* had a similar story on January 24, 1969, the same day it ran the "Jew boy" poem and its "Museum in the Crossfire" piece.

64. Thomas Mann, "Why I'm Not Going Back to Germany," *Aufbau*, September 28, 1946, p. 5.

65. "Letter to Joseph Campbell," January 6, 1941, in Thomas Mann, Richard Winston, Clara Winston, *The Letters of Thomas Mann, 1889–1955* (Berkeley: University of California Press, 1970), 277.

66. Thomas Mann, "The Exiled Writer's Relation to His Homeland," in Anderson, *Hitler's Exiles*, 263–68.

67. Jeffrey Meyers, "Thomas Mann in America," *Michigan Quarterly Review* 51, no. 4 (Fall 2012); "The Boss of the F.B.I.," *Aufbau*, February 17, 1950, p. 9.

68. "I Stand Firm: A Letter from Thomas Mann to the Readers of *Aufbau*," *Aufbau*, April 13, 1951, p. 1.

69. Meyers, "Thomas Mann in America."

70. Manfred George, "Politics in the Dark," *Aufbau*, February 14, 1947, p. 4; "McCarthy without Mask," *Aufbau*, March 19, 1954, p. 1.

71. Anthony Heilbut, *Exiled in Paradise: German Refugee Artists and Intellectuals in America From the 1930s to the Present* (Berkeley: University of California Press, 1983), 366.

72. W. C. H. (Wilfred C. Hulse), "Here and Today," *Aufbau*, August 8, 1941, p. 7.

73. Robert Weltsch, "Judenbetreuung in Bayern" [Care of Jews in Bavaria], in *Mitteilungsblatt* (Tel Aviv) 19 (May 1946). Weltsch wrote on postwar events for *Aufbau* (e.g., "A Political Curiosity," December 14, 1951) and in 1955 became one of the founders of the Leo Baeck Institute. There is also an interview with Weltsch in Manfred George, "A Great Journalist," *Aufbau*, September 28, 1951, p. 11.

74. Rudolf Callmann, "Problems of Accountability in Jewish Restitution," *Aufbau*, August 2, 1946, p. 7.

75. Sidney Zabludoff, "Restitution of Holocaust-Era Assets: Promises and Reality," *Jewish Political Studies Review* 19, no. 1–2 (Spring 2007).

76. Romika Company history, http://www.romika.co.uk/historie.html (accessed September 2016).

77. Fritz Blum, "The Story of My Parents' Lives, 1881–1992," memoir in the archives of the Leo Baeck Institute (2003).

78. Herman Lewy, "Disappointments of a Returnee," *Aufbau*, October 11, 1946, p. 1; Broh, "The History of the Newspaper *Aufbau*," 391.

79. Sergio Della Pergola, *Review of Relevant Demographic Information on World Jewry*, Final Report to the International Commission on Holocaust Era Insurance Claims (Jerusalem: Hebrew University of Jerusalem, 2003).

80. William Helmreich, "The Impact of Holocaust Survivors on American Society: A Socio-Cultural Portrait," in Jeffery S. Gurock, *American Jewish History* (New York: Routledge, 1998), 4:61.

81. Jack Wertheimer, "The German-Jewish Experience: Toward a Usable Past," in Peck, *The German-Jewish Legacy in America*, 236.

82. Jonas, "A German-Jewish Legacy," 55.

83. William Grimes, "Esther Jungreis, 80, Who Led Secular Jews to Study Torah," *New York Times*, August 28, 2016.

84. Patricia Ard and Michael Rockland, *The Jews of New Jersey: A Pictorial History* (New Brunswick, NJ: Rutgers University Press, 2002), 72.

85. Finkelstein, quoted in *Jewish Farmers*, http://jewishfarmers.blogspot.com/2012 /12/jewish-poultry-farming.html (accessed August 2016).

86. "Vineland" in *Jewish Virtual Library*, https://www.jewishvirtuallibrary.org /jsource/judaica/ejud_0002_0020_0_20433.html (accessed August 2016).

87. Valerie J. Nelson, "Nathan Shapell, 85; Builder Who Developed Porter Ranch Was Also Noted Philanthropist," *Los Angeles Times*, March 13, 2007.

88. Hans Salzmann, "From Soldiers into Civilians," *Aufbau*, July 6, 1945, p. 13; July 13, 1945, p. 32.

89. Boris Smolar, "The True Facts," *Aufbau*, February 1, 1946, p. 1.

90. E.g., "I'm Staying in the Army," U.S. Army Recruitment ad, *Aufbau*, December 7, 1945, p. 3.

91. GI Bill, "Education and Training" (Washington: Department of Veteran Affairs), http://www.benefits.va.gov/gibill/history.asp (accessed August 2016).

92. On "whiteness," David R. Roediger, *Working toward Whiteness: How America's Immigrants Became White* (New York: Basic Books, 2005).

93. Kurt Hellmer, "Who Gave Senator McCarthy the Information?," *Aufbau*, April 7, 1950, p. 1.

94. Sen. Pat McCarran, Cong. Rec., March 2, 1953, p. 1518.

95. "Texts of President Truman's Speeches at Cleveland and Buffalo," *New York Times*, October 10, 1952.

96. *McCarran-Walter Act of 1952*, Public Law 82-414, 82nd Congress, 2nd session, *U.S. Statutes at Large* 66 (1952), 163–282; *Internal Security Act of 1950*, U.S. Statutes at Large, 81st Cong., 2nd Sess., Chap. 1024, 998.

97. George, "Your Veto Is Needed!"; Jacob Javits, "Five Fundamental Defects"; Herbert Lehman, "This Law Is Unbelievable"; and John O'Grady, "Minority Groups, Beware," all *Aufbau*, June 20, 1952, p. 1.

98. Monroe R. Sheinberg, "Three Lies," *Aufbau*, June 27, 1952, p. 1.

99. "Under False Flags," *Aufbau*, June 27, 1952, p. 4.

100. George F. Custen, "Over 50 Years, a Landmark Loses Some of Its Luster," *New York Times*, November 16, 1997. Thomas, who was himself later convicted of taking kickbacks from friends he'd put on his congressional payroll, would serve in the same federal prison where some of the Hollywood Ten were incarcerated.

101. Manfred George, "Letter to Europe," *Aufbau*, July 24, 1953, p. 1.

102. Gert Niers, "Reagan Changes His Itinerary for His Stay in Germany," *Aufbau*, April 19, 1985; Henry Marx, "Can Hitler's Soldiers Be Equated with the Death Camp Victims?," *Aufbau*, April 26, 1985, p. 6; Henry Marx, "After Bitburg: The Controversy Continues," *Aufbau*, May 10, 1985, p. 1.

103. Literally, making good again.

104. "Restitution and Atonement in Europe," *Aufbau*, October 12, 1945, p. 6.

105. *Aufbau*, October 5, 1951, p. 1.

106. Manfred George, "A Good Start," *Aufbau*, October 5, 1951, pp. 1–2.

107. "Jews and Germans," letters section, *Aufbau*, November 16, 1951, p. 13.

108. Manfred George, "The Auerbach Justice Scandal," *Aufbau*, September 14, 1951, pp. 1–2.

109. Schenderlein, *Germany on Their Minds?*, 310 ff.

110. Strauss, "Interview with Felix Guggenheim," 46.

111. *Aufbau*, November 21, 1947, p. 8; *Aufbau*, June 11, 1948, p. 8.

112. E.g., "Problems of the *Wiedergutmachung*," *Aufbau*, June 22, 1951, p. 11; *Aufbau*, March 6, 1964, p. 29.

113. Kurt Grossmann, "825,000 Claims Still Unsettled," *Aufbau*, July 20, 1962, p. 29.

114. Claims Conference website, http://www.claimscon.org/about/history/ (accessed December 2017).

115. E.g., James M. Markham, "Company Linked to Nazi Slave Labor Pays $2 Million," *New York Times*, January 9, 1986.

116. Veronica Kaufman in an email to the author, September 19, 2016.

117. Strauss, "Interview with Felix Guggenheim," 45.

118. The Jewish Virtual Library, http://www.jewishvirtuallibrary.org/jsource/Holocaust/reparations.html (accessed September 2016).

119. Schenderlein, *Germany on Their Minds?*, 296.

120. Ibid., 297.

121. Strauss, "Interview with Felix Guggenheim," 46.

122. Schenderlein, *Germany on Their Minds?*, 307.

123. Manfred George, "Interview with President Heuss," *Aufbau*, July 20, 1951, p. 1.

124. Schenderlein, *Germany on Their Minds?*, 366–67.

125. Lowenstein, *Frankfurt on the Hudson*, 242, 328.

126. Schenderlein, *Germany on Their Minds?*, 326–27.

127. *Aufbau*, September 20, 1968, p. 35.

128. *Aufbau*, May 23, 1969, p. 6.

129. Henry Marx, "The Advancement of Relations between U.S. Jews and Germans," *Aufbau*, November 6, 1987, p. 1; Marx, "Bonn Conference Outlines Efforts toward Better Relations with US Jews," *Aufbau*, December 4, 1987, p. 1.

130. *Aufbau*, November 20, 1987, p. 11.

131. Atina Grossmann, "Family Files: Emotions and Stories of (Non-) Restitution," *German Historical Institute London Bulletin* 34, no. 1 (May 2012): 59–78.

132. Ibid.

133. See, e.g., *Aufbau*, July 6, 1951, p. 31.

134. Andrea Mink, "'Aufbau'—Reconstruction as a Mission," *LBI News* 93 (Winter 2013), https://www.lbi.org/2013/11/aufbau-reconstruction-as-mission/ (accessed September 2016).

135. *Aufbau*, May 15, 1964, p. 9.

136. *Aufbau*, December 4, 1987, p. 26.

137. Gert Niers, *Arrived at Last: An Immigrant Narrative* (Bloomington, IN: Author House, 2014), 121. Niers was *Aufbau*'s coeditor from 1985 to 1989.

138. Michael T. Kaufman, "About New York: Exiles Who Fled for Lives Sustain German Culture," *New York Times*, December 3, 1994.

139. Jonathan Mark, "*Aufbau*: Don't' Stop the Presses," *The Jewish Week*, April 15, 1999.

Chapter 5. Legacy

1. Jean-Michel Palmier, *Weimar in Exile: The Anti-Fascist Emigration in Europe and America* (New York and London: Verso, 2006), 456.

2. See, e.g., Atina Grossman, "German Jews as Provincial Cosmopolitans: Reflections from the Upper West Side," *Leo Baeck Year Book* 53 (2008): 157–68.

3. "The Yiddish Language in America," *Aufbau*, November 6, 1987, p. 17. According to one estimate, 85 percent of the Jews who died in the Holocaust were Yiddish speakers.

4. Mark Lilla, *The Shipwrecked Mind* (New York: New York Review of Books, 2016), quoted in Sam Tanenhaus, "The Right Idea," *New Yorker*, October 24, 2016, p. 79.

5. Palmier, *Weimar in Exile*, 480.

6. Jeffrey A. Lieberman, *Shrinks: The Untold Story of Psychiatry* (Boston: Little, Brown, 2015). This was yet another skirmish in the battle between the talking and the medicating shrinks. Lieberman, chair of the Department of Psychiatry at Columbia, was duly barraged for his own excessive faith in antipsychotic drugs.

7. Philip Roth, *Portnoy's Complaint* (New York: Random House, 1967), 274.

8. George L. Mosse, "The End Is Not Yet: A Personal Memoir of the German-Jewish Legacy in America," in Peck, *The German-Jewish Legacy in America*, 11–12.

9. Guy Stern, "German Culture, Jewish Ethics," 31.

10. http://www.today.com/popculture/steven-spielberg-i-was-put-earth-tell-story-holocaust-2D79619816 (accessed September 2016).

11. Author interview with Stuart Kaplan, Selfhelp chief executive officer, October 5, 2016.

12. "Germany Buys California House Built by Writer Thomas Mann," Reuters, November 17, 2016, https://www.reuters.com/article/us-germany-usa-mann/germany-buys-california-house-built-by-writer-thomas-mann-idUSKBN13C2W0 (accessed December 2017).

13. Matt Hamilton, "Germany Buys Thomas Mann's Former Pacific Palisades Home, Averting Demolition," *Los Angeles Times*, November 21, 2016.

14. Lucy Steinitz, "The German-Jewish Legacy in America: A Second-Generation Perspective," in Peck, *The German-Jewish Legacy in America*, 172.

15. Quoted in Szymanski, *"Aufbau: Our Common Diary."*

16. Heilbut, *Exiled in Paradise*, ix.

17. Peter Schrag, "The WASP-less Presidential Election and the End of the Establishment," *The Daily Beast*, August 16, 2012, http://www.thedailybeast.com/articles/2012/08/16/the-wasp-less-presidential-election-and-the-end-of-the-establishment.html (accessed September 2016). By fall of 2018, there were four Catholics on the court.

18. Jonas, "A German-Jewish Legacy," 56–57.

19. Benjamin Franklin, "Observations Concerning the Increase of Mankind, Peopling of Countries, etc." (1751), in Leonard W. Labaree, ed., *The Papers of Benjamin Franklin* (New Haven: Yale University Press, 1959), 4:234.

20. Thomas Jefferson, *Notes on the State of Virginia*, Query VIII (1782), pp. 211–12, from Electronic Text Center, University of Virginia Library, http://xroads.virginia.edu/~hyper/jefferson/cho8.html.

21. Wertheimer, "The German-Jewish Experience," 235.

22. Wilfred Hulse, "The Lost Son," *Aufbau*, July 31, 1941, p. 9; August 14, 1942, p. 5; August 21, 1942, p. 8.

23. Broh, "The History of the Newspaper *Aufbau*," 383. Also, e.g., Richard Dyck, "The Pan-European Idea on the March," *Aufbau*, May 2, 1947; Harold Ickes, "A United Europe—Guardian of the Peace," *Aufbau*, May 23, 1947, p. 4.

24. Alfred Einstein, "Words in Remembrance," *Aufbau*, April 27, 1945, p. 7.

25. Manfred George, "World Government?," *Aufbau*, March 29, 1946, p. 3.

26. "Letter to Heinrich Mann," June 19, 1939, in Mann, Winston, and Winston, *Letters of Thomas Mann*, 242.

27. Stock, "From the American Scene."

Index

Page references in italics indicate an illustration.